Microsoft Excel 5.0
for Windows™
Illustrated

F5 → go to
Ctl + Home → A1
double click on
    sheet # to name sheet
    = sum(C4:C10)

Microsoft® Excel 5.0
for Windows™
Illustrated

Elizabeth Eisner Reding

Course Technology, Inc. One Main Street, Cambridge, MA 02142
An International Thomson Publishing Company

I(T)P

Microsoft® Excel 5.0 for Windows Illustrated © 1995 Course Technology, Inc.

Managing Editor	Marjorie Schlaikjer
Product Manager	Nicole Jones
Developmental Editor	Katherine T. Pinard
Director of Production	Myrna D'Addario
Production Editor	Roxanne Alexander
Editorial Assistant	Ann Marie Buconjic
Composition	Gex, Inc.
Copyeditor	Jane Pedicini
Proofreader	Nancy Hannigan
Indexer	Alexandra Nickerson
Product Testing and Support Supervisor	Jeff Goding
Technical Reviewers	Godfrey Degamo
	Gopal Swamy
Prepress Production	Gex, Inc.
Manufacturing Manager	Elizabeth Martinez
Instructional Designer	Debbie Krivoy
Text Designer	Leslie Hartwell
Cover Designer	John Gamache
Technical Writer	Michael Halvorson

Microsoft® Excel 5.0 for Windows Illustrated © 1995 Course Technology, Inc.
An International Thomson Publishing Company

All rights reserved. This publication is protected by federal copyright law. No part of this publication may be reproduced, stored in a retrieval system, or transmitted in any form or by any means, electronic, mechanical, photocopying, recording, or otherwise, or be used to make any derivative work (such as translation or adaptation), without prior permission in writing from Course Technology, Inc.

Trademarks

Course Technology and the open book logo are registered trademarks of Course Technology, Inc.

I(T)P   The ITP logo is a trademark under license.

Microsoft is a registered trademark and Excel for Windows is a trademark of Microsoft Corporation in the United States of America and other countries.

Some of the product names used in this book have been used for identification purposes only and may be trademarks or registered trademarks of their respective manufacturers and sellers.

Disclaimer

Course Technology, Inc. reserves the right to revise this publication and make changes from time to time in its content without notice.

ISBN 1-56527-264-1

Printed in the United States of America

10 9 8 7 6 5

From the Publisher

At Course Technology, Inc., we believe that technology will transform the way that people teach and learn. We are very excited about bringing you, instructors and students, the most practical and affordable technology-related products available.

The Course Technology Development Process

Our development process is unparalleled in the higher education publishing industry. Every product we create goes through an exacting process of design, development, review, and testing.

Reviewers give us direction and insight that shape our manuscripts and bring them up to the latest standards. Every manuscript is quality tested. Students whose background matches the intended audience work through every keystroke, carefully checking for clarity, and pointing out errors in logic and sequence. Together with our technical reviewers, these testers help us ensure that everything that carries our name is error-free and easy to use.

Course Technology Products

We show both *how* and *why* technology is critical to solving problems in college and in whatever field you choose to teach or pursue. Our time-tested, step-by-step instructions provide unparalleled clarity. Examples and applications are chosen and crafted to motivate students.

The Course Technology Team

This book will suit your needs because it was delivered quickly, efficiently, and affordably. In every aspect of business, we rely on a commitment to quality and the use of technology. Every employee contributes to this process. The names of all our employees are listed below: Tim Ashe, David Backer, Stephen M. Bayle, Josh Bernoff, Ann Marie Buconjic, Jody Buttafoco, Kerry Cannell, Jim Chrysikos, Barbara Clemens, Susan Collins, John M. Connolly, Kim Crowley, Myrna D'Addario, Lisa D'Alessandro, Howard S. Diamond, Kathryn Dinovo, Joseph B. Dougherty, MaryJane Dwyer, Chris Elkhill, Don Fabricant, Kate Gallagher, Jeff Goding, Laurie Gomes, Eileen Gorham, Andrea Greitzer, Catherine Griffin, Tim Hale, Roslyn Hooley, Nicole Jones, Matt Kenslea, Susannah Lean, Suzanne Licht, Laurie Lindgren, Kim Mai, Elizabeth Martinez, Debbie Masi, Don Maynard, Dan Mayo, Kathleen McCann, Jay McNamara, Mac Mendelsohn, Lauric Michelangelo, Kim Munsell, Amy Oliver, Michael Ormsby, Kristine Otto, Debbie Parlee, Kristin Patrick, Charlie Patsios, Jodi Paulus, Darren Perl, Kevin Phaneuf, George J. Pilla, Cathy Prindle, Nancy Ray, Marjorie Schlaikjer, Christine Spillett, Michelle Tucker, David Upton, Mark Valentine, Karen Wadsworth, Anne Marie Walker, Renee Walkup, Tracy Wells, Donna Whiting, Janet Wilson, Lisa Yameen.

Preface

Course Technology, Inc. is proud to present this new book in its Illustrated Series. *Microsoft Excel 5.0 for Windows Illustrated* provides a highly visual, hands-on introduction to Microsoft Excel. The book is designed as a learning tool for Excel novices but will also be useful as a source for future reference.

Organization and Coverage

Microsoft Excel 5.0 for Windows Illustrated contains a Windows overview and seven units that cover basic Excel skills. In these units students learn how to plan, define, create, and modify worksheets. They work with charts and lists, and learn to automate woorksheet tasks using macros.

Approach

Microsoft Excel 5.0 for Windows Illustrated distinguishes itself from other textbooks with its highly visual approach to computer instruction.

Lessons: Information Displays

The basic lesson format of this text is the "information display," a two-page lesson that is sharply focused on a specific task. This sharp focus and the precise beginning and end of a lesson make it easy for students to study specific material. Modular lessons are less overwhelming for students, and they provide instructors with more flexibility in planning classes and assigning specific work. The units are also modular and can be presented in any order.

Each lesson, or "information display," contains the following elements:

Introduction — Concise text that introduces the basic principles discussed in the lesson and integrates the brief case study scenario. Procedures are easier to learn when concepts fit into a framework.

Numbered steps — Clear step-by-step directions explain how to complete the specific task. When students follow the numbered steps, they quickly learn how each procedure is performed and what the results will be.

Reference tables — These are quickly accessible summaries of key terms, toolbar buttons, or keyboard alternatives connected with the lesson material. Students can refer easily to this information when working on their own projects at a later time.

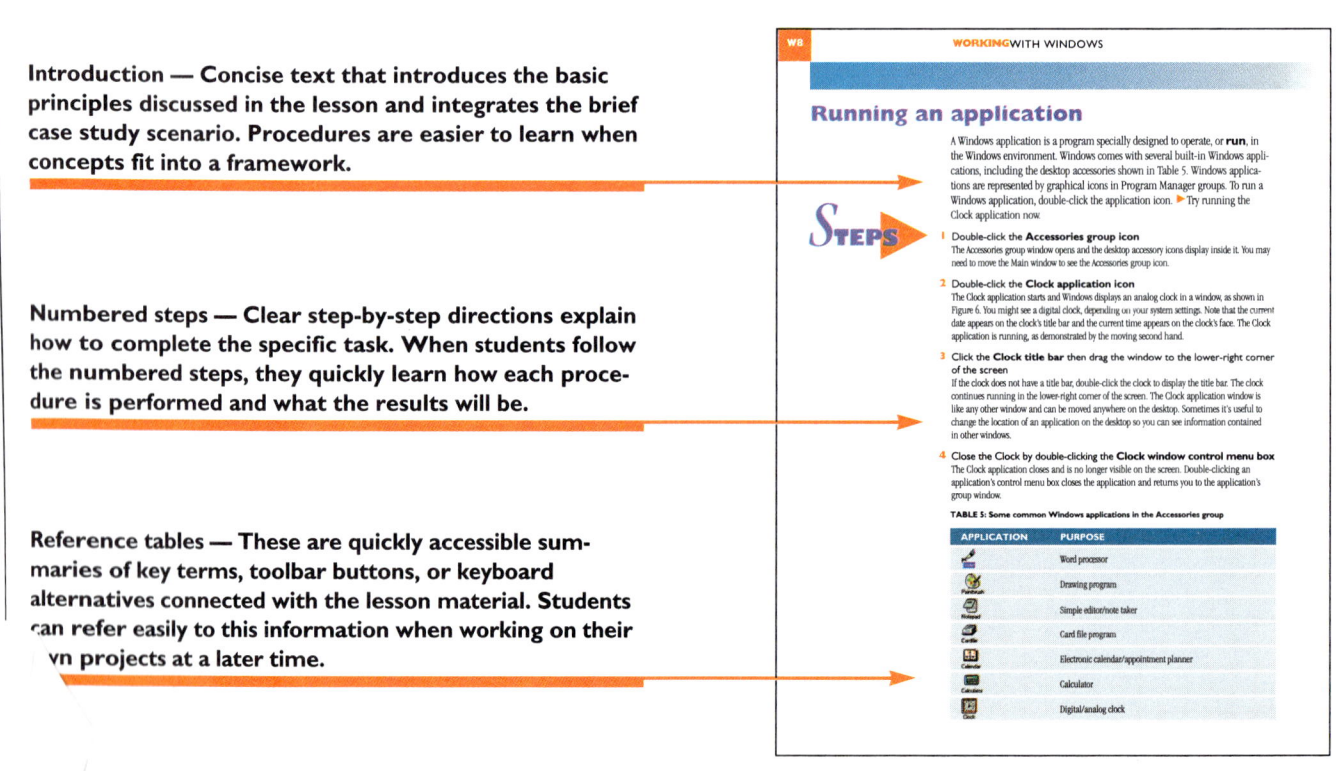

Features

Microsoft Excel 5.0 for Windows Illustrated is an exceptional textbook because it contains the following features:

- "Read This Before You Begin" Pages — These pages, one for the Windows section and one before Unit 1 provide essential information that both students and instructors need to know before they begin working through the units.

- Windows Overview — The "Working with Windows" section provides an overview so students can begin working in the Windows environment right away. This introductory section introduces students to the graphical user interface and helps them learn basic skills they can use in all Windows applications.

- Real-World Case — The case study used throughout the textbook is designed to be "real-world" in nature and representative of the kinds of activities that students will encounter when working with spreadsheet software. With a real-world case, the process of solving the problem will be more meaningful to students.

- End of Unit Material — Each unit concludes with a meaningful Concepts Review that tests students' understanding of what they learned in the unit. The Concepts Review is followed by an Applications Review, which provides students with additional hands-on practice of the skills they learned in the unit. The Applications Review is followed by Independent Challenges, which pose case problems for students to solve. The Independent Challenges allow students to learn by exploring, and develop critical thinking skills.

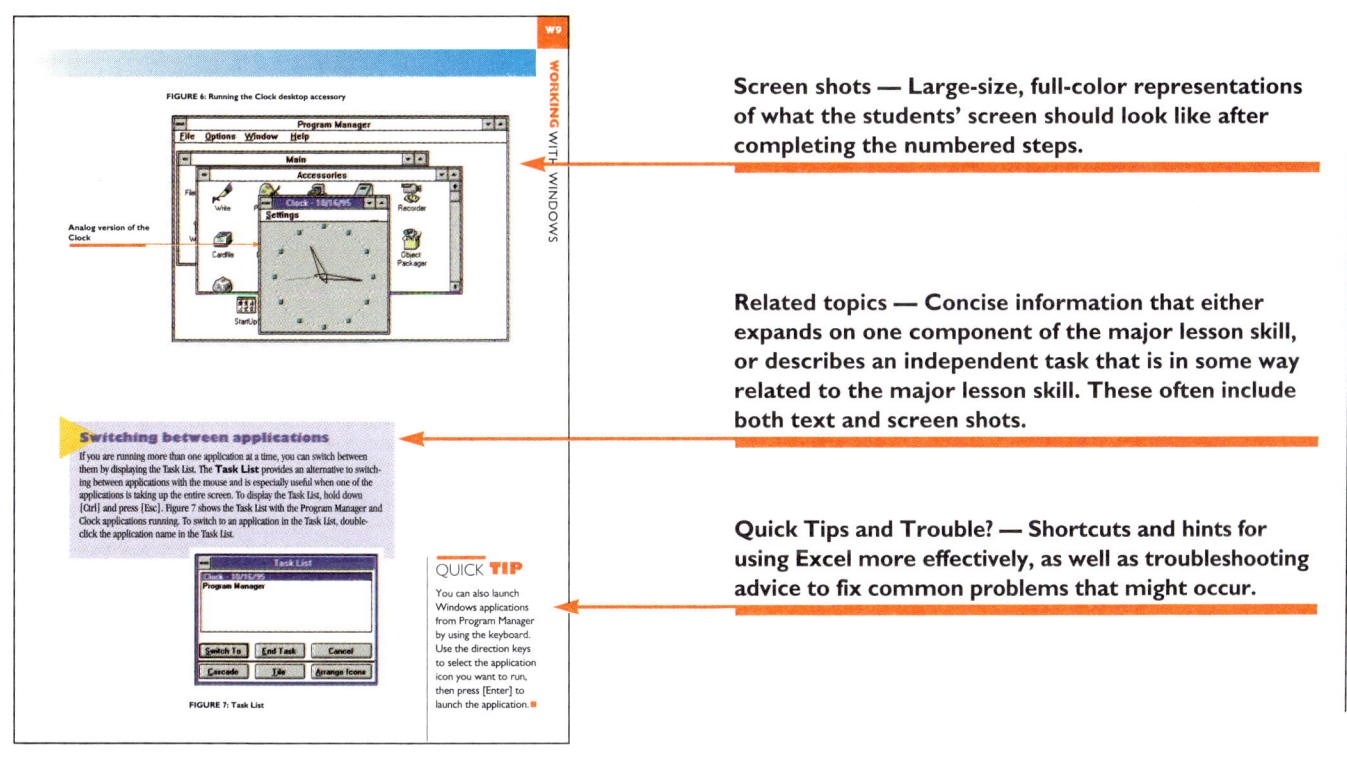

The Student Disk

The Student Disk bundled with the instructor's copy of this book contains all the data files students need to complete the step-by-step lessons.

Adopters of this text are granted the right to post the Student Disk on any standalone computer or network used by students who have purchased this product.

For more information on the Student Disk, see the section in this book called "Read This Before You Begin Excel 5.0."

The Supplements

Instructor's Manual — The Instructor's Manual is quality assurance tested. It includes:

- Solutions to all lessons, Concept Reviews, Application Reviews, and Independent Challenges
- A disk containing solutions to all of the lessons, Concept Reviews, Application Reviews, and Independent Challenges
- Unit notes, which contain tips from the author about the instructional progression of each lesson
- Extra problems
- Transparency masters of key concepts

Test Bank — The Test Bank contains approximately 50 questions per unit in true/false, multiple choice, and fill-in-the-blank formats, plus two essay questions. Each question has been quality assurance tested by students to achieve clarity and accuracy.

Electronic Test Bank — The Electronic Test Bank allows instructors to edit individual test questions, select questions individually or at random, and print out scrambled versions of the same test to any supported printer.

Acknowledgments

This book was made possible due to the extreme persistence and devotion of the Course Technology team, especially Nicole Jones, Kitty Pinard, Marjorie Schlaikjer, and Roxanne Alexander.

I would also like to acknowledge my Dad, who instilled in me the qualities of drive, attention to detail, and personal integrity.

Brief Contents

	From the Publisher	*v*
	Preface	*vi*
	Read This Before You Begin Working with Windows	*xvi*
	Working with Windows	**W1**
	Read This Before You Begin Microsoft Excel 5.0	*2*
UNIT 1	**Getting Started with Microsoft Excel 5.0 for Windows**	*3*
UNIT 2	**Building a Worksheet**	*25*
UNIT 3	**Revising a Worksheet**	*49*
UNIT 4	**Enhancing a Worksheet**	*69*
UNIT 5	**Working with Charts**	*87*
UNIT 6	**Working with Databases**	*107*
UNIT 7	**Automating Worksheet Tabs**	*127*
	Glossary	*141*
	Index	*145*

Contents

From the Publisher	*v*
Preface	*vi*
Read This Before You Begin *Working with Windows*	*xvi*

Working with Windows   *W1*

Starting Windows	W2
The Windows desktop	W3
Using the Mouse	W4
Using Program Manager groups	W6
Scroll bars	W7
Running an application	W8
Switching between applications	W9
Resizing a window	W10
Changing the dimension of a window	W11
Using menus and dialog boxes	W12
Saving a file	W14
Using File Manager	W16
Arranging windows and icons	W18
Exiting Windows	W20
Exiting Windows with the Program Manager control menu box	W21
Concepts Review	W22
Applications Review	W24
Independent Challenge	W24

Read This Before You Begin *Microsoft Excel 5.0*	*2*

UNIT 1 — Getting Started with Microsoft Excel 5.0 for Windows — 3

Defining spreadsheet software	4
Starting Microsoft Excel 5.0 for Windows	6
Viewing the Excel screen	8
Working with Excel menus and dialog boxes	10
Using keyboard shortcuts	10
Working with tools	12
Repositioning toolbars	13
Getting Help	14
Moving around the worksheet	16
Naming a Sheet	18
Moving sheets	19
Closing a workbook and exiting Excel	20
Concepts Review	22
Applications Review	23
Independent Challenges	24

UNIT 2 — Building a Worksheet — 25

Planning and designing a worksheet	26
Entering labels	28
Entering values	30
Editing cell entries	32
Using the Cancel button	33
Working with ranges	34
Using range names to move around a workbook	35
Entering formulas	36
Order of precedence in Excel formulas	39
Using Excel functions	40
Using the Function Wizard	41
Saving a workbook	42
Creating backup files	43
Previewing and printing a worksheet	44
Using Zoom in print preview	45

Concepts Review	46
Applications Review	47
Independent Challenges	48

UNIT 3 — Revising a Worksheet — 49

Opening an existing worksheet	50
Inserting and deleting rows and columns	52
Using dummy columns and rows	53
Copying and moving cell entries	54
Adding and deleting worksheets	55
Copying and moving formulas	56
Filling ranges with series of labels	57
Using Find & Replace to edit a worksheet	59
Copying formulas with absolute cell references	60
Adjusting column widths	62
Specifying row height	63
Checking spelling	64
Modifying the dictionary	65
Concepts Review	66
Applications Review	67
Independent Challenges	68

UNIT 4 — Enhancing a Worksheet — 69

Formatting values	70
Using the Format Painter tool	71
Formatting cell data with fonts and point sizes	72
Using the Formatting toolbar to change fonts and sizes	73
Formatting cell data with attributes and alignment	74
Formatting non-contiguous ranges	75
Customizing the toolbar	76
Using colors, patterns, and borders	78
Using color to organize a worksheet	79
Using AutoFormat	80
Integrating graphic images	81

	Freezing rows and columns	82
	Concepts Review	84
	Applications Review	85
	Independent Challenges	86

UNIT 5 — Working with Charts — 87

Planning and designing a chart	88
Creating a chart	90
Editing a chart	92
Rotating a chart	93
Moving and resizing a chart	94
Viewing multiple worksheets	95
Changing the appearance of a chart	96
Enhancing a chart	98
Changing text font and alignment in charts	99
Adding text annotations to a chart	100
Pulling out a pie slice	101
Previewing and printing charts	102
Concepts Review	104
Applications Review	105
Independent Challenges	106

UNIT 6 — Working with Databases — 107

Planning a list	108
Creating a list	110
Maintaining the quality of information in a list	111
Adding records	112
Finding and deleting records	114
Deleting records without using the data form	115
Sorting records	116
Finding records using AutoFilter	118
Using "And" or "Or"	119
Using the PivotTable Wizard	120

	Dramatize PivotTable data with a chart	123
	Concepts Review	124
	Applications Review	125
	Independent Challenges	125

UNIT 7   Automating Worksheet Tasks   *127*

Planning a macro	128
Recording a macro	130
Using the Personal Macro Workbook	131
Running a macro	132
Using step mode	133
Editing a macro	134
Adding comments to code	135
Adding macros to a menu and a toolbar	136
Creating and using templates	137
Concepts Review	138
Applications Review	139
Independent Challenges	140

TABLES

Table 1: Elements of the Windows desktop	W2
Table 2: Basic mouse techniques	W4
Table 3: Common mouse pointer shapes	W5
Table 4: Standard Windows groups	W6
Table 5: Some common Windows applications in the Accessories group	W8
Table 6: Buttons for managing windows	W10
Table 7: Typical items on menus and dialog boxes	W13
Table 8: Directory window icons	W17
Table 1-1: Common business spreadsheet uses	5
Table 1-2: Commonly used tools	12
Table 1-3: The Help buttons	15
Table 1-4: Getting around the worksheet window	17
Table 2-1: Confirming cell entries	29
Table 2-2: Understanding the mode indicator	32
Table 2-3: Excel arithmetic operators	37
Table 2-4: The difference between the Save and Save As commands	43
Table 2-5: Worksheet printing guidelines	44
Table 3-1: Cut, Copy, Paste, and Undo shortcuts	58
Table 3-2: Format Column commands	62
Table 4-1: Types of formatting	72
Table 4-2: Formatting tools	75
Table 4-3: Border tools	79
Table 5-1: Commonly used chart types	89
Table 5-2: Chart type tools	92
Table 5-3: Chart enhancement tools	96
Table 6-1: Field naming guidelines	110
Table 6-2: Sort Options	116
Table 6-3: Arithmetic operators used to find records	118
Table 6-4: Query and Pivot tools	121

Read This Before You Begin Working with Windows

To the Student

The Working with Windows section gives you practice using the main features of Windows, the control program that lets you work easily with your computer and many programs you run. You need a copy of the Student Disk to complete this section.

Your instructor might provide you with your own copy of the Student Disk, or might make the Student Disk files available to you over a network in your school's computer lab. See your instructor or your technical support person for further information.

To the Instructor

Student Disk
The instructor's copy of this book is bundled with the Student Disk, which contains all the files your students need to complete the step-by-step lessons in this book. Your students will not need the Student Disk files to complete this Working with Windows section, but they will need the disk itself to create a practice directory called MY_FILES.

If you choose to make the Student Disk files available to students over a network, then be sure to tell students where you want them to create the MY_FILES directory. For more information on the Student Disk, refer to the Read This Before You Begin Microsoft Excel 5.0 page.

Screens
This Working with Windows section assumes students will use the default Windows setup. If you want your students' screen to look like those in the figures, set up the Program Manager window to look like Figure 1, and make sure the Clock accessory is in analog mode with the title bar displayed at the top.

OBJECTIVES

▶ Start Windows

▶ Use the mouse

▶ Use Program Manager groups

▶ Run an application

▶ Resize a window

▶ Use menus and dialog boxes

▶ Save a file

▶ Use File Manager

▶ Arrange windows and icons

▶ Exit Windows

Working WITH WINDOWS

Microsoft Windows 3.1 is the **graphical user interface** (GUI) that works hand in hand with MS-DOS to control the basic operation of your computer and the programs you run on it. Windows is a comprehensive control program that helps you run useful, task-oriented programs known as **applications**. ▶ This introduction will help you to learn basic skills that you can use in all Windows applications. First you'll learn how to start Windows and how to use the mouse in the Windows environment. Next you'll get some hands-on experience with Program Manager, and you'll learn how to work with groups, run an application, resize a window, use menus and dialog boxes, save files, use File Manager, and arrange windows and icons. Then you'll learn how to exit a Windows application and exit Windows itself. ▶

WORKING WITH WINDOWS

Starting Windows

Windows is started, or **launched**, from MS-DOS with the Win command. Once started, Windows takes over most of the duties of MS-DOS and provides a graphical environment in which you run your applications. Windows has several advantages over MS-DOS. As a graphical interface, it uses meaningful pictures and symbols known as **icons** to replace hard-to-remember commands. Windows lets you run more than one application at a time, so you can run, for example, a word processor and a spreadsheet at the same time and easily share data between them. ▶ Each application is represented in a rectangular space called a **window**. The Windows environment also includes several useful desktop accessories, including Clock and Notepad, which you can use for day-to-day tasks. ▶ Try starting Windows now.

1. **Turn on your computer**
   The computer displays some technical information as it starts up and tests its circuitry. MS-DOS starts automatically, then displays the **command prompt** (usually C:\>). The command prompt gives you access to MS-DOS commands and applications. If your computer is set up so that it automatically runs Windows when it starts, the command prompt will not display. You can then skip Step 2.

2. **Type win then press [Enter]**
   This command starts Windows. The screen momentarily goes blank while the computer starts Windows. An hourglass displays, indicating Windows is busy processing a command. Then the Windows Program Manager displays on your screen, as shown in Figure 1. Your screen might look slightly different depending on which applications are installed on your computer.

TABLE 1:
Elements of the Windows desktop

DESKTOP ELEMENT	DESCRIPTION
Program Manager	The main control program of Windows. All Windows applications are started from the Program Manager.
Window	A rectangular space framed by a double border on the screen. The Program Manager is framed in a window.
Application icon	The graphic representation of a Windows application.
Title bar	The area directly below the window's top border that displays the name of a window or application.
Sizing buttons	Buttons in the upper-right corner of a window that you can use to minimize or maximize a window.
Menu bar	The area under the title bar on a window. The menu bar provides access to most of an application's commands.
Control menu box	A box in the upper-left corner of each window; provides a menu used to resize, move, maximize, minimize, or close a window. Double-clicking this box closes a window or an application.
Mouse pointer	An arrow indicating the current location of the mouse on the desktop.

FIGURE 1: Program Manager window

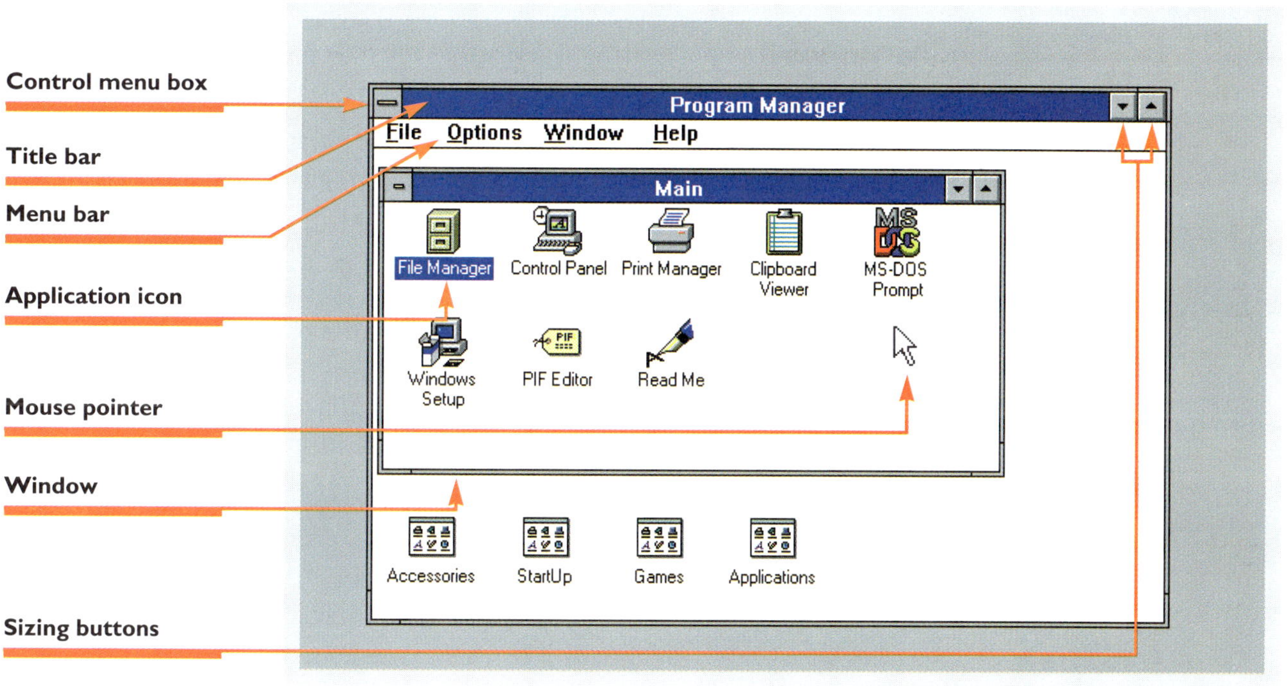

- Control menu box
- Title bar
- Menu bar
- Application icon
- Mouse pointer
- Window
- Sizing buttons

The Windows desktop

The entire screen area on the monitor represents the Windows desktop. The **desktop** is an electronic version of a desk that provides workspace for different computing tasks. Windows allows you to customize the desktop to support the way you like to work and to organize the applications you need to run. Use Table 1 to identify the key elements of the desktop, referring to Figure 1 for their locations. Because the Windows desktop can be customized, your desktop might look slightly different.

Using the mouse

The **mouse** is a handheld input device that you roll on your desk to position the mouse pointer on the Windows desktop. When you move the mouse on your desk, the **mouse pointer** on the screen moves in the same direction. The buttons on the mouse are used to select icons and choose commands, and to indicate the work to be done in applications. Table 2 lists the four basic mouse techniques. Table 3 shows some common mouse pointer shapes. ▶ Try using the mouse now.

1. **Locate the mouse pointer on the Windows desktop and move the mouse across your desk**
   Watch how the mouse pointer moves on the Windows desktop in response to your movements. Try moving the mouse pointer in circles, then back and forth in straight lines.

2. **Position the mouse pointer over the Control Panel icon in the Main group window**
   Positioning the mouse pointer over an icon is called **pointing**. The Control Panel icon is a graphical representation of the Control Panel application, a special program that controls the operation of the Windows environment. If the Control Panel icon is not visible in the Main group window, point to any other icon. The Program Manager is customizable so the Control Panel could be hidden from view.

3. **Press and release the left mouse button**
   Pressing and releasing the mouse button is called **clicking**. When you position the mouse pointer on an icon in Program Manager then click, you **select** the icon. When the Control Panel icon is selected, its title is highlighted, as shown in Figure 2. If you clicked an icon that caused a menu to open, click the icon again to close the menu. You'll learn about menus later. Now practice a mouse skill called **dragging**.

4. **With the icon selected, press and hold the left mouse button and move the mouse down and to the right**
   The icon moves with the mouse pointer, as shown in Figure 3. When you release the mouse button, the icon relocates in the group window.

5. **Drag the Control Panel icon back to its original position**

TABLE 2:
Basic mouse techniques

TECHNIQUE	HOW TO DO IT
Pointing	Move the mouse pointer to position it over an item on the desktop.
Clicking	Press and release the mouse button.
Double-clicking	Press and release the mouse button twice quickly.
Dragging	Point at an item, press and hold the mouse button, move the mouse to a new location, then release the mouse button.

FIGURE 2: Selecting an icon

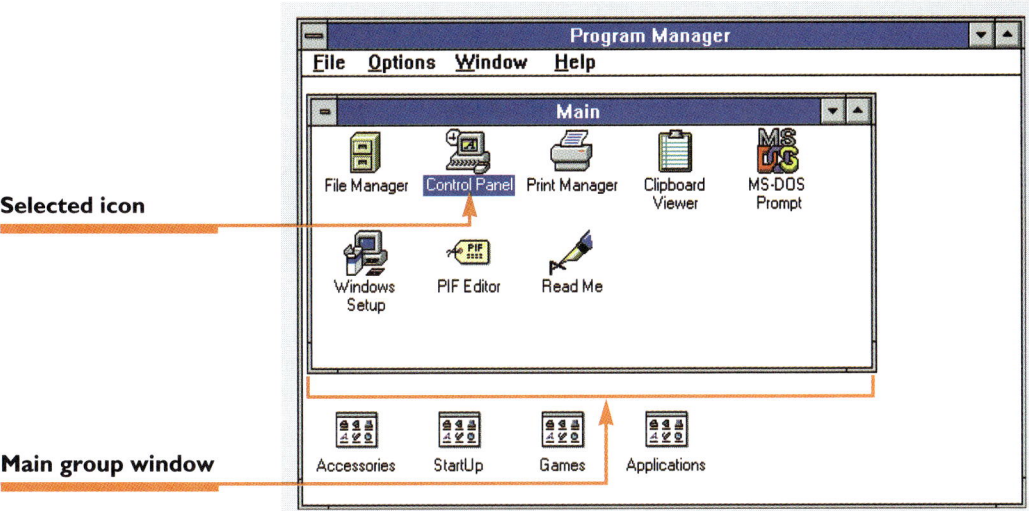

Selected icon

Main group window

FIGURE 3: Dragging an icon

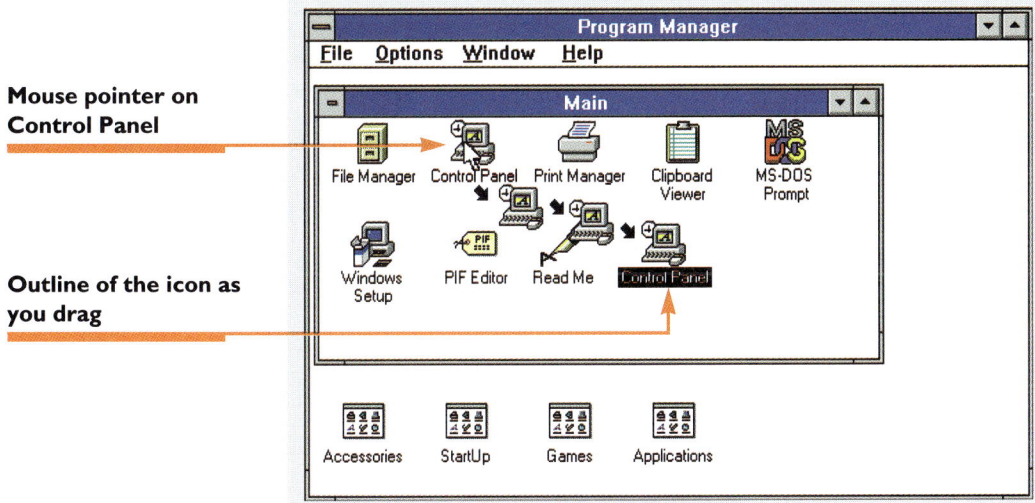

Mouse pointer on Control Panel

Outline of the icon as you drag

TABLE 3: Common mouse pointer shapes

SHAPE	USED TO
▶	Select items, choose commands, start applications, and work in applications.
I	Position mouse pointer for editing or inserting text. This icon is called an insertion point.
⌛	Indicate Windows is busy processing a command.
⟷	Change the size of a window. This icon appears when mouse pointer is on the border of a window.

Using Program Manager groups

In Program Manager, you launch applications and organize your applications into windows called groups. A **group** can appear as an open window or as an icon in the Program Manager window. Each group has a name related to its contents, and you can reorganize the groups to suit your needs. The standard Windows groups are described in Table 4. ▶ Try working with groups now.

1. **If necessary, double-click the Main group icon to open the Main group window**
   The Main group icon is usually located at the bottom of the Program Manager window.

2. **Double-click the Accessories group icon**
   When you double-click the Accessories group icon, it expands into the Accessories group window, as shown in Figure 4. Now move the Accessories group window to the right.

3. **Click the Accessories group window title bar and drag the group window to the right**
   An outline of the window moves to the right with the mouse. When you release the mouse button, the Accessories group window moves to the location you've indicated. Moving a window lets you see what is beneath it. Any window in the Windows environment can be moved with this technique.

4. **Click the title bar of the Main group window**
   The Main group window becomes the **active window**, the one you are currently working in. Other windows, including the Accessories group window, are considered background windows. Note that the active window has a highlighted title bar. Program Manager has a highlighted title bar because it is the **active application**.

5. **Activate the Accessories group window by clicking anywhere in that window**
   The Accessories group window moves to the foreground again. Now try closing the Accessories group window to an icon.

6. **Double-click the control menu box in the Accessories group window**
   When you double-click this box, the Accessories group window shrinks to an icon and the Main group window becomes the active window. Double-clicking the control menu box is the easiest way to close a window or an application.

TABLE 4:
Standard Windows groups

GROUP NAME	CONTENTS
Main	Applications that control how Windows works; the primary Windows group.
Accessories	Useful desktop accessories for day-to-day tasks.
StartUp	Programs that run automatically when Windows is started.
Games	Game programs for Windows.
Applications	Group of applications found on your hard disk.

FIGURE 4: Accessories group expanded into a window

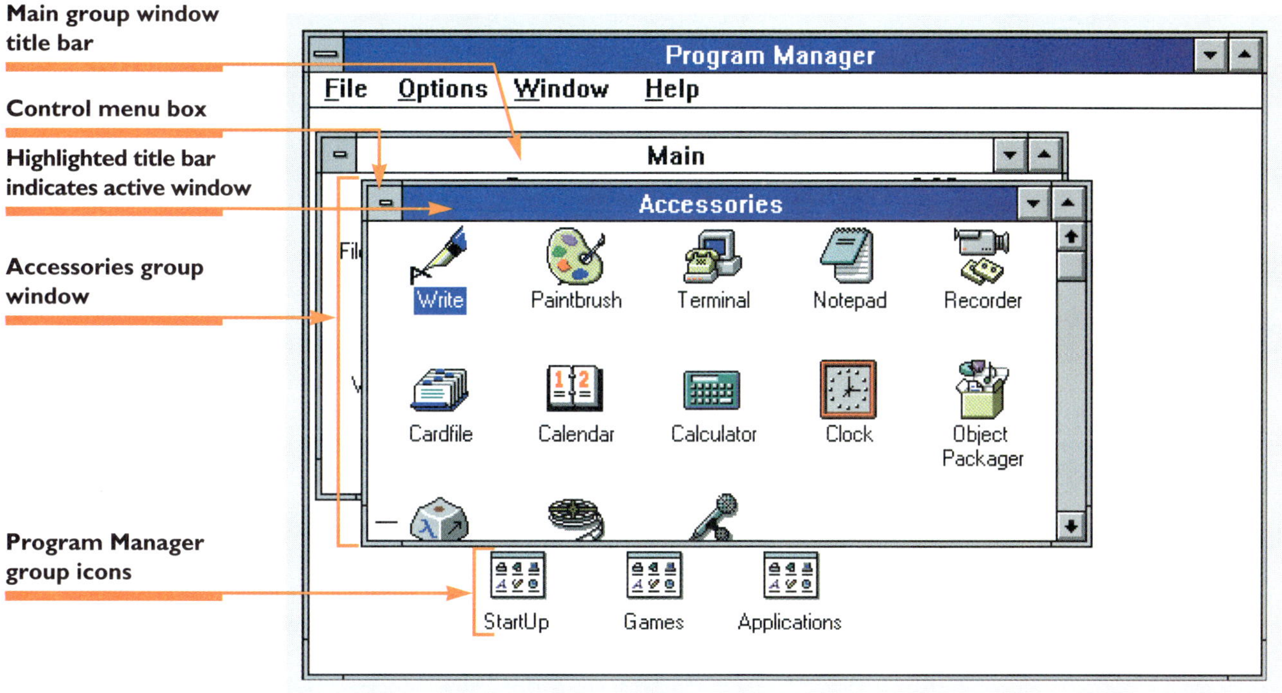

- Main group window title bar
- Control menu box
- Highlighted title bar indicates active window
- Accessories group window
- Program Manager group icons

Scroll bars

If a group contains more icons than can be displayed at one time, **scroll bars** appear on the right and/or bottom edges of the window to give you access to the remaining icons, as shown in Figure 5. Vertical or horizontal arrows appear at the ends of the bars. To use scroll bars, click the vertical or horizontal arrows that point in the direction you want the window to scroll or drag the scroll box along the scroll bar. Scroll bars appear whenever there is more information than can fit in a window. You'll see them in many Windows applications.

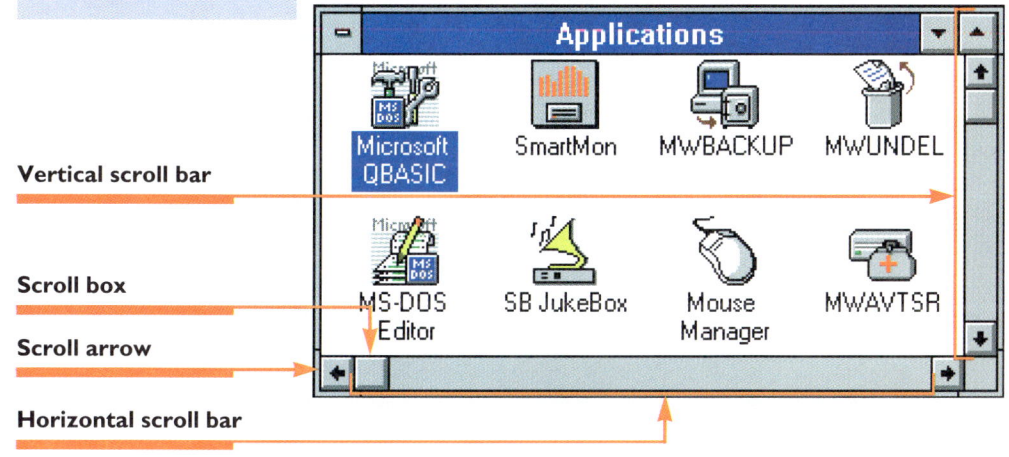

- Vertical scroll bar
- Scroll box
- Scroll arrow
- Horizontal scroll bar

FIGURE 5: Vertical and horizontal scroll bars on a window

You can use the direction keys on the keyboard to scroll the contents of the active window. To scroll vertically, press [↑] or [↓]. To scroll horizontally, press [←] or [→].

WORKING WITH WINDOWS

WORKING WITH WINDOWS

Running an application

A Windows application is a program specially designed to operate, or **run**, in the Windows environment. Windows comes with several built-in Windows applications, including the desktop accessories shown in Table 5. Windows applications are represented by graphical icons in Program Manager groups. To run a Windows application, double-click the application icon. ▶ Try running the Clock application now.

1 Double-click the Accessories group icon
The Accessories group window opens and the desktop accessory icons display inside it. You may need to move the Main window to see the Accessories group icon.

2 Double-click the Clock application icon
The Clock application starts and Windows displays an analog clock in a window, as shown in Figure 6. You might see a digital clock, depending on your system settings. Note that the current date appears on the clock's title bar and the current time appears on the clock's face. The Clock application is running, as demonstrated by the moving second hand.

3 Click the Clock title bar then drag the window to the lower-right corner of the screen
If the clock does not have a title bar, double-click the clock to display the title bar. The clock continues running in the lower-right corner of the screen. The Clock application window is like any other window and can be moved anywhere on the desktop. Sometimes it's useful to change the location of an application on the desktop so you can see information contained in other windows.

4 Close the Clock by double-clicking the Clock window control menu box
The Clock application closes and is no longer visible on the screen. Double-clicking an application's control menu box closes the application and returns you to the application's group window.

TABLE 5: Some common Windows applications in the Accessories group

APPLICATION	PURPOSE
Write	Word processor
Paintbrush	Drawing program
Notepad	Simple editor/note taker
Cardfile	Card file program
Calendar	Electronic calendar/appointment planner
Calculator	Calculator
Clock	Digital/analog clock

FIGURE 6: Running the Clock desktop accessory

Analog version of the Clock

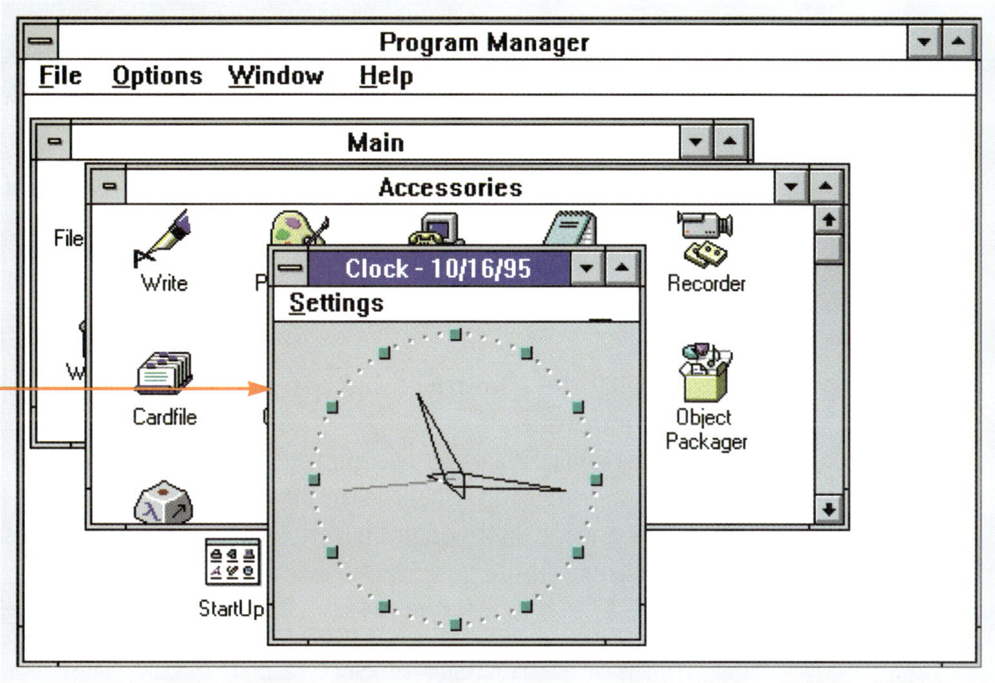

Switching between applications

If you are running more than one application at a time, you can switch between them by displaying the Task List. The **Task List** provides an alternative to switching between applications with the mouse and is especially useful when one of the applications is taking up the entire screen. To display the Task List, hold down [Ctrl] and press [Esc]. Figure 7 shows the Task List with the Program Manager and Clock applications running. To switch to an application in the Task List, double-click the application name in the Task List.

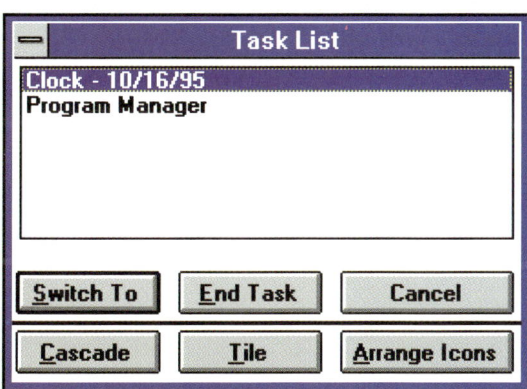

FIGURE 7: Task List

Resizing a window

The Windows desktop can get cluttered with icons and windows if you use lots of applications. Each window is surrounded by a standard border and sizing buttons that allow you to minimize, maximize, and restore windows as needed. The sizing buttons are shown in Table 6. They help you keep the desktop organized. ▶ Try sizing the Clock window now.

1 Double-click the **Clock application icon**
The Clock application restarts.

2 Click the **Minimize button** in the upper-right corner of the Clock window
The Minimize button is the sizing button on the left. When you **minimize** the clock, it shrinks to an icon at the bottom of the screen, as shown in Figure 8. Notice that the Clock icon continues to show the right time, even as an icon. Windows applications continue to run after you minimize them.

3 Double-click the **Clock icon** to restore the Clock window to its original size
The clock is restored to its original size, and the application continues to run.

4 Click the **Maximize button** in the upper-right corner of the Clock window
The Maximize button is the sizing button to the right of the Minimize button. When you **maximize** the clock, it takes up the entire screen, as shown in Figure 9. Although it's unlikely you'll want to maximize this application very often, you'll find the ability to maximize other Windows applications very useful.

5 Click the **Restore button** in the upper-right corner of the Clock window
The Restore button, as shown in Figure 9, is located to the right of the Minimize button *after* an application has been maximized. The Restore button returns an application to its original size.

6 Double-click the **Clock window control menu box** to close the application

TABLE 6:
Buttons for managing windows

BUTTON	PURPOSE
▼	Minimizes an application to an icon on the bottom of the screen.
▲	Maximizes an application to its largest possible size.
⬍	Restores an application, returning it to its original size.

FIGURE 8:
Minimized Clock application as an icon

Minimize button

Maximize button

Minimized clock with current time and date

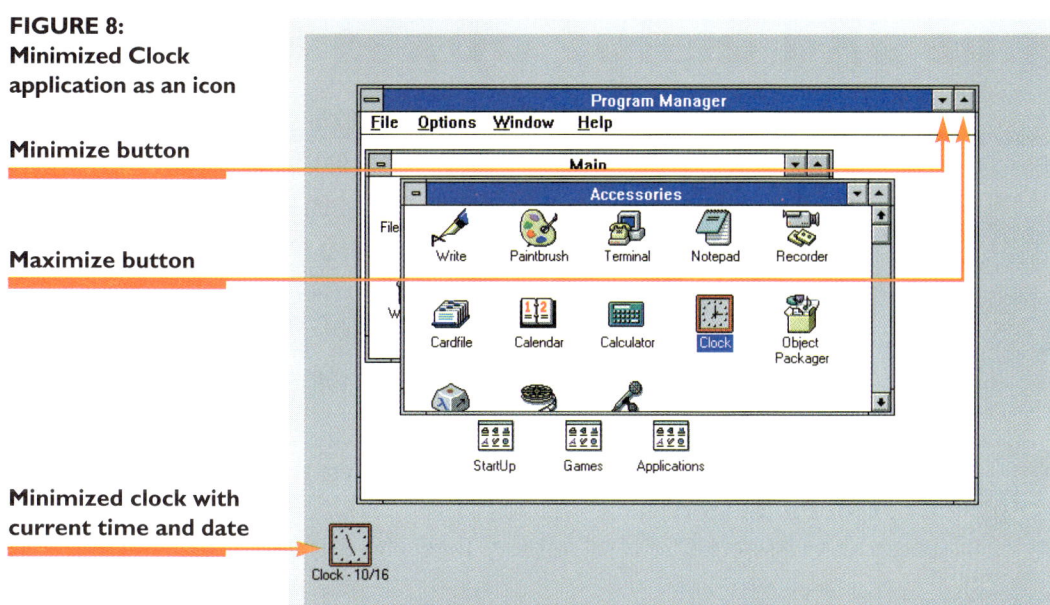

FIGURE 9:
Maximized clock filling entire screen

Restore button appears after a window has been maximized

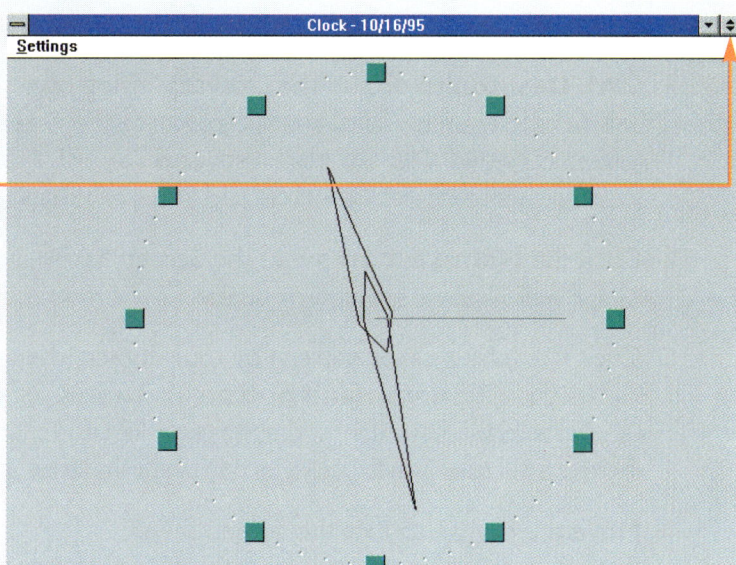

Changing the dimension of a window

The dimension of a window can also be changed, but the window will always be a rectangle. To change the dimension of a window, position the mouse pointer on the window border you want to modify. The mouse pointer changes to ⇔. Drag the border in the direction you want to change. Figure 10 shows the width of the Clock window being increased, which will make the clock face larger.

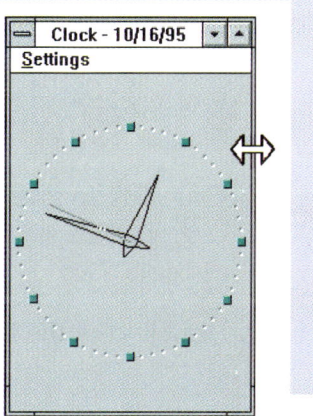

FIGURE 10: Increasing the width of the Clock window

Using menus and dialog boxes

A **menu** is a list of commands that you can use to accomplish certain tasks. Each Windows application has its own set of menus, which are listed on the **menu bar** along the top of the application window. Sometimes when you select a command from a menu, the application needs more information before it can complete the task, in which case a **dialog box** opens, giving you more options. See Table 7 for some of the typical conventions used on menus and dialog boxes. ▶ Try using the Control Panel which lets you customize your Windows desktop.

1. Click the **Main group window** to make it active, then double-click the **Control Panel icon**
   Drag other windows out of the way, if necessary. The Control Panel window opens.

2. Click **Settings** on the menu bar
   A menu displays listing all the commands that let you adjust different aspects of your desktop. See Table 7.

3. Click **Desktop** to display the Desktop dialog box
   This dialog box provides options to customize your desktop. See Figure 11. Next, locate the Screen Saver section of the dialog box. A **screen saver** is a moving pattern that fills your screen after your computer has not been used for a specified amount of time.

4. Click the **Name list arrow** in the Screen Saver section
   A list of available screen saver patterns displays.

5. Click the screen saver pattern of your choice, then click **Test**
   The Test button is a **command button**. The two most common command buttons are OK and Cancel which you'll see in almost every dialog box. The screen saver pattern you chose displays. It will remain on the screen until you move the mouse or press a key.

6. Move the mouse to exit the screen saver
   Next, you'll adjust the cursor blink rate in the Cursor Blink Rate section. The **cursor** is the vertical line that shows you where you are on the screen. See Figure 11.

7. Drag the scroll box all the way to the right of the scroll bar, then click the **left arrow** in the scroll bar a few times
   By moving the scroll box between Slow and Fast on the scroll bar, you can adjust the cursor blink rate to suit your needs.

8. Click **OK** to save your changes and close the dialog box
   Clicking OK accepts your changes; clicking Cancel rejects your changes. Now you can exit the Control Panel.

9. Double-click the **Control Panel control menu box** to close this window

FIGURE 11:
Desktop dialog box

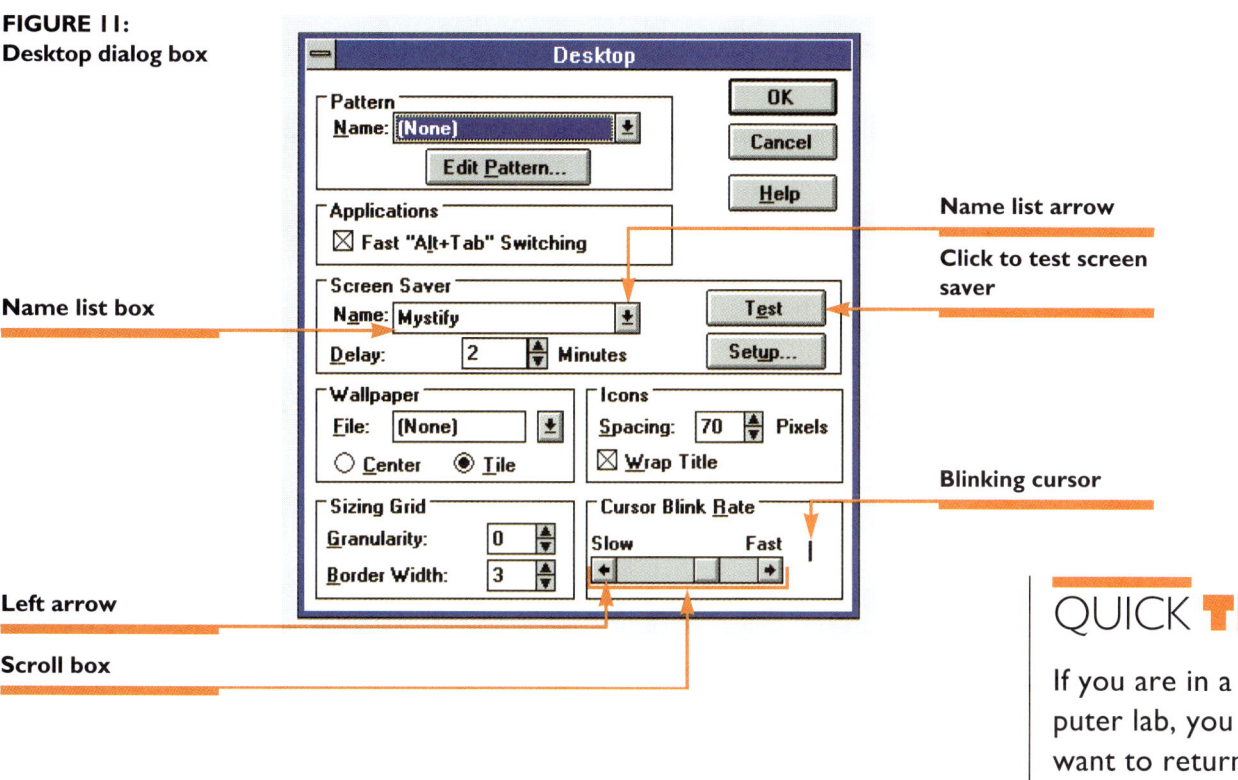

TABLE 7: Typical items on menus and dialog boxes

QUICK TIP

If you are in a computer lab, you might want to return the desktop settings you changed to their original state.

ITEM	MEANING	EXAMPLE
Dimmed command	A menu command that is not currently available.	Undo
Ellipsis	Choosing this menu command opens a dialog box that asks for further information.	Paste Special...
Triangle	Clicking this button opens a cascading menu containing an additional list of menu commands.	Axis ▶
Keyboard shortcut	A keyboard alternative for executing a menu command.	Cut Ctrl+X
Underlined letter	Pressing the underlined letter executes this menu command.	Copy Right
Check box	Clicking this square box turns a dialog box option on or off.	☒ Wrap Title
Text box	A box in which you type text.	tours.wk4
Radio button	Clicking this small circle selects a single dialog box option.	⦿ Tile
Command button	Clicking this button executes this dialog box command.	OK
List box	A box containing a list of items. To choose an item, click the list arrow, then click the desired item.	c: ms-dos_5

Saving a file

The documents you create using a computer are stored in the computer's random access memory (RAM). **RAM** is temporary storage space that is erased when the computer is turned off. To store a document permanently, you need to save it to a disk. You can either save your work to a 3.5-inch or a 5.25-inch disk that you insert into the disk drive of your computer (i.e., drive A or B), or a hard disk, which is a disk built into the computer (usually drive C). Your instructor has provided you with a Student Disk to use as you proceed through the lessons in this book. This book assumes that you will save all of your files to your Student Disk. Refer to the Read This Before You Begin page immediately preceding this section for more information on your Student Disk. ▶ In this lesson, you'll create a simple document using Notepad, then you will save the document to your Student Disk. **Notepad** is a simple text editor that lets you create memos, record notes, or edit text files. A **text file** is a document containing words, letters, or numbers, but no special computer instructions, such as formatting.

1. Insert your Student Disk into drive A or drive B
   Check with your instructor if you aren't sure which drive you should use.

2. Click the **Accessories group window** to activate it

3. Double-click the **Notepad application icon** to start Notepad
   The Notepad application starts, and the Notepad window displays. Now, enter some text.

4. Type **Today I started working with Notepad.** then press **[Enter]**
   Your screen should look like Figure 12.

5. Click **File** on the Notepad menu bar, then click **Save**
   The Save As dialog box displays, as shown in Figure 13. In this dialog box you enter a name for your file and specify where you want to save it.

6. Type **MYNOTES** in the File Name text box
   Your entry replaces the highlighted (selected) *.txt. Notepad will automatically add the extension when you click OK. Now you need to specify the drive where your Student Disk is located.

7. Click the **Drives list arrow** to display the drives on your computer, then click **a:** or **b:**, depending on which drive contains your Student Disk
   Notice that the list of files that are on your Student Disk displays below the File Name text box.

8. Click **OK**
   The Save As dialog box closes and MYNOTES is now saved on your Student Disk.

9. Click **File** on the Notepad menu bar, then click **Exit** to close Notepad

FIGURE 12: Notepad window with text entered

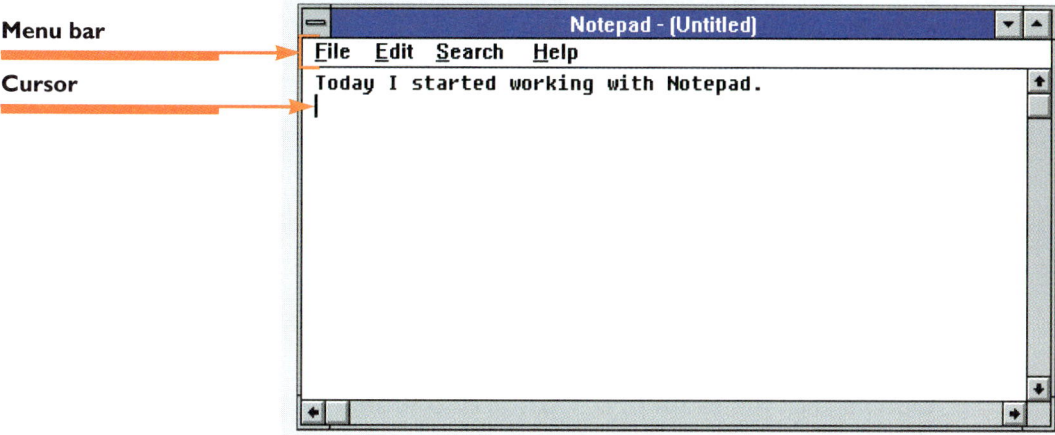

Menu bar
Cursor

FIGURE 13: Save As dialog box

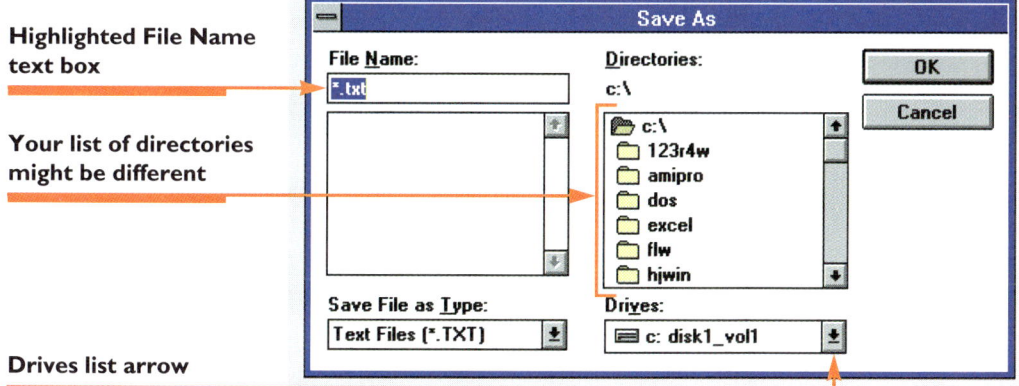

Highlighted File Name text box

Your list of directories might be different

Drives list arrow

WORKING WITH WINDOWS

Save your work often, at least every 15 minutes and before printing.

Using File Manager

File Manager is an application included with Windows that can help you organize files and directories. A **directory** is like a file folder—it is a part of a disk where you can store a group of related files. For example, you might want to create a directory called PROJECT1 and store all of the files relating to a particular project in that directory. You can use File Manager to create the directory, then move the related files into it.

▶ Use File Manager to create a directory called MY_FILES on your Student Disk and then move the Notepad file you created and saved in the previous lesson into that directory. Make sure your Student Disk is in drive A or drive B before beginning the steps.

1 Double-click the **Main program group icon**, or if it is already open, click the **Main group window** to activate it

2 Double-click the **File Manager application icon** in the Main group window
   File Manager opens to display the directory window, as shown in Figure 14. Your File Manager will contain different files and directories. The directory window is divided by the split bar. The left side of the window displays the structure of the current drive, or the directory tree. The right side of the window displays a list of files in the selected directory. See Table 8 for a description of the various icons used in the directory window. The status bar displays the information about the current drive and directory and other information to help you with file management tasks.

3 Click the **drive icon** that corresponds to the drive containing your Student Disk
   The contents of your Student Disk displays. Now create a directory on this disk.

4 Click **File** on the menu bar, then click **Create Directory**
   The Create Directory dialog box displays listing the current directory, which in this case is the top level directory indicated by the backslash (\). You will type a new directory name in the text box provided. Directory names can have up to 11 characters but cannot include spaces, commas, or backslashes.

5 Type **MY_FILES** in the Name text box, then click **OK**
   You can type in the directory name in either uppercase or lowercase letters. The new directory appears in both sides of the directory window.

6 Press and hold the mouse button to select MYNOTES.TXT, then drag the file into the MY_FILES directory on the left side of the window
   The mouse pointer changes as you drag the file, as shown in Figure 15. Don't worry if you move a file to the wrong place; simply drag it again to the correct location. (You can drag it to the MY_FILES directory in either the left or right side of the window.)

7 Click **Yes** in the Confirm Mouse Operation dialog box
   Notice that the file no longer appears in the list of files. Now check that the file is in the newly created directory.

8 Double-click the **MY_FILES icon**
   The file appears in the list of files. If you want, you can use this directory throughout this book to store the files that you save. Now that you have created a directory and moved a file into it, you can exit File Manager.

9 Double-click the **control menu box** to exit File Manager

WORKING WITH WINDOWS

FIGURE 14: File Manager

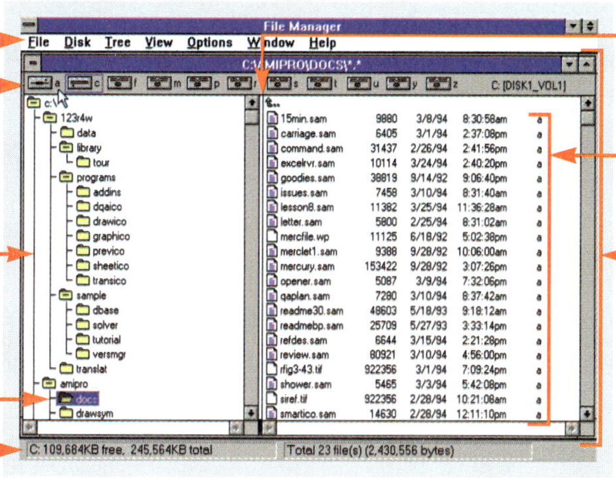

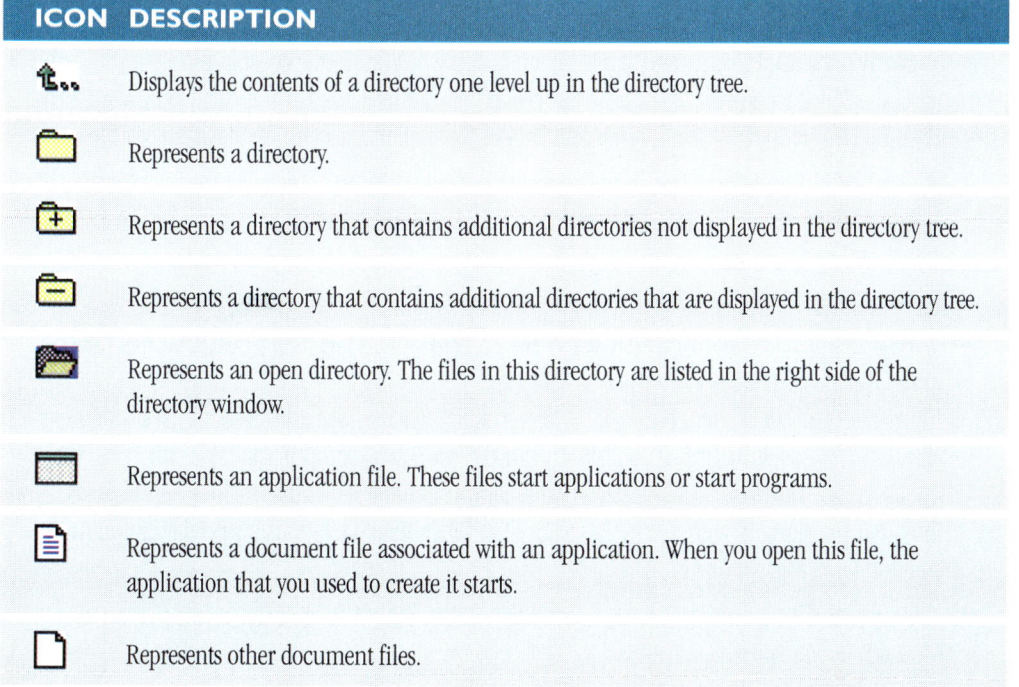

Labels: Menu bar, Drive icons, Directory tree, Selected directory, Status bar, Split bar, List of files, Directory window

FIGURE 15: Dragging a file to a new location

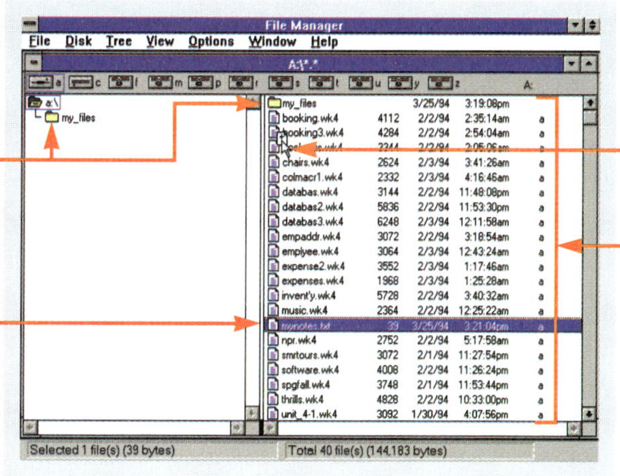

Labels: New directory, Select this file and drag it into the new directory, Mouse pointer changes as you are dragging the file, Your list of files might be different

TABLE 8: Directory window icons

ICON	DESCRIPTION
⬆..	Displays the contents of a directory one level up in the directory tree.
📁	Represents a directory.
📁+	Represents a directory that contains additional directories not displayed in the directory tree.
📁-	Represents a directory that contains additional directories that are displayed in the directory tree.
📂	Represents an open directory. The files in this directory are listed in the right side of the directory window.
🗔	Represents an application file. These files start applications or start programs.
📄	Represents a document file associated with an application. When you open this file, the application that you used to create it starts.
📄	Represents other document files.

QUICK TIP

To select a group of files, click the first file, then press [Shift] and click the last file. To select noncontiguous files (files not next to each other in the file list), click the first file, then press [Ctrl] and click each additional file. ■

Arranging windows and icons

If your desktop contains many groups that you open regularly, you might find that the open windows clutter your desktop. The Tile and Cascade commands on the Window menu let you view all your open group windows at once in an organized arrangement. You can also use the Window menu to open all the program groups installed on your computer. ▶ Once you are comfortable working with Windows, you might decide to reorganize your group windows. You can easily move an icon from one group window to another by dragging it with the mouse. In the following steps, you'll drag the Clock icon from the Accessories group window to the StartUp group window. The StartUp group window contains programs that automatically start running when you launch Windows.

1. Click the **Program Manager Maximize button** to maximize this window, then click **Window** on the menu bar
   The Window menu opens, as shown in Figure 16, displaying the commands Cascade, Tile, and Arrange Icons, followed by a numbered list of the program groups installed on your computer. You might see a check mark next to one of the items, indicating that this program group is the active one. Locate StartUp on the numbered list. If you don't see StartUp, click More Windows at the bottom of the list, then double-click StartUp in the dialog box that displays. If you still can't find StartUp, see your instructor or technical support person for assistance.

2. Click **StartUp**
   The StartUp group window opens. Depending on how your computer is set up, you might see some program icons already in this window. At this point, your screen is getting cluttered with three program group windows open (Main, Accessories, and StartUp). Use the Cascade command to arrange them in an orderly way.

3. Click **Window** on the menu bar, then click **Cascade**
   The windows display in a layered arrangement, with the title bars of each showing. This formation is neatly organized and shows all your open group windows, but it doesn't allow you to easily drag the Clock icon from the Accessories group window to the StartUp group window. The Tile command arranges the windows so that the contents of all the open windows are visible.

4. Click **Window** on the menu bar, then click **Tile**
   The windows are now positioned in an ideal way to copy an icon from one window to another. Before continuing to step 5, locate the Clock icon in the Accessories group window. If you don't see the icon, use the scroll bar to bring it into view.

5. Drag the Clock application icon from the Accessories group window to the StartUp group window
   Your screen now looks like Figure 17. The Clock application will automatically start the next time Windows is launched. If you are working on your own computer and want to leave the Clock in the StartUp group, skip Step 6 and continue to the next lesson, "Exiting Windows." If you are working in a computer lab, move the Clock icon back to its original location in the Accessories group window.

6. Drag the Clock application icon from the StartUp group window to the Accessories group window
   The Clock icon is now back in the Accessories group.

FIGURE 16:
Window menu

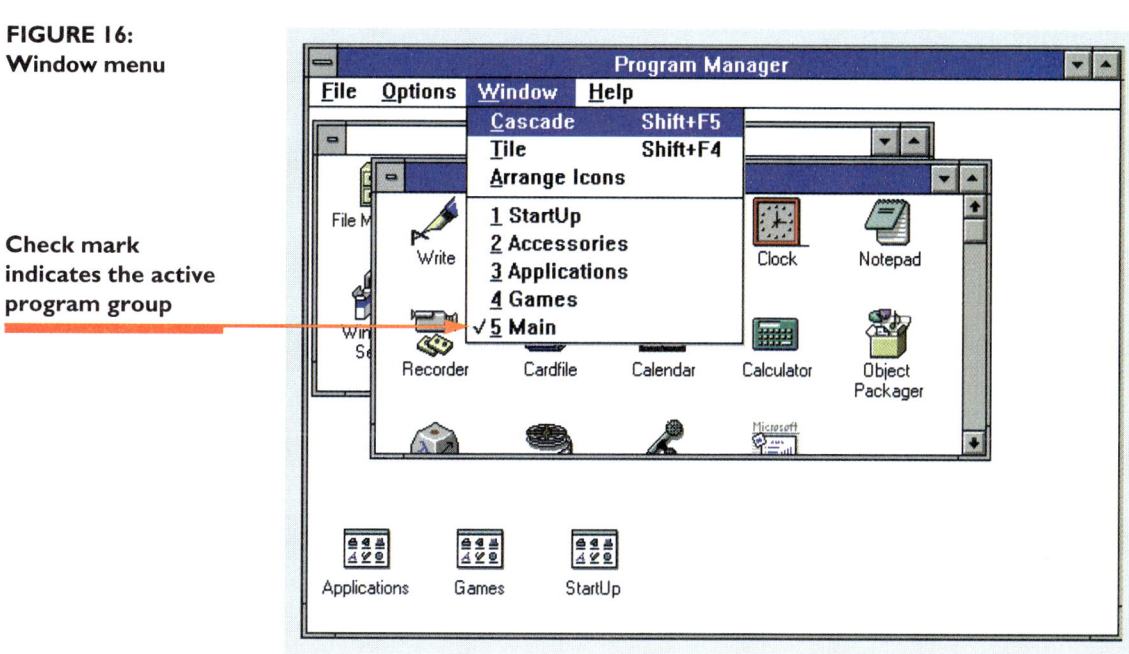

Check mark indicates the active program group

FIGURE 17:
Tiled group windows

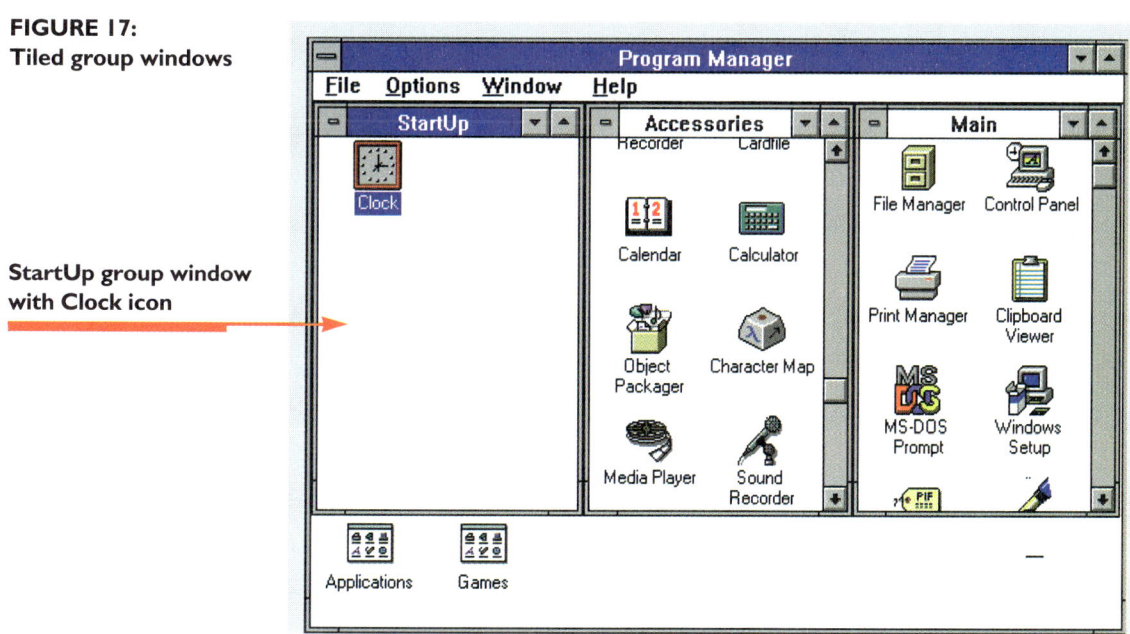

StartUp group window with Clock icon

QUICK TIP

To move a copy of an icon from one group window to another, hold down [Ctrl] as you drag the icon.∎

Exiting Windows

When you are finished working with Windows, close all the applications you are running and exit Windows. Do not turn off the computer while Windows is running; you could lose important data if you turn off your computer too soon. ▶ Now try closing all your active applications and exiting Windows.

1. **Close any active applications or group windows by double-clicking the control menu boxes of the open windows, one at a time**
   The windows close. If you have any unsaved changes in your application, a dialog box displays, asking if you want to save them.

2. **Click File on the Program Manager menu bar**
   The File menu displays, as shown in Figure 18.

3. **Click Exit Windows**
   Program Manager displays the Exit Windows dialog box, as shown in Figure 19. You have two options at this point: Click OK to exit Windows, or click Cancel to abort the Exit Windows command and return to the Program Manager.

4. **Click OK to exit Windows**
   Windows finishes its work and the MS-DOS command prompt appears. You can now safely turn off the computer.

FIGURE 18: Exiting Windows using the File menu

Menu bar →

Exit Windows command →

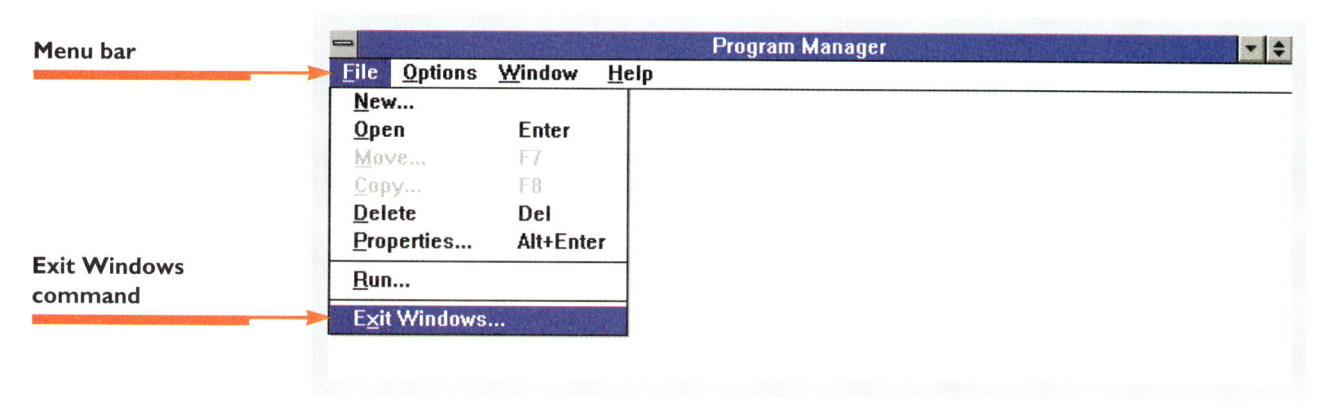

FIGURE 19: Exit Windows dialog box

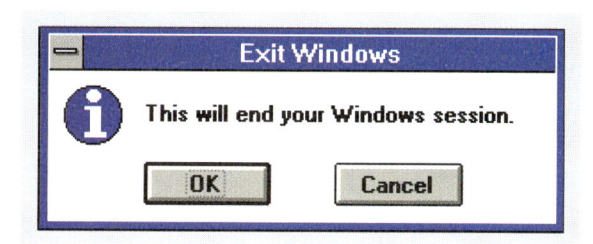

Exiting Windows with the Program Manager control menu box

You can also exit Windows by double-clicking the control menu box in the upper-left corner of the Program Manager window, as shown in Figure 20. After you double-click the control menu box, you see the Exit Windows dialog box. Click OK to exit Windows.

Double-click the control menu box →

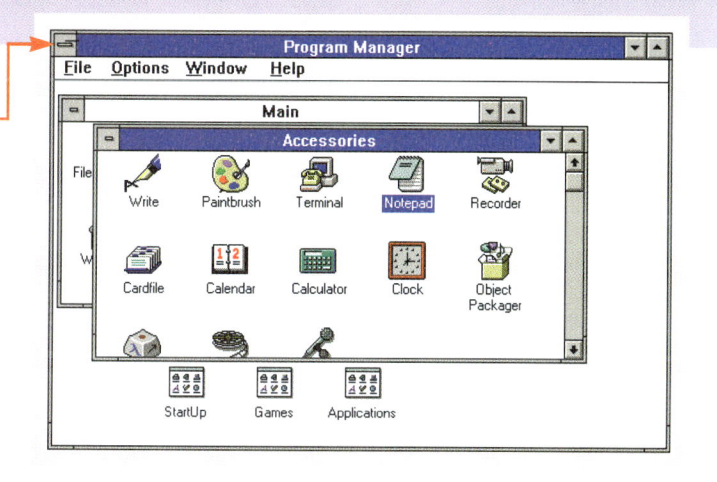

FIGURE 20: Exiting Windows with the Program Manager control menu box

TROUBLE?

If you do not exit from Windows before turning off the computer, you might lose data from the applications you used while you were running Windows. Always close your applications and exit from Windows before turning off your computer. Do not turn off the computer if you are in a computer lab.

CONCEPTS REVIEW

Label each of the elements of the Windows screen shown in Figure 21.

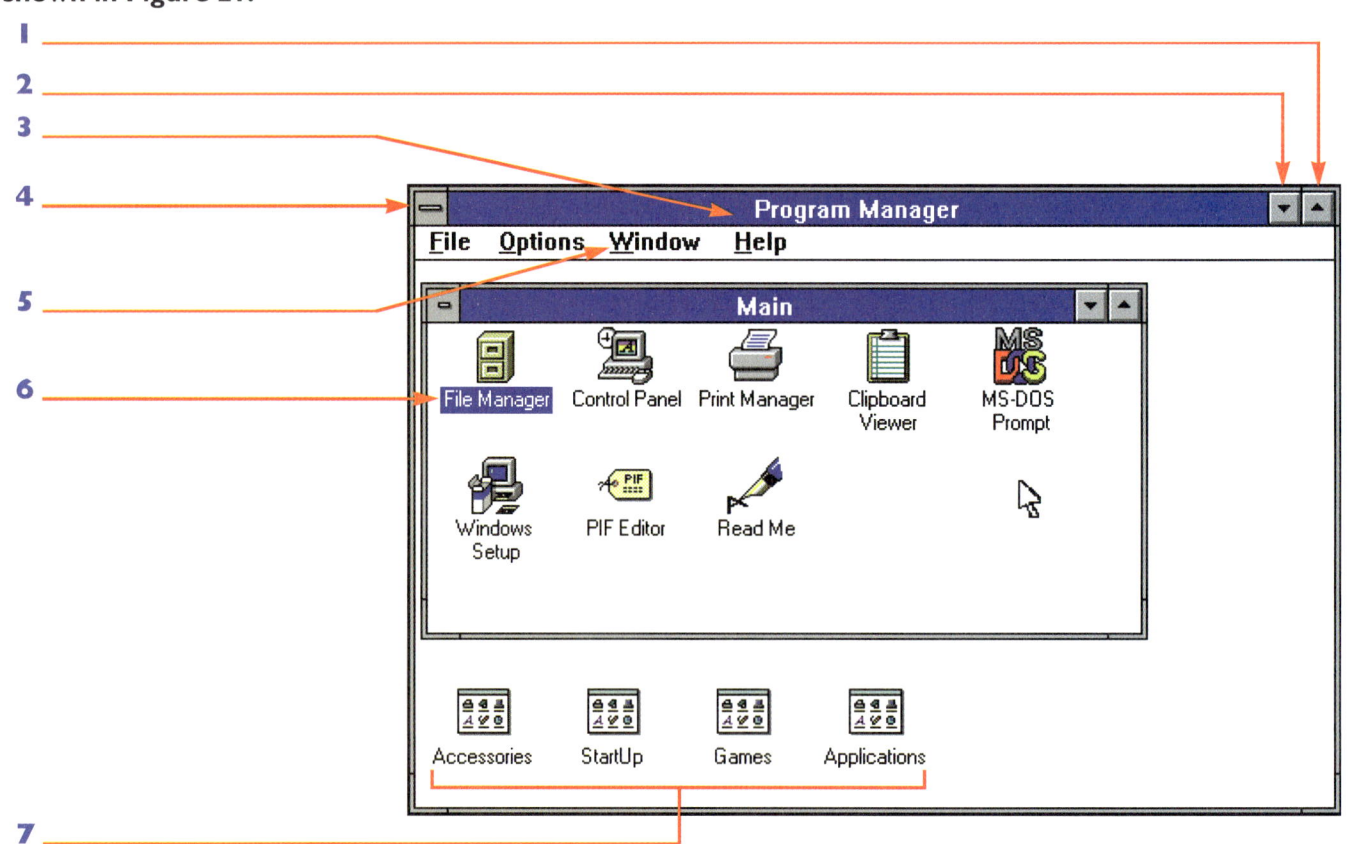

1. _____
2. _____
3. _____
4. _____
5. _____
6. _____
7. _____

FIGURE 21

Match each of the statements with the term it describes.

8. Shrinks an application window to an icon
9. Displays the name of the window or application
10. Serves as a launching pad for all applications
11. Requests more information that you supply before executing command
12. Lets the user point at screen menus and icons

a. Program Manager
b. Dialog box
c. Mouse
d. Title bar
e. Minimize button

Select the best answer from the list of choices.

13. The acronym GUI means:
    a. Grayed user information
    b. Group user icons
    c. Graphical user interface
    d. Group user interconnect

14. The term for starting Windows is:
    a. Prompting
    b. Launching
    c. Applying
    d. Processing

15 The small pictures that represent items such as applications are:
   a. Icons
   b. Windows
   c. Buttons
   d. Pointers

16 All of the following are examples of using a mouse, EXCEPT:
   a. Clicking the Maximize button
   b. Pressing [Enter]
   c. Pointing at the control menu box
   d. Dragging the Games icon

17 When Windows is busy performing a task, the mouse pointer changes to a(n):
   a. Hand
   b. Arrow
   c. Clock
   d. Hourglass

18 The term for moving an item to a new location on the desktop is:
   a. Pointing
   b. Clicking
   c. Dragging
   d. Restoring

19 The Clock, Notepad, and Calendar applications in Windows are known as:
   a. Menu commands
   b. Control panels
   c. Sizing buttons
   d. Desktop accessories

20 The Maximize button is used to:
   a. Return a window to its original size
   b. Expand a window to fill the computer screen
   c. Scroll slowly through a window
   d. Run programs from the main menu

21 What appears if a window contains more information than can be displayed in the window?
   a. Program icon
   b. Cascading menu
   c. Scroll bars
   d. Check box

22 A window is active when its title bar is:
   a. Highlighted
   b. Dimmed
   c. Checked
   d. Underlined

23 What is the term for changing the dimensions of a window?
   a. Selecting
   b. Resizing
   c. Navigating
   d. Scrolling

24 The menu bar provides access to an application's functions through:
   a. Icons
   b. Scroll bars
   c. Commands
   d. Control menu box

25 File Manager is a Windows application that lets you:
   a. Select a different desktop wallpaper
   b. Move a file from one location to another
   c. Type entries into a text file
   d. Determine what programs begin automatically when you start Windows

26 When your desktop is too cluttered, you can organize it by all the following methods, EXCEPT:
   a. Double-clicking the control menu box to close unneeded windows
   b. Using the Tile command to view all open group windows
   c. Using the Cascade command to open group window title bars
   d. Clicking File, clicking Exit Windows, then clicking OK

27 You can exit Windows by double-clicking the:
   a. Accessories group icon
   b. Program Manager control menu box
   c. Main window menu bar
   d. Control Panel application

APPLICATIONS REVIEW

1 Start Windows and identify items on the screen.

   a. Turn on the computer, if necessary.

   b. At the command prompt, type "WIN," then press [Enter]. After Windows loads, the Program Manager displays.

   c. Try to identify as many items on the desktop as you can, without referring to the lesson material. Then compare your results with Figure 1.

2 Minimize and restore the Program Manager window.

   a. Click the Minimize button. Notice that the Program Manager window reduces to an icon at the bottom of the screen. Now try restoring the window.

   b. Double-click the minimized Program Manager icon. The Program Manager window opens.

   c. Practice minimizing and restoring other windows on the desktop.

3 Resize and move the Program Manager window.

   a. Click anywhere inside the Program Manager window to activate the window.

   b. Move the mouse pointer over the lower-right corner of the Program Manager window. Notice that the mouse pointer changes to a double-ended arrow.

   c. Press and hold the mouse button and drag the corner of the window up and to the right until the Program Manager takes up the top third of your screen.

   d. Drag the Program Manager title bar to reposition the window at the bottom of the screen.

4 Practice working with menus and dialog boxes.

   a. Click Window on the Program Manager menu bar, then click Accessories (if you can't find it in the menu, click More Windows, then double-click it from the list that appears, scrolling if necessary).

   b. Double-click the Calculator icon to open the Calculator application.

   c. Click numbers and operators as you would on a handheld calculator to perform some simple arithmetic operations, like 22 multiplied by 3.99, to see how much it would cost to take a bus of 22 employees on the way back from a conference to a fast-food place for a quick lunch. (Multiplication is indicated by an asterisk *.)

   d. Double-click the Calculator control menu box when you are finished.

5 Practice working with files:

   a. Open File Manager from the Main group window.

   b. Be sure your Student Disk is in drive A or drive B, then double-click the drive icon containing your Student Disk.

   c. Double-click the drive C icon, then choose Tile from the Window menu. The open drive windows display, one above the other. If you have more windows open, double-click their control menu boxes to close them, then choose Tile again.

   d. Double-click the c:\ folder icon on the left side of the drive C window, then scroll down the left side of the drive C window using the vertical scroll bar to see the available directories. When you see the Windows folder icon, double-click it to see the directories and files available in the Windows folder.

   e. Scroll down the right side of the drive C window using the vertical scroll bar to see the files contained in the Windows folder. If you needed to copy a file from the Windows folder to your Student Disk, you could drag it from the list of files in the drive C window to the drive A window, but don't do so now.

6 Exit Windows.

   a. Close any open application by double-clicking the application's control menu box.

   b. Double-click the control menu box in the upper-left corner of the Program Manager window. The Exit Windows dialog box displays.

   c. Click OK. Windows closes and the DOS command prompt displays.

INDEPENDENT CHALLENGE

Windows 3.1 provides an on-line tutorial which can help you master essential Windows controls and concepts. The tutorial features interactive lessons that teach you how to use Windows elements such as the mouse, Program Manager, menus, and icons. The tutorial also covers how to use Help.

The tutorial material you should use depends on your level of experience with Windows. Some users might want to review the basics of the Windows work area. Others might want to explore additional Windows topics, such as managing files and customizing windows.

Ask your instructor or technical support person about how to use the Windows tutorial.

Microsoft® Excel 5.0
for Windows™

UNIT 1	Getting Started with Microsoft Excel 5.0 for Windows
UNIT 2	Building a Worksheet
UNIT 3	Revising a Worksheet
UNIT 4	Enhancing a Worksheet
UNIT 5	Working with Charts
UNIT 6	Working with Databases
UNIT 7	Automating Worksheet Tasks

Read This Before You Begin
Microsoft Excel 5.0

To the Student

The lessons and exercises in this book feature several ready-made Excel files provided to your instructor. To complete the step-by-step lessons, Applications Reviews, and Independent Challenges in this book, you must have a Student Disk. Your instructor will do one of the following: 1) provide you with your own copy of the disk; 2) have you copy it from the network onto your own floppy disk; or 3) have you copy the lesson files from a network into your own subdirectory on the network. Always use your own copies of the lesson and exercise files. See your instructor or technical support person for further information.

Using Your Own Computer

If you are going to work through this book using your own computer, you need a computer system running Microsoft Windows 3.1, Microsoft Excel 5.0 for Windows, and a Student Disk. *You will not be able to complete the step-by-step lessons in this book using your own computer until you have your own Student Disk.* This book assumes the default settings under a standard installation of Microsoft Excel 5.0 for Windows.

To the Instructor

Bundled with the instructor's copy of this book is a Student Disk. The Student Disk contains all the files your students need to complete the step-by-step lessons in the units, Applications Reviews, and Independent Challenges. As an adopter of this text, you are granted the right to distribute the files on the Student Disk to any student who has purchased a copy of the text. You are free to post all these files to a network or standalone workstations, or simply provide copies of the disk to your students. The instructions in this book assume that the students know which drive and directory contain the Student Disk, so it's important that you provide disk location information before the students start working through the units.

UNIT 1

OBJECTIVES

- Define spreadsheet software
- Start Microsoft Excel 5.0 for Windows
- View the Excel screen
- Work with Excel menus and dialog boxes
- Work with tools
- Get Help
- Move around the worksheet
- Name a sheet
- Close a workbook and exit Excel

Getting Started
WITH MICROSOFT EXCEL 5.0

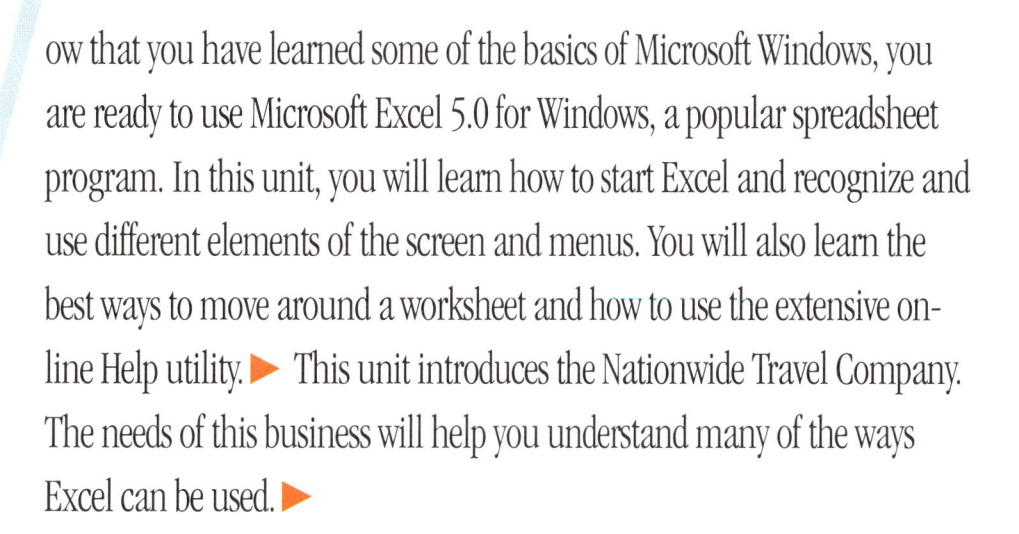

Now that you have learned some of the basics of Microsoft Windows, you are ready to use Microsoft Excel 5.0 for Windows, a popular spreadsheet program. In this unit, you will learn how to start Excel and recognize and use different elements of the screen and menus. You will also learn the best ways to move around a worksheet and how to use the extensive on-line Help utility. ▶ This unit introduces the Nationwide Travel Company. The needs of this business will help you understand many of the ways Excel can be used. ▶

Defining spreadsheet software

Excel is an electronic spreadsheet that runs on Windows computers. An **electronic spreadsheet** uses a computer to perform numeric calculations rapidly and accurately. See Table 1-1 for common ways spreadsheets are used in business. Like traditional paper-based spreadsheets, an electronic spreadsheet contains a **worksheet** area that is divided into columns and rows. The intersection of a column and a row, or **cell**, can contain text, numbers, formulas or a combination of all three. ▶ Cathy Martinez works in the Accounting Department at Nationwide Travel Company where they recently switched to Excel from a paper-based system. Figure 1-1 shows a budget worksheet that Cathy created using pencil and paper. Figure 1-2 shows the same worksheet that Cathy created using Excel. Cathy likes working with Excel more than the paper system for the following reasons:

STEPS

1. **Enter data quickly and accurately**. *With Excel, Cathy can enter information faster and more accurately than she could using the pencil and paper method. With Excel, she needs to enter only data and formulas, and Excel calculates the results.*

2. **Recalculate easily**. *Fixing errors using Excel is easy, and any results based on a changed entry are recalculated automatically.*

3. **Perform What-if Analysis**. *One of most powerful decision-making features of Excel is the ability to change data and then quickly recalculate changed results. Anytime you use a worksheet to answer the question "what if," you are performing a* **what-if analysis**. *For instance, if the advertising budget for May were increased to $3,000, Cathy could enter the new figure into the spreadsheet and immediately find out the impact on the overall budget.*

4. **Change the appearance of information**. *Excel provides powerful features for enhancing a spreadsheet so that information is visually appealing and easy to understand.*

5. **Create charts**. *Excel makes it easy to create charts based on information in a worksheet. With Excel, charts are automatically updated as data changes. The worksheet in Figure 1-2 shows a pie chart that graphically shows the distribution of expenses for the second quarter.*

6. **Share information with other users**. *It's easy for Cathy to share information with her colleagues who also use Excel. If she wants to use the data from someone else's worksheet, she accesses their files through the network or by disk.*

7. **Create new worksheets from existing ones quickly**. *It's easy for Cathy to take an existing Excel worksheet and quickly modify it to create a new one.*

8. **Organize information into a list**. *Cathy can take advantage of the Excel list feature to effectively organize information. A* **list**—*or database—is a collection of related information. Cathy now maintains a list of all employee names and addresses at Nationwide Travel so that she can keep track of personnel information.*

FIGURE 1-1:
Traditional paper worksheet

```
              Nationwide Travel Company

              Qtr 1    Qtr 2    Qtr 3    Qtr 4    Total

Net Sales    48,000   76,000   64,000   80,000   268,000

Expenses:

Salary        8,000    8,000    8,000    8,000    32,000
Interest      4,800    5,600    6,400    7,200    24,000
Rent          2,400    2,400    2,400    2,400     9,600
Ads           3,600    8,000   16,000   20,000    47,600
COG          16,000   16,800   20,000   20,400    73,200

Total Exp    34,800   40,800   52,800   58,000   186,400

Net Income   13,200   35,200   11,200   22,000    81,600
```

FIGURE 1-2:
Excel worksheet

Worksheet area

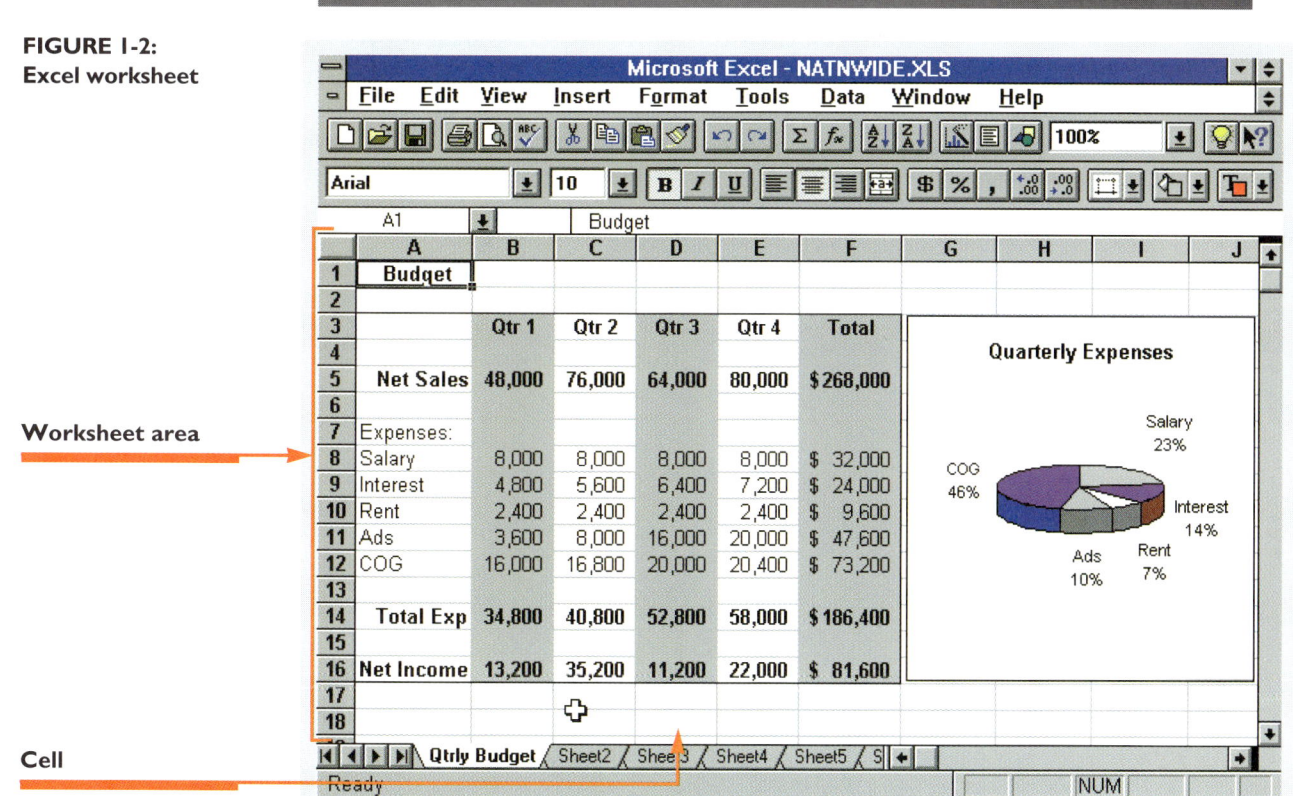

Cell

TABLE 1-1: Common business spreadsheet uses

USE	EXAMPLE
Maintain and analyze values	Calculating totals, averages, percentages, etc.
Visually represent values	Creating a chart based on worksheet values
Manipulate lists of data	Sorting, filtering, and analyzing data

EXCEL 5 UNIT I **GETTING STARTED** WITH MICROSOFT EXCEL 5.0

5

Starting Microsoft Excel 5.0 for Windows

To use Excel, you must first turn on the computer, access Microsoft Windows from the DOS prompt, then double-click the Microsoft Excel icon. A slightly different procedure might be required for computers on a network and those that use utility programs to enhance Microsoft Windows. ▶ Try starting Excel now.

Steps

1. **Make sure your computer and monitor are on and you are in the Windows Program Manager**
   If you need help, refer to the lesson "Starting Windows" in the Working with Windows section.

2. **Locate the Microsoft Office group icon, probably at the bottom of your screen**
   See Figure 1-3. The Microsoft Office group icon on your screen might already be maximized. If you have a window titled Microsoft Office on your screen, as shown in Figure 1-4, skip Step 3.

3. **Double-click the Microsoft Office group icon**
   The Microsoft Office group window opens and the Microsoft Excel icon displays, as shown in Figure 1-4. Your screen will probably look different depending on which applications are installed on your computer.

4. **Double-click the Microsoft Excel application icon**
   Excel opens and a blank worksheet appears. In the next lesson, you will familiarize yourself with the elements of a worksheet.

FIGURE 1-3: Microsoft Office group icon

Your desktop might look different, depending on the applications installed on your computer

Microsoft Office group icon

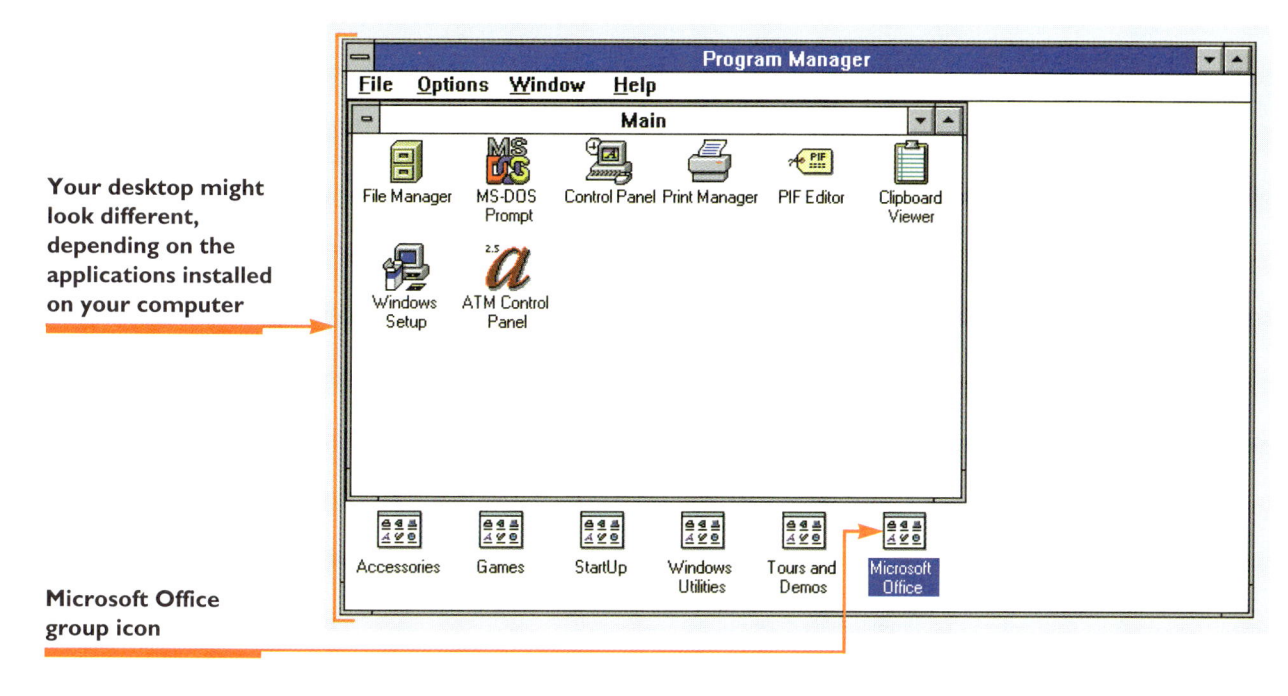

FIGURE 1-4: Microsoft Excel application icon in group window

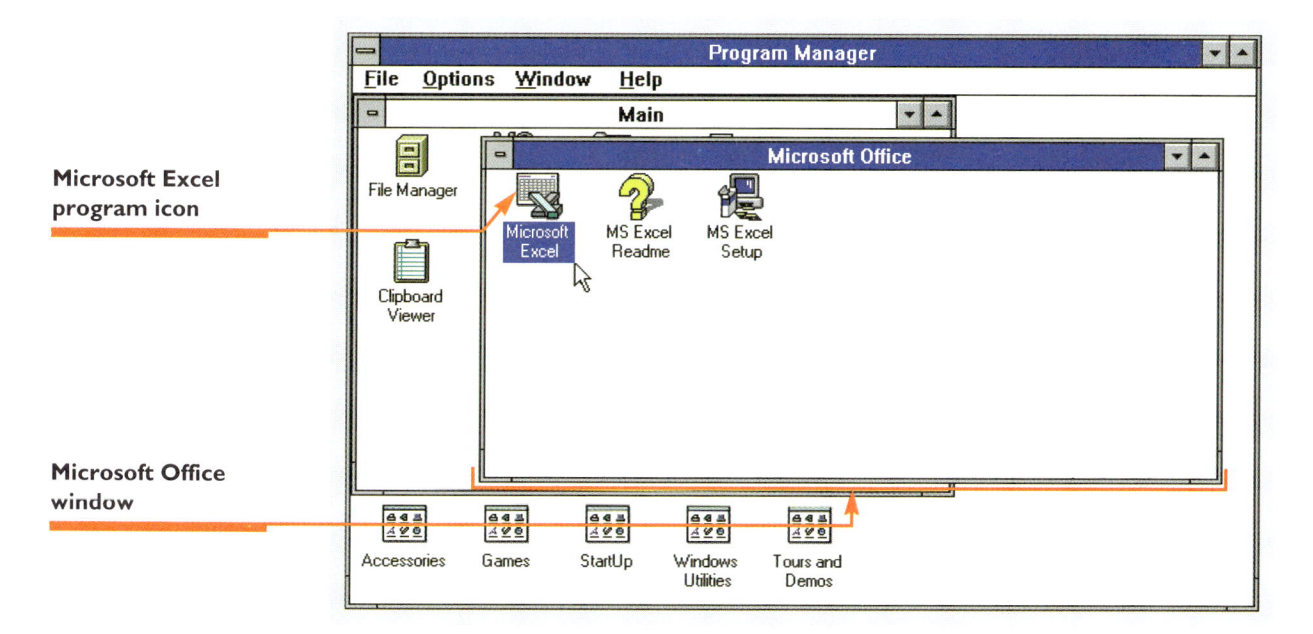

Microsoft Excel program icon

Microsoft Office window

TROUBLE?

If you don't have a Microsoft Office group icon, look for one called Microsoft Excel or a similar name.∎

EXCEL 5   UNIT 1   **GETTING STARTED** WITH MICROSOFT EXCEL 5.0

Viewing the Excel screen

When you start Excel, the computer displays both the **worksheet window**, the area where you enter data, and Excel screen elements. The screen elements enable you to create and work with worksheets. ▶ Familiarize yourself with the Excel worksheet window and screen elements by comparing the descriptions below to Figure 1-5.

- The **worksheet window** contains a grid of columns and rows. Columns are labeled alphabetically (A, B, C, etc.) and rows are labeled numerically (1, 2, 3 etc.). The worksheet window only displays a tiny fraction of the whole worksheet, which has a total of 256 columns and 16,384 rows. The intersection of a column and a row is a **cell**. Every cell has its own unique location, or **cell address**, which is identified by the coordinates of the intersecting column and row. For example, the cell address of the cell in the left-most corner of a worksheet is A1.

- The **cell pointer** is a dark border that highlights the cell in which you are working, or the **active cell**. In Figure 1-5, the cell pointer is located at A1, so A1 is the active cell. To make another cell active, click any other cell or press one of the pointer-movement keys on your keyboard.

- The **title bar** displays the application name (Microsoft Excel) and the filename of the open worksheet (in this case, Book1). The title bar also contains a control menu box and resizing buttons, which you learned about in the Working with Windows section.

- The **main menu bar** contains menus from which you choose Excel commands. As with all Windows applications, you can choose a menu command by clicking it with the mouse or by pressing [Alt] plus the underlined letter in the menu name.

- The **name box** displays the active cell address. In Figure 1-5, A1 displays in the name box, which means that A1 is the active cell.

- The **formula bar** allows you to enter or edit data in the worksheet.

- **Tools** are located on toolbars and provide easy access to a variety of commonly used Excel commands. To choose a tool, simply click it with the left mouse button. The face of any tool has a graphic representation of its function; for instance, the Print tool has a printer on it.

- **Sheet tabs** below the worksheet enable you to keep your work in collections called **workbooks**. Each workbook contains 16 worksheets, or sheets by default and can contain a maximum of 255 sheets. Sheet tabs can be given meaningful names. **Sheet tab scrolling buttons** help you move from one sheet to another.

- The **status bar** is located at the bottom of the Excel screen. The left side of the status bar provides a brief description of the active command or task in progress. The right of the status bar shows the status of important keys, such as the Caps Lock key and the Num Lock key.

FIGURE 1-5: Excel worksheet window and screen elements

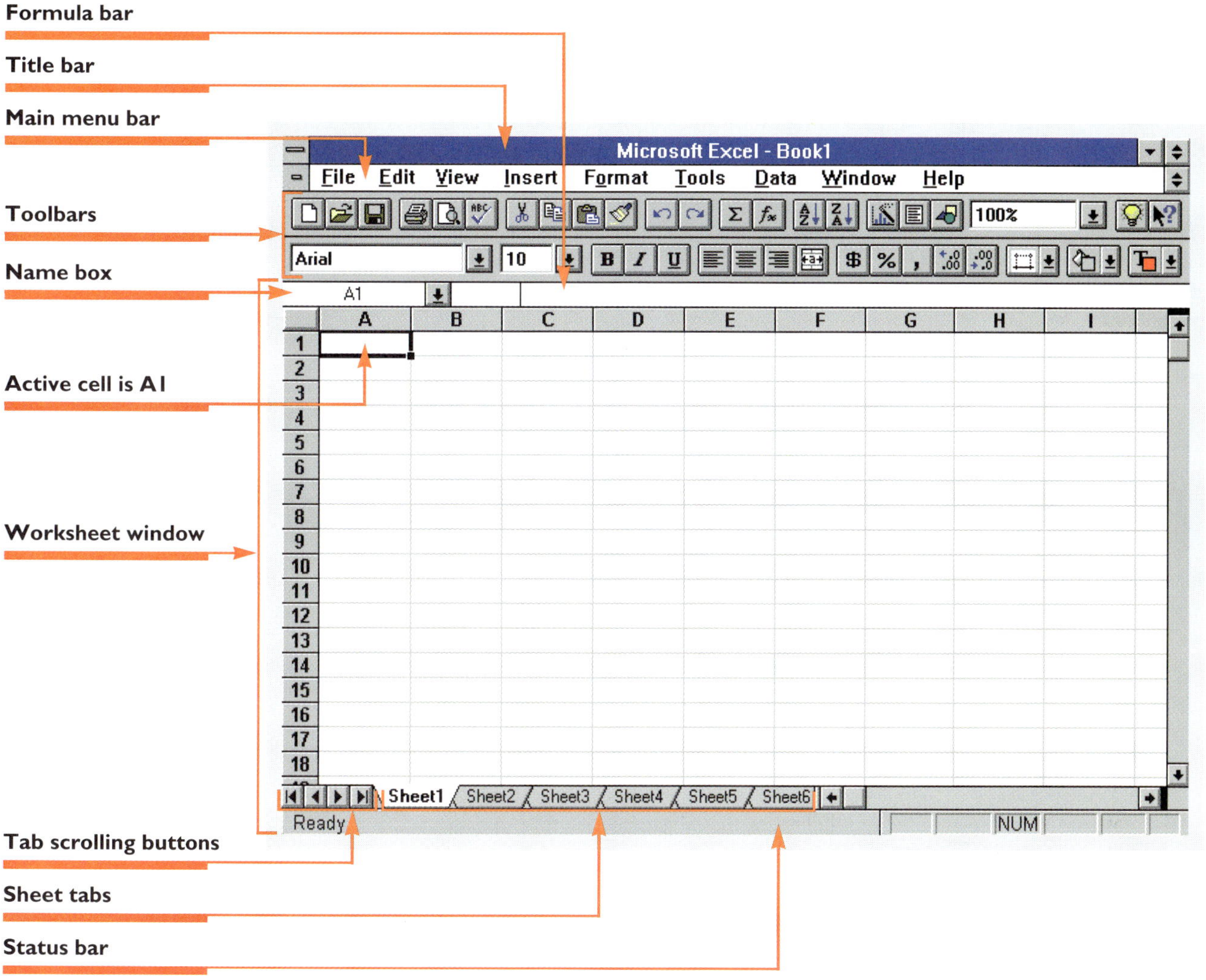

- Formula bar
- Title bar
- Main menu bar
- Toolbars
- Name box
- Active cell is A1
- Worksheet window
- Tab scrolling buttons
- Sheet tabs
- Status bar

EXCEL 5 UNIT 1 **GETTING STARTED** WITH MICROSOFT EXCEL 5.0

TROUBLE?

If your worksheet does not fill the screen as shown in Figure 1-5, click the maximize button. ■

Working with Excel menus and dialog boxes

Like other Windows applications, you choose many commands in Excel using menus that display dialog boxes. ▶ Use menu and dialog box commands to enter the title for Cathy Martinez's budget worksheet that you saw in Figure 1-2, earlier in this unit.

STEPS

1 Click cell **A1** to make it the active cell
The cell pointer surrounds cell A1, and "A1" displays in the name box.

2 Type **Budget** then press **[Enter]**
The word "Budget" appears in cell A1 aligned on the left side of the cell. To center this text in the cell, you will use a command from the Format menu.

3 Click cell **A1**, then click **Format** on the menu bar
The Format menu opens, displaying a list of commands relating to the appearance of the worksheet. See Figure 1-6. You also could have pressed [Alt][O] to open the Format menu. Notice that a description of the highlighted menu command displays in the status line.

4 Click **Cells**
The Format Cells dialog box displays. See Figure 1-7. Many dialog boxes in Excel have tabs similar to sheet tabs. These tabs separate the various formatting options into separate sub-dialog boxes. The sub-dialog box used last is the front-most tab. Your screen might show a different sub-dialog box than the one in Figure 1-7.

5 Click the **Alignment tab**
The Alignment tab moves to the front of the dialog box, providing options for changing the alignment of the text in the active cell. See Figure 1-8. One of the elements you'll see in Excel dialog boxes is the **check box**. Check boxes turn an option on or off.

6 In the Horizontal section, click the round circle next to the word Center
The round circle is called a **radio button**. Radio buttons display when only one option can be chosen in a dialog box.

7 Click **OK** or press **[Enter]**
If a command button in a dialog box has a dark border around it, you can press [Enter] to execute the command. The dialog box closes and the word Budget is centered in cell A1.

Using keyboard shortcuts

Pointer-movement keys can be used to make choices within a dialog box or menu. To choose a menu from the keyboard, press [Alt] and the underlined letter in the menu you want to select. To choose a command from a menu, use [↑] or [↓], then press [Enter], or press the underlined letter of the command you want to select. To open a new menu, use [→] or [←]. To move within a dialog box, press the underlined letter of the command you want to execute.

EXCEL 5 UNIT 1 **GETTING STARTED** WITH MICROSOFT EXCEL 5.0

Ellipsis (...) indicates a dialog box will display

FIGURE 1-6: Worksheet with Format menu open

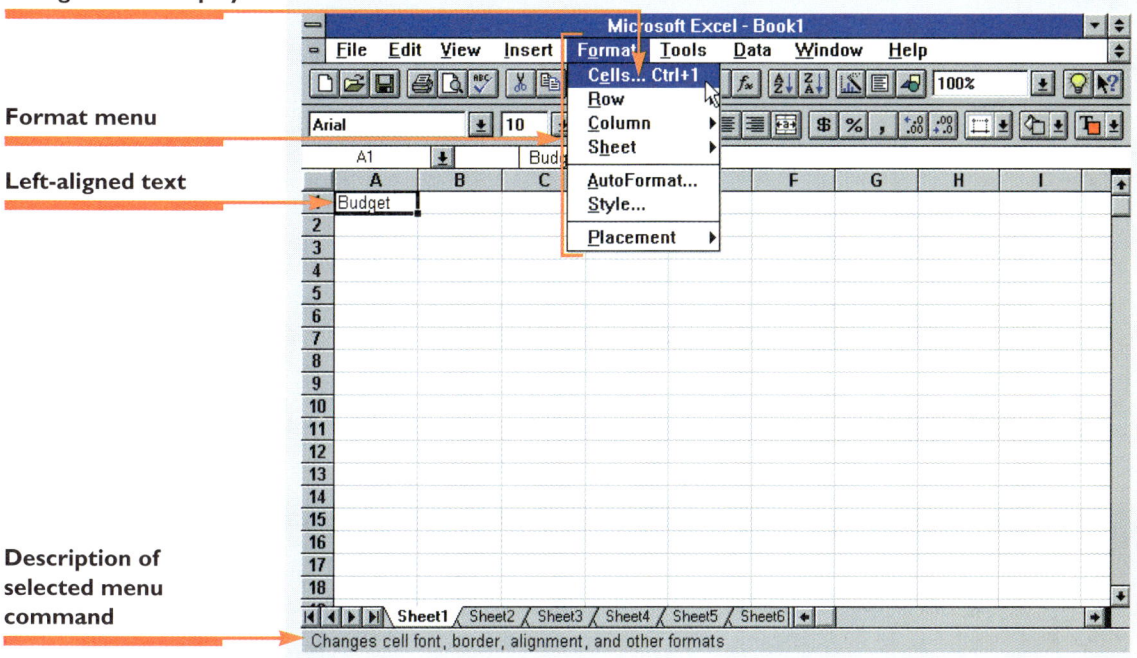

Format menu

Left-aligned text

Description of selected menu command

FIGURE 1-7: Format Cells dialog box

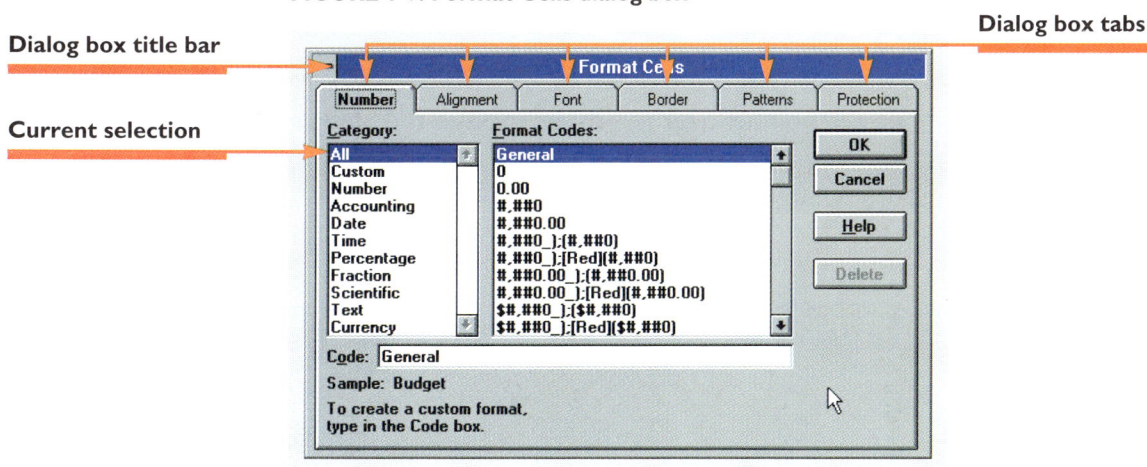

Dialog box title bar

Dialog box tabs

Current selection

FIGURE 1-8: Alignment tab in Format dialog box

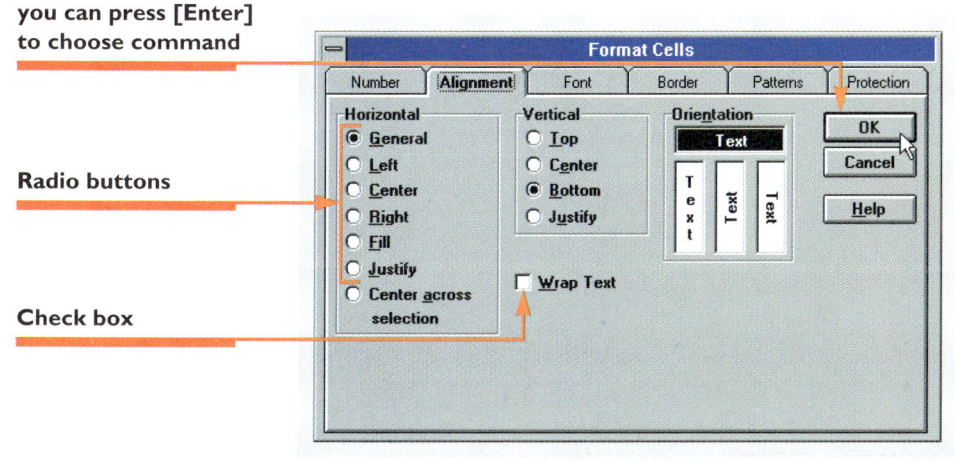

Dark border means you can press [Enter] to choose command

Radio buttons

Check box

QUICK TIP

To close a menu without choosing a command, click anywhere outside the menu, or press [Esc].

Working with tools

Buttons, or **tools**, give you easy access to a variety of commonly used Excel commands. Clicking a tool to execute a command offers a faster alternative to clicking a menu name and then clicking a command. Tools are organized in **toolbars**, as shown in Figure 1-9. The Standard and Formatting toolbars appear below the menu bar as part of the installation process. In addition to these toolbars, Excel provides toolbars that contain tools for specific purposes, such as charting (these will be discussed in future units). You can also customize the toolbars so they contain the tools for the commands you use most often. See Table 1-2 for a description of commonly used tools. ▶ Use the Bold tool to format your worksheet title, then explore some of the other tools.

STEPS

1. **Move the pointer over the Bold tool** [B], *but do not click the mouse button*
   When you move the pointer over a tool, the ToolTip associated with that tool displays the name of the tool under the pointer and a description of the tool displays in the status bar. See Figure 1-10.

2. **Click cell A1 to make it the active cell, then click** [B]
   The word Budget becomes bold. The Bold tool is a **toggle button**, which means that if you clicked the Bold tool again, you would remove the bold formatting. Notice that the Center and Bold tools appear depressed indicating that the cell contents are bold and centered.

3. **Move the pointer over the other tools in the Standard and Formatting toolbars to see the names of these tools**
   Notice how much can be accomplished using tools.

TABLE 1-2: Commonly used tools

TOOL	NAME	DESCRIPTION
	Open	Opens a file
	Save	Saves a file
	Print	Displays the Print dialog box
	Print Preview	Shows the worksheet as it will appear when it is printed
	Spelling	Checks the spelling in the current workbook
	Cut	Cuts the selected range to the Clipboard
	Copy	Copies the selected range to the Clipboard
	Paste	Pastes Clipboard contents into the current workbook at the location of the cell pointer
	Bold	Adds/removes bold formatting

FIGURE 1-9: Standard and Formatting toolbars

Standard toolbar
Formatting toolbar

FIGURE 1-10: Bold ToolTip

Text centered
ToolTip
Center tool

Description of selected tool

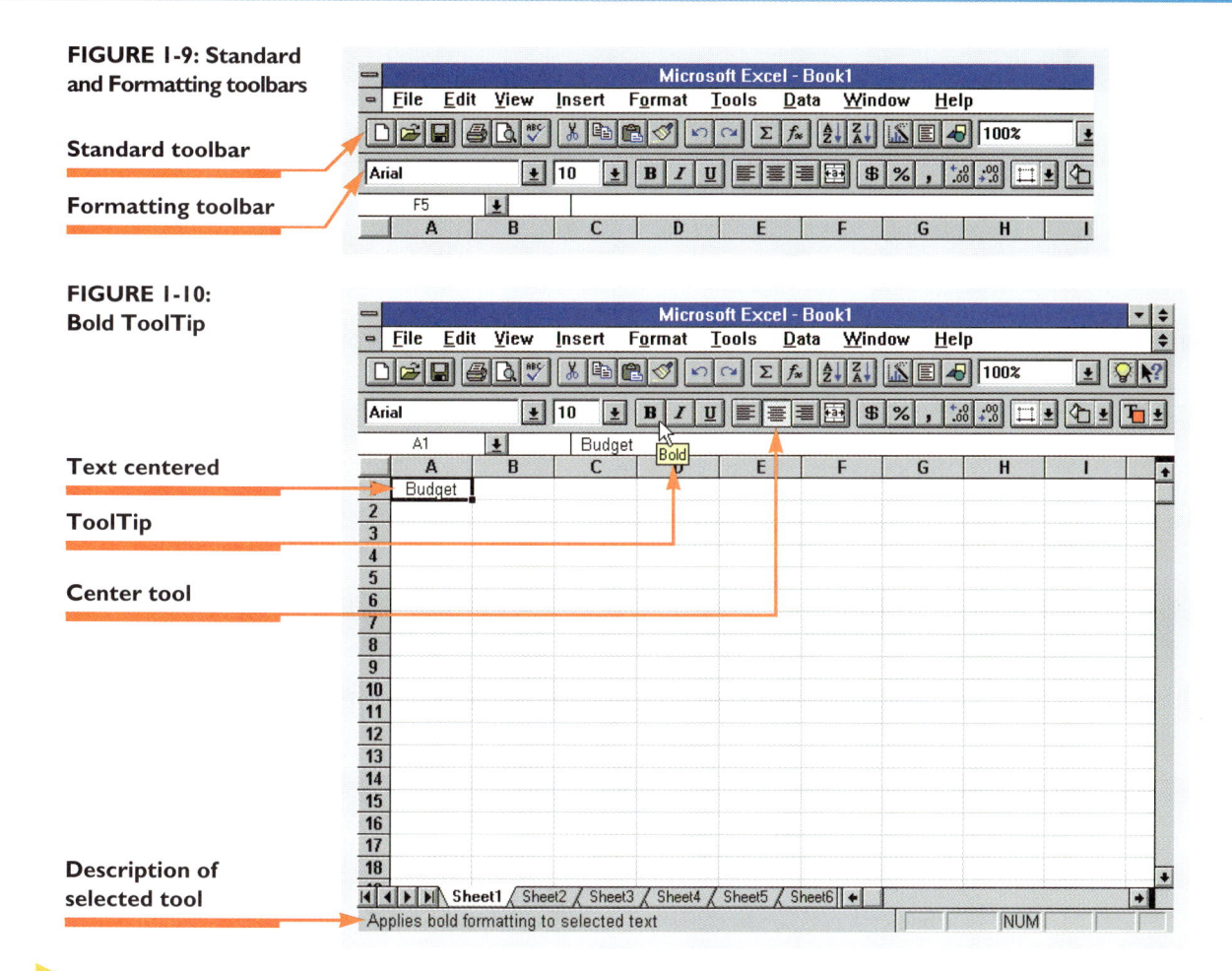

Repositioning toolbars

To allow you to make the best use of your work area, toolbars can be moved and resized. Each toolbar can be positioned along the top of the window, as shown in Figure 1-10, or it can float within its own window. To change a toolbar's location, click and hold the pointer in the gray area around the edge of the toolbar and drag the toolbar to a new location. To resize a **floating toolbar**, a toolbar that displays in the worksheet area, move the pointer over the edge of the toolbar window until it becomes ↕, then drag the pointer until the window is the size you want. In Figure 1-11, the Standard toolbar is floating. Compare Figure 1-11 with Figure 1-10.

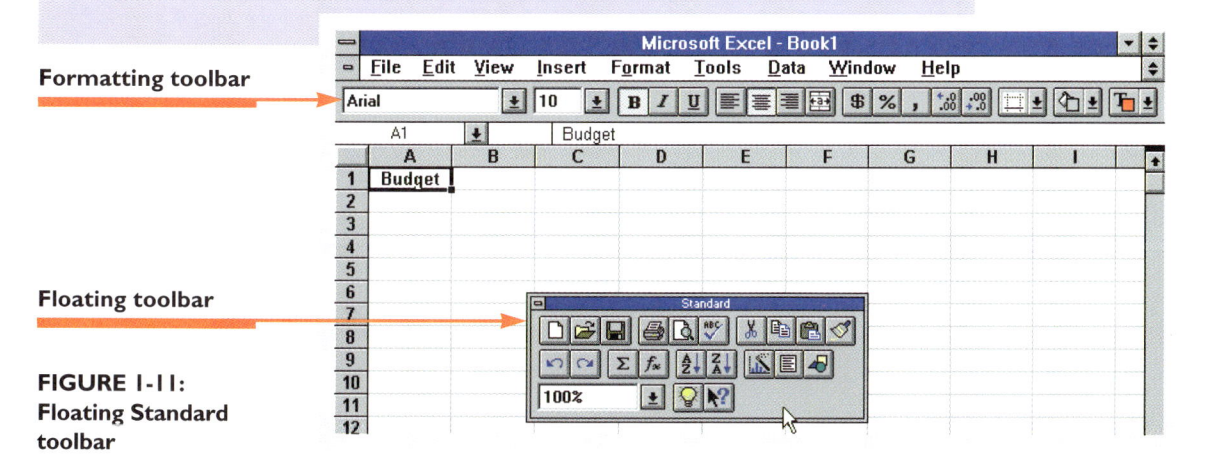

Formatting toolbar

Floating toolbar

FIGURE 1-11: Floating Standard toolbar

EXCEL 5 UNIT 1 **GETTING STARTED** WITH MICROSOFT EXCEL 5.0

Getting Help

Excel features an extensive on-line Help utility, which gives you immediate access to definitions, explanations, and useful tips. Help information displays in a separate window that you can resize and refer to as you work. ▶ Use Help now to find out more about toolbars.

STEPS

1 Click **Help** on the menu bar, then click **Search for Help on**
The Search dialog box displays. See Figure 1-12. You use this dialog box to look up a specific topic or feature.

2 In the search text box, type **too**
Notice as you type each letter, the alphabetically arranged topics scroll in the list box below the text box. After you type the second o, topics beginning with "too" appear in the list box.

3 Click **toolbars**, then click **Show Topics**
A list of related topics displays in the box at the bottom of the dialog box.

4 Scroll down the related topics list, click the topic **Moving and resizing toolbars**, then click **Go To**
Two windows open: Help and How To. If the How To window opens under the Help window, click within its border to make the How To window active. See Figure 1-13. Depending on the type and size of your monitor, the two windows might appear on different sides of the screen. The Help window contains buttons that will lead you through different sets of instructions for Excel. The Help buttons located under the Help menu bar are described in Table 1-3. The How To window displays information about moving and resizing toolbars, the topic you selected. You can click the green underlined words to open a window with more information about that topic.

5 Move the pointer to the green underlined topic floating toolbar until the pointer changes to 👆, then click the topic
A Help window containing a definition of a floating toolbar opens.

6 After reading the information, click anywhere outside the window or press **[Esc]** to close it
Clicking the Overview button will display general information about customizing toolbars in the Microsoft Excel Help window. You can use the Example and Practice button to see examples of the topic you've selected or to practice performing a task.

7 Click the **Overview button**
See Figure 1-14.

8 After reading the information in the window, click **File** in the Help window menu bar, then click **Exit**
The Help utility closes and you return to your worksheet.

EXCEL 5 UNIT 1 **GETTING STARTED** WITH MICROSOFT EXCEL 5.0

FIGURE 1-12:
Search dialog box

Type topic you want to search for

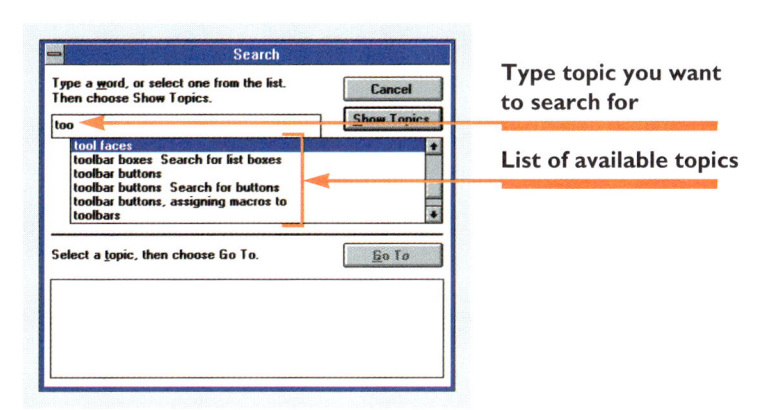

List of available topics

FIGURE 1-13:
How To window

Example and Practice button

Overview button

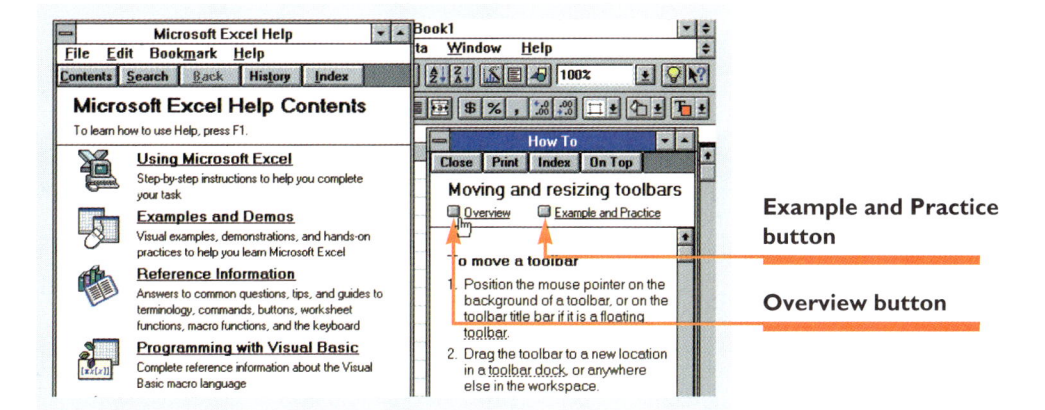

FIGURE 1-14:
Overview of Customizing Toolbars window

Example and Practice button

How To window

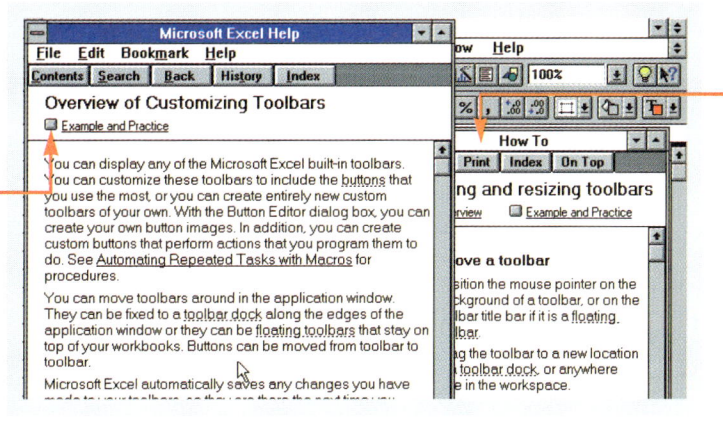

TABLE 1-3:
The Help buttons

BUTTON	DESCRIPTION
Contents	Displays the contents of the Help file by subject grouping
Search	Provides a dialog box where you can type the word or command you want help with
Back	Returns you to the previous topic
History	Displays a list of Help topics that you referred to recently
Index	Displays an alphabetical listing of topics

QUICK TIP

If you need help while you are working on a particular topic, click the Help tool on the Standard toolbar. The mouse pointer changes to . Point to a part of the worksheet or a command on a menu and then click the mouse button. Excel's Help utility displays context-sensitive information about your current location.

Moving around the worksheet

With over a billion cells available to you, it's important to know how to move around, or navigate, the worksheet. If you want to move up, down, or over one or two cells, you can simply press the pointer-movement keys ([↑], [↓], [←], [→]). To move longer distances within the worksheet window, you might prefer to use the mouse and click the desired cell address. If the desired cell address is not visible within the worksheet window, you can use the scroll bars or the Go To command to move the location into view. Table 1-4 lists helpful shortcuts for moving around the worksheet. ▶ Try navigating the worksheet now using a combination of methods.

1 Click cell **I18**
The cell pointer highlights cell I18 in the lower-right corner of your worksheet window.

2 Press **[→]**
The cell pointer moves over one cell to J18, moving the entire worksheet over one column. Notice that cell A1, which contains the word "Budget," is no longer visible in the worksheet window.

3 On the vertical scroll bar, click the **down arrow** once
The worksheet window scrolls down one row so that row 1 scrolls off the top of the window. You can move a window's contents one row or column at a time by clicking on the vertical or horizontal scroll bar arrows. You can move one screenful at a time by clicking on either side of a scroll box.

4 Click to the right of the horizontal scroll box
Columns K through S should appear in your worksheet window. If you need to travel a great distance across a worksheet, you can use the Go To command.

5 Click **Edit** on the menu bar, then click **Go To**
The Go To dialog box displays. See Figure 1-15. You could also press [F5] to display the Go To dialog box.

6 Type **Z1000** in the Reference text box

7 Click **OK** or press **[Enter]**
The cell pointer highlights cell Z1000 in the lower-right corner of the worksheet window. You could use the Go To command or the scroll bars to move the cell pointer back to the beginning of the worksheet, but there is a faster way to move the cell pointer directly to A1.

8 Press **[Ctrl][Home]**
The cell pointer highlights cell A1.

FIGURE 1-15: Go To dialog box

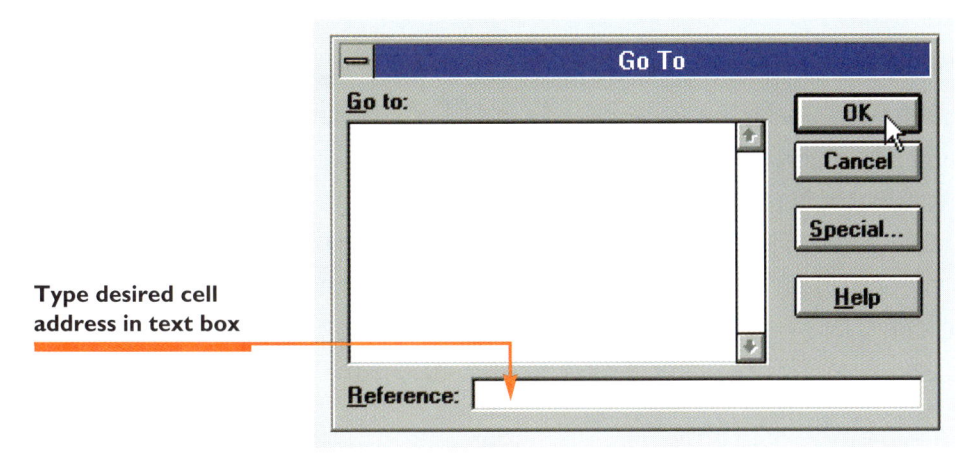

Type desired cell address in text box

TABLE 1-4: Getting around the worksheet window

TO MOVE	DO THIS
Up one row	Press [↑]
Down one row	Press [↓]
Left one cell	Press [←]
Right one cell	Press [→]
Up one screenful	Press [PgUp]
Down one screenful	Press [PgDn]
Left one screenful	Press [Alt][PgUp]
Right one screenful	Press [Alt][PgDn]
Left one column	Click the left arrow on the horizontal scroll bar
Right one column	Click the right arrow on the horizontal scroll bar
Cell A1	Press [Ctrl][Home]
Column A in current row	Press [Home]
Last active column in current row	Press [End]

Naming a sheet

Each workbook initially contains 16 worksheets. When the workbook is first open, the first worksheet is the active sheet. To move from sheet to sheet, click the desired sheet tab, located at the bottom of the worksheet window. Tab scrolling buttons, located to the left of the sheet tabs, allow rapid movement among the sheets. ▶ To make it easier to identify the sheets in a workbook, you can name each sheet. The name appears on the sheet tab. For instance, sheets within a single workbook could be named for individual sales people to better track performance goals. ▶ Cathy practices moving from sheet to sheet and decides to name a sheet in her workbook.

Steps

1 Click the Sheet2 tab
Sheet2 becomes active. Its tab moves to the front while the tab for Sheet1 moves to the background. The word "Budget" disappears from view because it is in cell A1 of Sheet1.

2 Click the Sheet5 tab
Sheet5 becomes active. Now you'll rename Sheet1 so it has a name that is easily remembered.

3 Double-click the Sheet1 tab
The Rename Sheet dialog box displays with the sheet name (Sheet1) selected in the Name text box. Double-clicking a sheet tab opens the Rename Sheet dialog box. You could also click Format in the menu bar, click Sheet, and then click Rename to display the Rename Sheet dialog box.

4 Type Qtrly Budget in the Name text box
See Figure 1-16. The new name automatically replaced the default name in the Name text box. Worksheet names can have up to 31 characters including spaces and punctuation.

5 Click OK or press [Enter]
Notice that the first sheet tab is now named "Qtrly Budget." See Figure 1-17.

6 Double-click Sheet2 and rename this sheet Additional Info

FIGURE 1-16: Rename Sheet dialog box

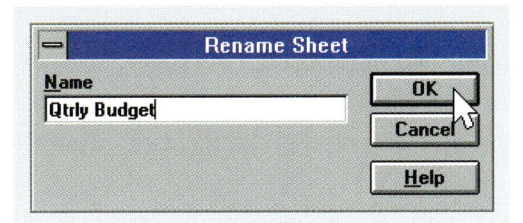

FIGURE 1-17: Renamed sheet tab

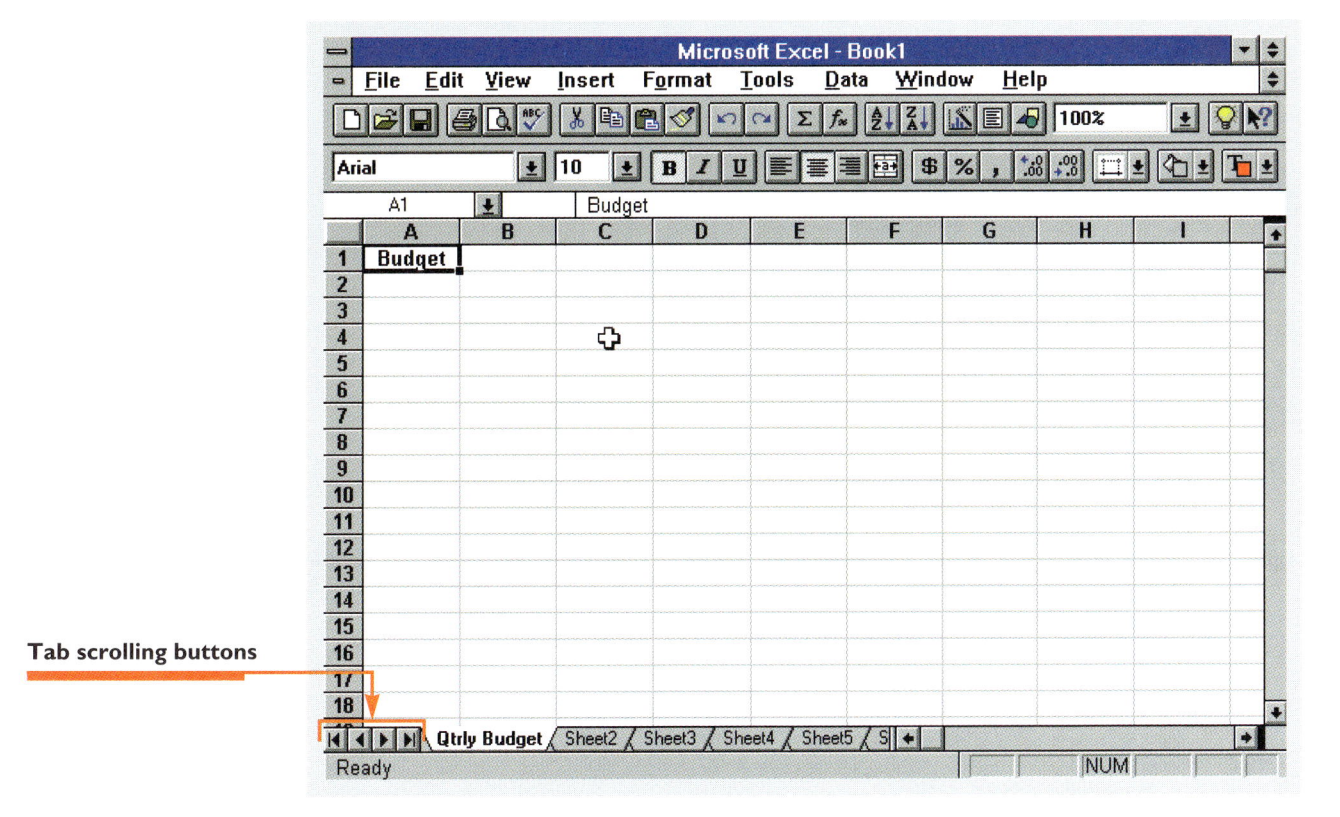

Tab scrolling buttons

Moving sheets

You can easily rearrange worksheets in a workbook. To move a sheet, move the mouse pointer to its tab, click and hold the mouse button, then drag the sheet tab to its new location. A small arrow and an icon of a document just above the sheet names indicate the new location of the worksheet, as shown in Figure 1-18.

New location indicator

FIGURE 1-18: Moving Sheet3 after Qtrly Budget sheet

EXCEL 5 UNIT 1 GETTING STARTED WITH MICROSOFT EXCEL 5.0

Closing a workbook and exiting Excel

When you have finished working on a workbook, you need to save the file and close it. To close a file, click Close on the File menu. ▶ When you have completed all your work in Excel, you need to exit the application. To exit Excel, click Exit on the File menu.

Steps

1 Click **File** on the menu bar
See Figure 1-19.

2 Click **Close**
You could also double-click the workbook control menu box instead of choosing File Close. The Close dialog box displays, asking if you want to save changes in "Book1" before closing. See Figure 1-20. Because this was only a practice session, there is no need to save the file.

3 Click **No**
Excel closes the workbook you were working in and displays a blank worksheet window. Notice that the menu bar contains only the File and Help menu choices.

4 Click **File**, then click **Exit**
You could also double-click the application control menu box. Excel closes and computer memory is freed up for other computing tasks.

5 Click the Minimize button in the Excel or Microsoft Office group window to reduce the window to a group icon

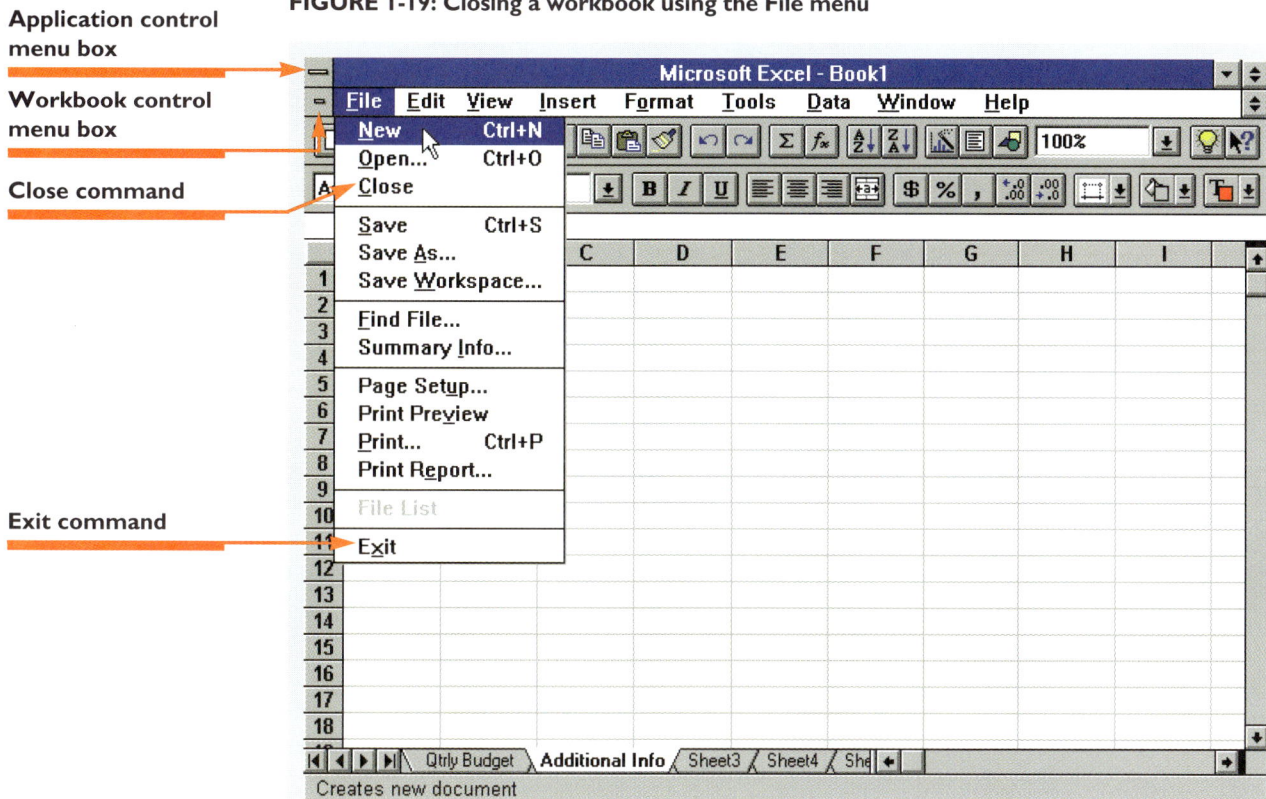

FIGURE 1-19: Closing a workbook using the File menu

Application control menu box

Workbook control menu box

Close command

Exit command

FIGURE 1-20: Save Changes dialog box

QUICK TIP

To exit Excel and close several files at once, choose Exit from the File menu. Excel will prompt you to save changes to each workbook before exiting.■

EXCEL 5 UNIT 1 **GETTING STARTED** WITH MICROSOFT EXCEL 5.0

21

EXCEL 5 UNIT I GETTING STARTED WITH MICROSOFT EXCEL 5.0

CONCEPTSREVIEW

Label each of the elements of the Excel worksheet window shown in Figure 1-21.

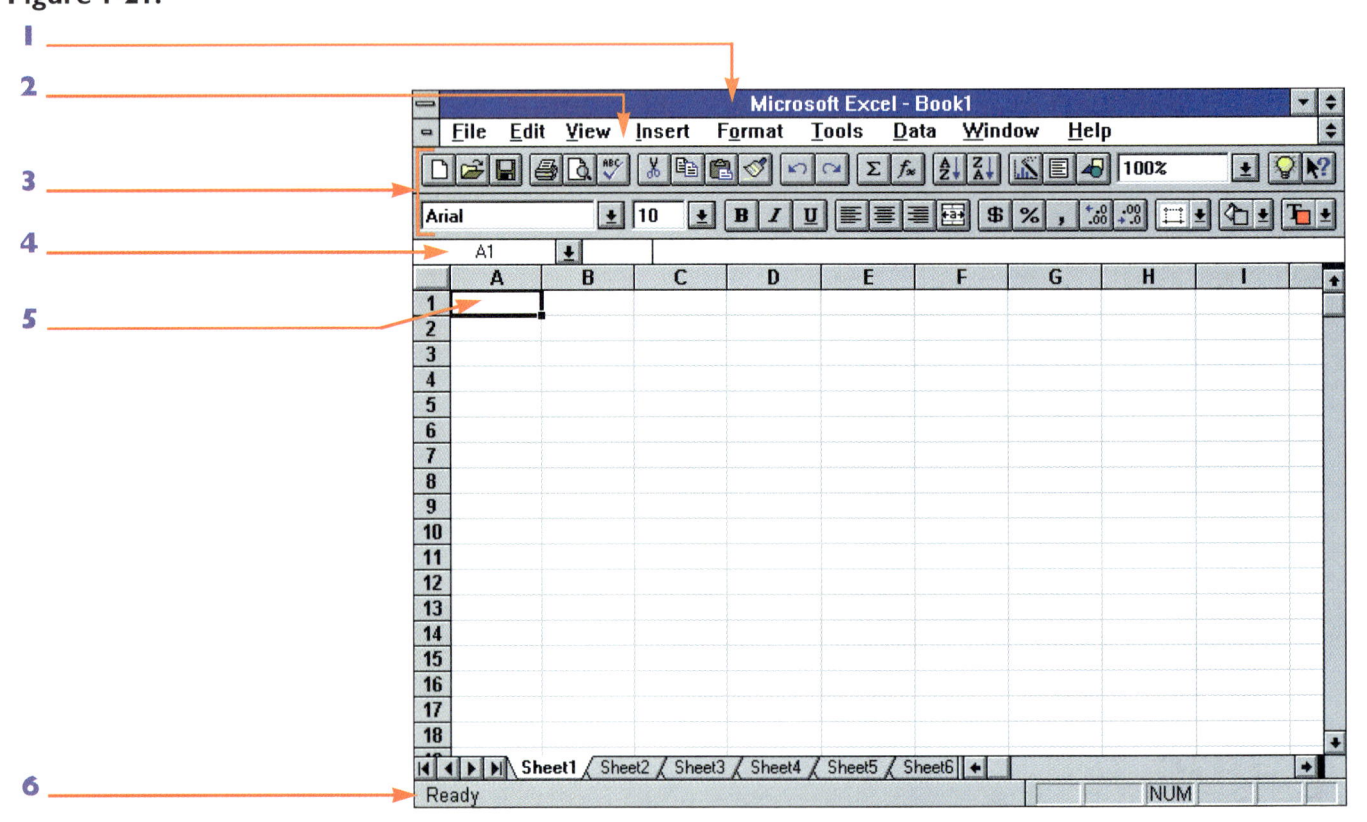

1. _____
2. _____
3. _____
4. _____
5. _____
6. _____

FIGURE 1-21

Match each of the terms with the statement that describes its function.

7. Sheet that contains a grid of columns and rows
8. The intersection of a column and row
9. Graphic symbol that depicts a task or function
10. Area that displays the worksheet name
11. Rectangle that indicates the worksheet cell you are currently working in

a. Cell pointer
b. Tool
c. Worksheet
d. Cell
e. Title bar

Select the best answer from the list of choices.

12. An electronic spreadsheet can perform all of the following tasks, *except*:
    a. Displaying information visually
    b. Calculating data accurately
    c. Planning worksheet objectives
    d. Recalculating updated information

13. You can move one screenful to the right by pressing:
    a. [PgUp]
    b. [Alt][PgDn]
    c. [Ctrl][PgUp]
    d. [Up Arrow]

14 Which key(s) do you press to move quickly to cell A1?

   a. [Ctrl][Home]

   b. [Alt]

   c. [Esc][Home]

   d. [Enter]

15 You can get Excel Help any of the following ways, *except*:

   a. Clicking Help on the menu bar

   b. Pressing [F1]

   c. Clicking the Help tool on the Standard toolbar

   d. Minimizing the application window

16 How do you move the worksheet to the right one column?

   a. Press [Enter]

   b. Click the right arrow on the horizontal scroll bar.

   c. Press [Esc]

   d. Press [Alt][R]

APPLICATIONS REVIEW

1 Launch Excel and identify items on the worksheet.

   a. Make sure your computer is on and Windows is running.

   b. Double-click the Microsoft Office group icon if the window is not maximized.

   c. Double-click the Microsoft Excel application icon.

   d. Try to identify as many items on the worksheet as you can, without referring to the lesson material.

2 Explore Excel menus.

   a. Click Edit on the menu bar. Notice that a description of the highlighted Undo command displays in the status bar.

   b. Drag through the commands on the Edit menu so that you can review brief descriptions in the status bar.

   c. Click Format on the menu bar.

   d. Move through the commands using [↓] and review the descriptions in the status bar.

   e. Review other commands on the Excel menu bar in the same fashion.

3 Practice moving the cell pointer in the worksheet.

   a. Press [Ctrl][Home]. The cell pointer moves to the upper-left corner of the worksheet. This is cell A1, as shown in the name box.

   b. Press [→] once to move the cell pointer right one column. The name box displays B1.

   c. Press [↓] twice. Watch the cell pointer move down two rows to cell B3.

   d. Click the right arrow on the horizontal scroll bar. The screen shifts the column display to the right by one column.

   e. Click the left arrow on the horizontal scroll bar. The screen shifts back to its original column display.

4 Practice moving within a workbook and naming a sheet.

   a. Double-click the Sheet3 sheet tab.

   b. Type "March" in the Rename Sheet dialog box.

   c. Click the Sheet4 tab.

   d. Click the Sheet2 tab.

   e. Double-click the Sheet1 tab.

   f. Type "January" in the Rename Sheet dialog box.

5 Explore Excel Help.

   a. Click Help on the menu bar.

   b. Click Search for Help on. The Search dialog box displays.

   c. Identify all of the buttons that appear in the Search dialog box.

d. Click the down arrow on the topics list box scroll bar to view available topics.

e. Select a topic from the list box, then click Show Topics.

f. Select a topic to read, then click Go To.

g. Click File on the Help window menu bar, then click Exit.

6 Practice minimizing and restoring the worksheet window.

a. Click the Minimize button in the worksheet window. Make sure you click the worksheet Minimize button and not the application Minimize button. The worksheet window minimizes to an icon on the screen.

b. Double-click the Book1 workbook icon to restore it to its original size.

7 Close the workbook and exit Excel.

a. Click File on the menu bar then click Close. The Save Changes dialog box asks if you want to save any changes. You do not want to save this worksheet file.

b. Click No to close the dialog box.

c. If necessary, close any other worksheets you may have opened. Follow the steps above to do so.

d. Click File on the menu bar then click Exit. Excel closes.

INDEPENDENT CHALLENGES

Excel provides on-line Help that explains procedures and gives you examples and demos. Covered are such elements as the active cell, status bar, tools, and dialog boxes. Help provides detailed information about Excel commands and options. Learn to explore on-line Help by clicking Examples and Demos from the Help menu. Read all topics within "Using Toolbars" and "Selecting Cells, Choosing Commands." Use "Search for Help on" dialog boxes, active cell, and status bar. Return to your workbook when finished.

Spreadsheet software has many possible uses that can effect the way work is done. Some examples of how Excel can be used are discussed in the beginning of this unit. Use your own personal or business experiences to come up with ten different examples of how Excel could be used in a business setting.

To complete this independent challenge:

1 Think of five different business functions which would be more efficient if done in a worksheet.

2 Illustrate each function in a sketch. See Figure 1-22 for an example of a payroll worksheet.

3 Hand in each of these sketches.

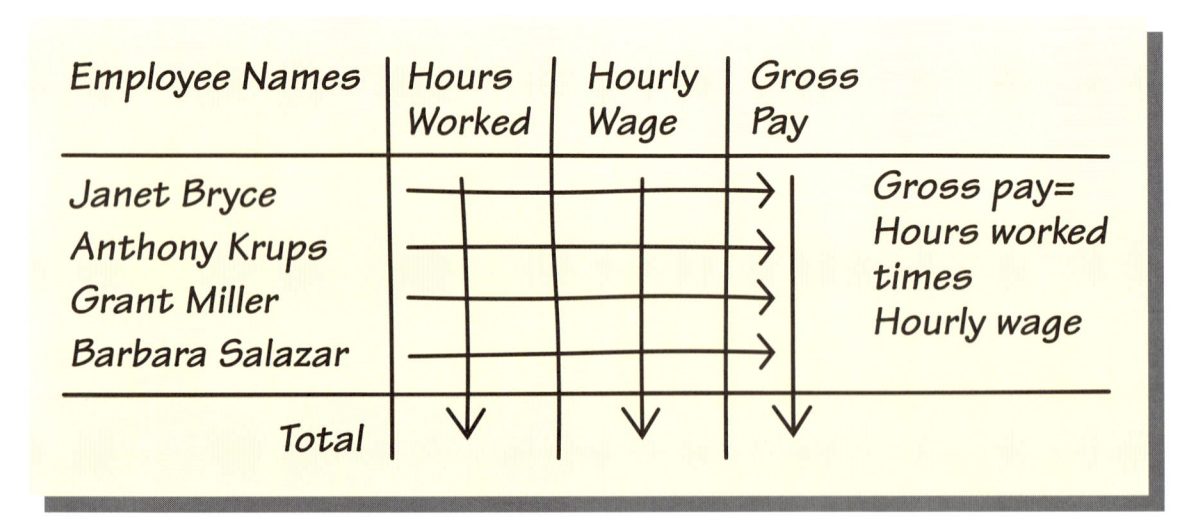

Employee Names	Hours Worked	Hourly Wage	Gross Pay	
Janet Bryce			→	Gross pay= Hours worked times Hourly wage
Anthony Krups			→	
Grant Miller			→	
Barbara Salazar			→	
Total	↓	↓	↓	

FIGURE 1-22

UNIT 2

OBJECTIVES

▶ Plan and design a worksheet

▶ Enter labels

▶ Enter values

▶ Edit cell entries

▶ Work with ranges

▶ Enter formulas

▶ Use Excel funtions

▶ Save a workbook

▶ Preview and print a worksheet

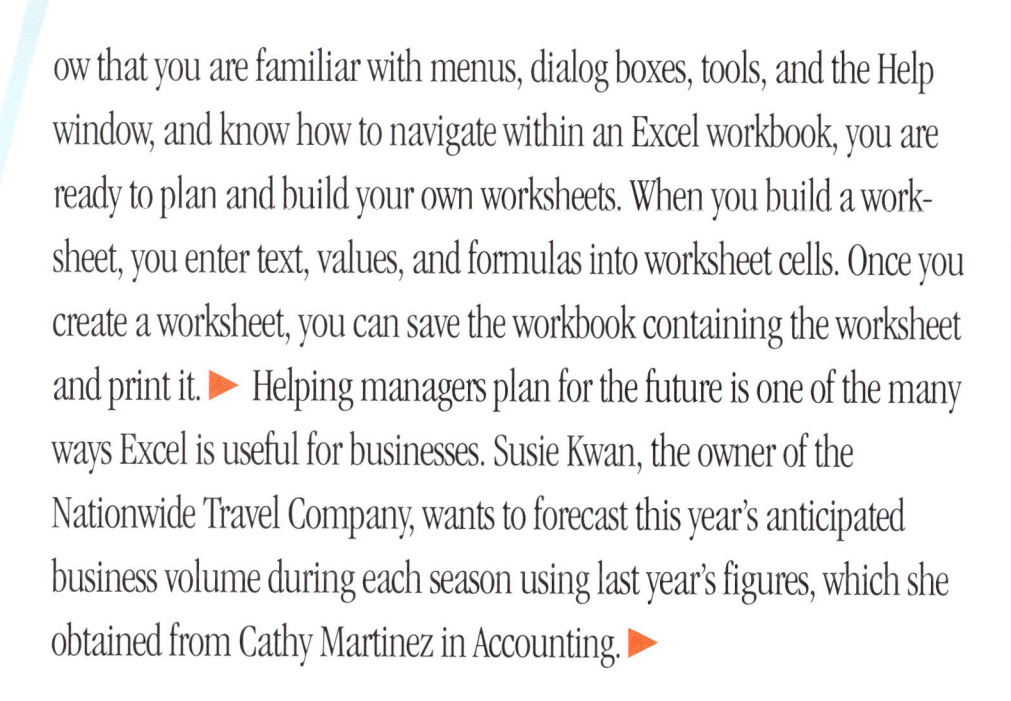

Building
A WORKSHEET

Now that you are familiar with menus, dialog boxes, tools, and the Help window, and know how to navigate within an Excel workbook, you are ready to plan and build your own worksheets. When you build a worksheet, you enter text, values, and formulas into worksheet cells. Once you create a worksheet, you can save the workbook containing the worksheet and print it. ▶ Helping managers plan for the future is one of the many ways Excel is useful for businesses. Susie Kwan, the owner of the Nationwide Travel Company, wants to forecast this year's anticipated business volume during each season using last year's figures, which she obtained from Cathy Martinez in Accounting. ▶

Planning and designing a worksheet

Before you start entering data into a worksheet, you need to know the goal and approximate appearance of the worksheet. At the Nationwide Travel Company, Susie decides to forecast summer tour sales for 1995 first. Susie's sales goal for the 1995 summer season is to increase the 1994 summer sales totals by 20%. Susie's sketch of her worksheet is shown in Figure 2-1. Susie uses the worksheet sketch and the following planning guidelines to plan her worksheet.

1. **Determine the purpose of the worksheet and give it a meaningful title.**
   Susie needs to forecast summer tours sales for 1995. Susie titles the worksheet "1995 Summer Tour Sales Forecast."

2. **Determine your worksheet's desired results, sometimes called output.**
   Susie needs to determine what the 1995 sales totals will be if sales increased by 20% over 1994 sales.

3. **Collect all the information, sometimes called input, that will produce the results you want to see.**
   Susie gathers together her sales data for the 1994 summer tour season. The season runs from June through August. The types of tours sold in these months include Bike, Raft, Horse, and Bus.

4. **Determine the calculations, or formulas, necessary to achieve the desired results.**
   First, Susie needs to total the number of tours sold for each month of the 1994 season. Then she needs to add these totals together to determine the grand total of 1994 summer tour sales. Finally, the 1994 monthly totals and grand total must be multiplied by 1.2 to calculate a 20% increase for the following year.

5. **Draw a rough sketch on paper to decide how the worksheet will look, that is, where the labels and values will go. Labels are text entries that describe and help you understand the data in a worksheet. Values are the numbers used in calculations.**
   Susie decides to put tour types in the rows, and the months in the columns. She enters the tour sales data in her sketch and indicates where the monthly sales totals and the grand total should go. Below the totals, she writes out the formula for determining a 20% increase in sales for 1995.

FIGURE 2-1: Worksheet sketch showing labels, values, and calculations

	June	July	August	Totals
\multicolumn{5}{c}{1995 Summer Tours Sales Forecast}				
Bike	14	10	6	3 month total
Raft	7	8	12	
Horse	12	7	6	
Bus	1	2	9	↓
Totals	June Total	July Total	August Total	Grand Total for 1994
1995 Sales	Total x 1.2	→		

Entering labels

Labels are used to identify the data in the rows and columns of a worksheet. They are also used to make your worksheet readable and understandable. For these reasons, you should enter all labels in your worksheet first. Labels can contain text and numerical information not used in calculations such as dates, times, or address numbers. Labels are left-aligned by default. ▶ Using Susie's sketch as a guide, start building her worksheet by entering the labels.

STEPS

1. **Start Excel as described in Unit 1 and make sure you have an empty workbook on your screen**

2. **Click cell B4 to make it the active cell**
   Notice that the cell address B4 displays in the name box. Now enter the worksheet title.

3. **Type 1995 Summer Tours Sales Forecast, then click the Enter button** ✓
   You must click ✓ or use one of the other methods shown in Table 2-1 to confirm your entry. Notice that the title does not fit in cell B4 and spreads across several columns. See Figure 2-2. If a label does not fit in a cell, Excel displays the remaining characters in the next cell as long as it is empty. Otherwise, the label is cut off. The contents of B4 display in the formula bar. Whenever a cell contains both text and numbers, Excel recognizes the entry as a label. If you want to enter a value as a label, you type an apostrophe (') before the first number.

4. **Click cell A6, type Bike, then press [Enter] to complete the entry and move the cell pointer to cell A7; type Raft in cell A7, then press [Enter]; type Horse in cell A8, then press [Enter]; type Bus in cell A9, then press [Enter]**
   Now enter the labels for the rows containing the totals and the 1995 sales forecast.

5. **Click cell A11, type Total, then press [Enter]; click cell A13, type 1995 Sales, then press [Enter]**
   Now enter the first label for the summer month sales.

6. **Click cell B5, type June, then click the Enter button** ✓**; click cell C5, type July, then click** ✓**; click cell D5, type August, then click** ✓

7. **Click cell E5, type Total, then click** ✓
   All the labels for Susie's worksheet are now entered. See Figure 2-3.

FIGURE 2-2: Worksheet with title entered

- Enter button
- Formula bar
- Title spreads across columns

FIGURE 2-3: Worksheet with labels entered

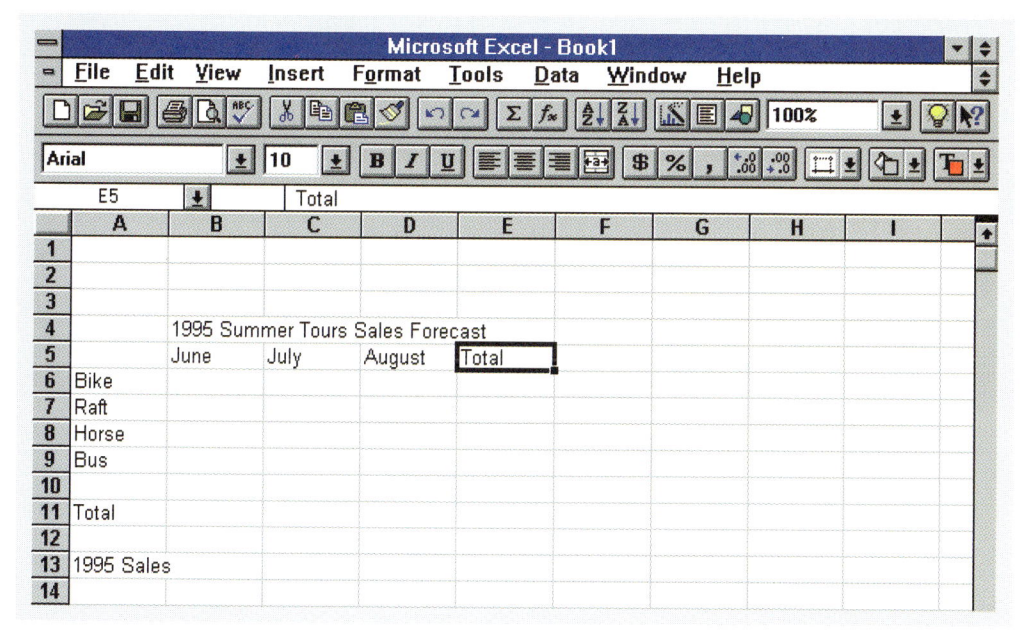

TABLE 2-1:
Confirming cell entries

ACTION	CONFIRMS ENTRY THEN
Click ✓	Cell pointer stays in current cell
Press [Enter]	Moves the cell pointer one row down
Press [Shift][Enter]	Moves the cell pointer one row up
Press [Tab]	Moves the cell pointer one column to the right
Press [Shift][Tab]	Moves the cell pointer one column to the left
Click in another cell	Moves the cell pointer to the cell that is clicked

TROUBLE?

Cell entries can be edited after they have been confirmed. Select the cell you want to edit and press [F2]. Use [Backspace] and [Delete] to make any corrections, then click the Enter button ✓ or press [Enter] to confirm the corrected entry.■

EXCEL 5 UNIT 2 BUILDING A WORKSHEET

29

Entering Values

Values, which include numbers, formulas, and functions, are used in calculations. Excel recognizes an entry as a value when it is a number or begins with one of these symbols +, -, =, @, #, or $. All values are right-aligned by default.

▶ Enter the sales data from the 1994 summer season into Susie's worksheet.

STEPS

1. Click cell **B6**, type **14**, then press **[Enter]**; type **7** in cell B7, then press **[Enter]**; type **12** in cell B8, then press **[Enter]**; type **1** in cell B9, then press **[Enter]**

   All the tour sales for the month of June are now entered. Now enter the sales for the month of July.

2. Click cell **C6**, type **10**, then press **[Enter]**; type **8** in cell C7, then press **[Enter]**; type **7** in cell C8, then press **[Enter]**; type **2** in cell C9, then press **[Enter]**

   Next enter the tour sales for August.

3. Click cell **D6**, type **6**, then press **[Enter]**; type **12** in cell D7, then press **[Enter]**; type **6** in cell D8, then press **[Enter]**; type **9** in cell D9, then press **[Enter]**

   All the labels and data are entered. Compare your worksheet to Figure 2-4.

FIGURE 2-4: Worksheet with labels and values entered

Labels →
Values →

QUICK TIP

To enter a number, such as the year 1995, as a label so it will not be included in a calculation, type an apostrophe (') before the number. ■

EXCEL 5 UNIT 2 **BUILDING** A WORKSHEET

31

Editing cell entries

You can change the contents of any cells at any time. To edit the contents of a cell, you first select the cell you want to edit, then click the formula bar, double-click the selected cell, or press [F2]. This puts Excel into Edit mode. To make sure you are in Edit mode, check the mode indicator on the left side of the status bar. Refer to Table 2-2 for more information on the mode indicator. ▶ After checking her worksheet, Susie notices that she entered the wrong value for the June bus tours and she forgot to include the canoe tours. She will fix the bus tours figure, and she decides to add the canoe sales data to the raft sales figures.

STEPS

1. **Click cell B9**
   This cell contains June bus tours, which Susie needs to change to 2.

2. **Click anywhere on the formula bar**
   Excel goes into Edit mode, and the mode indicator displays "Edit." A blinking **insertion point** appears in the formula bar, and if you move the mouse pointer to the formula bar, it changes to I. See Figure 2-5.

3. **Press [Backspace], type 2, then press [Enter] or click the Enter button**
   Susie now needs to add "/Canoe" to the Raft label.

4. **Click cell A7, then press [F2]**
   Excel is in Edit mode again, but the blinking insertion point is in the cell.

5. **Type /Canoe then press [Enter]**
   The label changes to Raft/Canoe, which is a little too long to fit in the cell. Don't worry about this. You will learn how to change the width of a column in the next unit.

6. **Double-click cell B7**
   Double-clicking a cell also puts Excel into Edit mode with the insertion point in the cell.

7. **Press [Delete], then type 9**
   See Figure 2-6.

8. **Click the Enter button to confirm the entry**

TABLE 2-2:
Understanding the mode indicator

MODE	DESCRIPTION
Edit	You are editing a cell entry.
Enter	You are entering data.
Error	You have made an entry Excel cannot understand; click the Help tool on the Standard toolbar or click OK.
Point	You have specified a range without a formula.
Ready	Excel is ready for you to enter data or choose a command.
Wait	Excel is completing a task.

EXCEL 5 UNIT 2 BUILDING A WORKSHEET

FIGURE 2-5: Worksheet in Edit mode

Insertion point in formula bar

Mouse pointer changes to I-bar

Edit mode indicator

FIGURE 2-6: Worksheet with edits completed

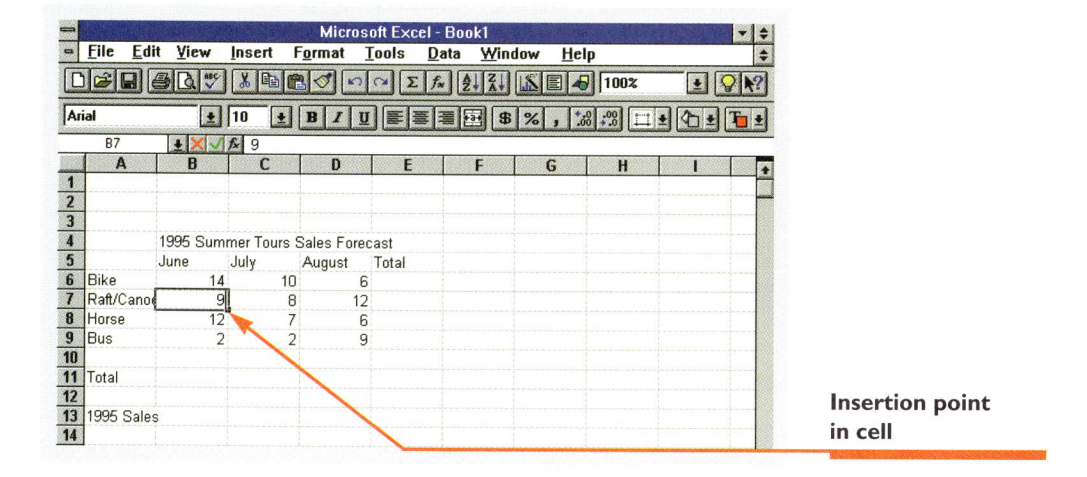

Insertion point in cell

Using the Cancel button

When you enter data into a cell, the Cancel button ☒ appears to the left of the Enter button ☑ in the formula bar, as shown in Figure 2-7. If you make a mistake entering data or editing a cell entry, you can click the Cancel button instead of confirming the entry to remove the data entered and revert to the original contents. This is especially useful when editing a complex formula in the formula bar.

Cancel button

Enter button

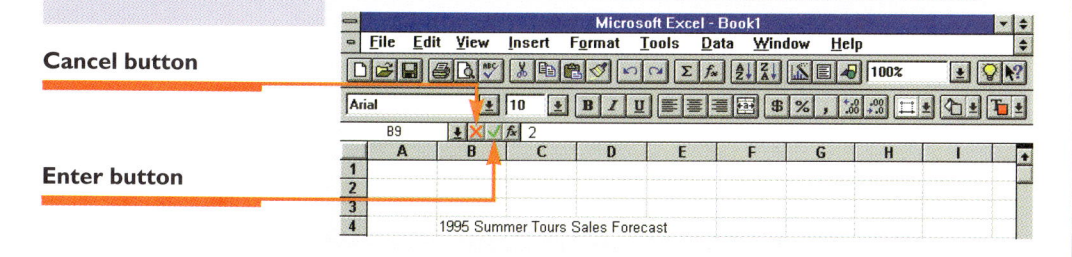

FIGURE 2-7: Cancel button

QUICK TIP

If you make a mistake, click the Undo tool ↶ on the Standard toolbar or choose Undo from the Edit menu before doing anything else.∎

Working with ranges

Any group of cells (two or more) is called a range. To select a range, click the first cell and drag to the last cell you want included in the range. The range address is defined by noting the first and last cells in the range. Figure 2-8 shows a selected range whose address is B6:C9. Ranges can be given meaningful names that can then be used in formulas. Named ranges are usually easier to remember than cell addresses. ▶ To make her forecasting worksheet easier to understand, Susie decides to use named ranges in her worksheet.

Steps

1. Click cell **B6** and drag to cell **B9** to select the range B6:B9

2. Click the **name box** to select the cell address B6

3. Type **June**, then press **[Enter]**
   Now whenever cells B6:B9 are selected, the range name "June" will appear in the name box.

4. Click cell **C6** and drag to cell **C9** to select the range C6:C9; click the **name box**, type **July**, then press **[Enter]**

5. Click cell **D6** and drag to cell **D9** to select the range D6:D9; click the **name box**, type **August**, then press **[Enter]**
   Next, you will name the four ranges containing the data for each type of tour.

6. Select the range **B6:D6**, click the **name box**, type **Bike**, then press **[Enter]**

7. Name range B7:D7 RaftCanoe, range B8:D8 Horse, and range B9:D9 Bus

8. Click the **name box list arrow** to see the list of range names in this worksheet
   Notice that the named ranges are in alphabetical order. See Figure 2-9. Click anywhere outside the range name list to close it.

FIGURE 2-8: Worksheet showing selected range of cells

Name box →

FIGURE 2-9: List of range names

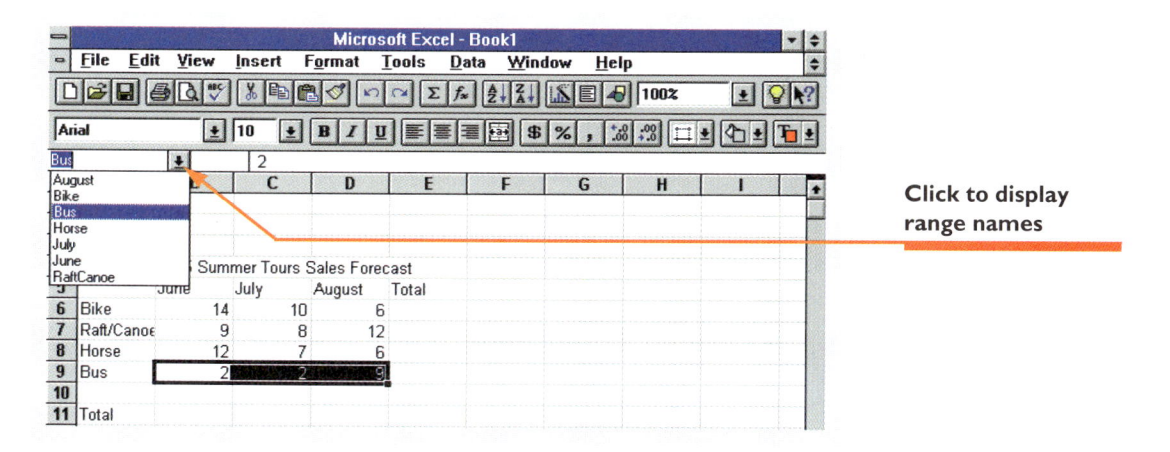

Click to display range names

Using range names to move around a workbook

You can use range names to move around a workbook quickly. Click the name box list arrow, then click the name of the range you want to go to (Figure 2-10). The cell pointer moves immediately to that range in the workbook.

August range →

Cell pointer moves to selected range →

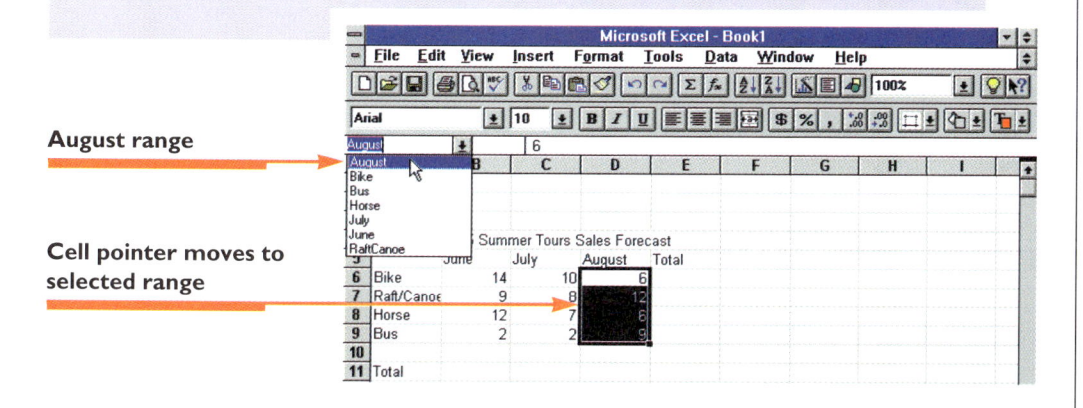

FIGURE 2-10: Moving the cell pointer using range names

TROUBLE?

If you make a mistake selecting and naming a range, click Insert in the menu bar, click Name, then click Define. In the Define Name dialog box, highlight the range name you need to redefine, click Delete, then click Close. Select and name the range again. ∎

EXCEL 5 UNIT 2 **BUILDING** A WORKSHEET

Entering formulas

Formulas are used to perform numeric calculations such as adding, multiplying and averaging. Formulas in an Excel worksheet start with an equal sign (=). All formulas use **arithmetic operators** to perform calculations. See Table 2-3 for a list of Excel operators. Formulas often contain cell addresses and range names. Using a cell address or range name in a formula is called **cell referencing**. Using cell references keeps your worksheet up-to-date and accurate. If you change a value in a cell, any formula containing that cell reference will be automatically recalculated using the new value. ▶ Use formulas to add the total tours for June, July, and August in Susie's worksheet.

Steps

1 Click cell **B11**
This is the cell where Susie wants to put the calculation that will total the June sales.

2 Type **=** (equal sign)
The equal sign at the beginning of an entry tells Excel that a formula is about to be entered rather than a label or a value. The total June sales is equal to the sum of the values in cells B6, B7, B8, and B9.

3 Type **b6+b7+b8+b9** then press **[Enter]**
The result, 37, appears in cell B11, and the formula displays in the formula bar. Next, add the number of tours in July.

4 Click cell **C11**, type **=c6+c7+c8+c9**, then press **[Enter]**
The result of 27 is shown in cell C11. Finally, enter the formula to calculate the August tour sales.

5 Click cell **D11**, type **=d6+d7+d8+d9**, then click the **Enter button**
The total tour sales for August displays in cell D11. Compare your results with Figure 2-11.

FIGURE 2-11: Worksheet showing formula and result

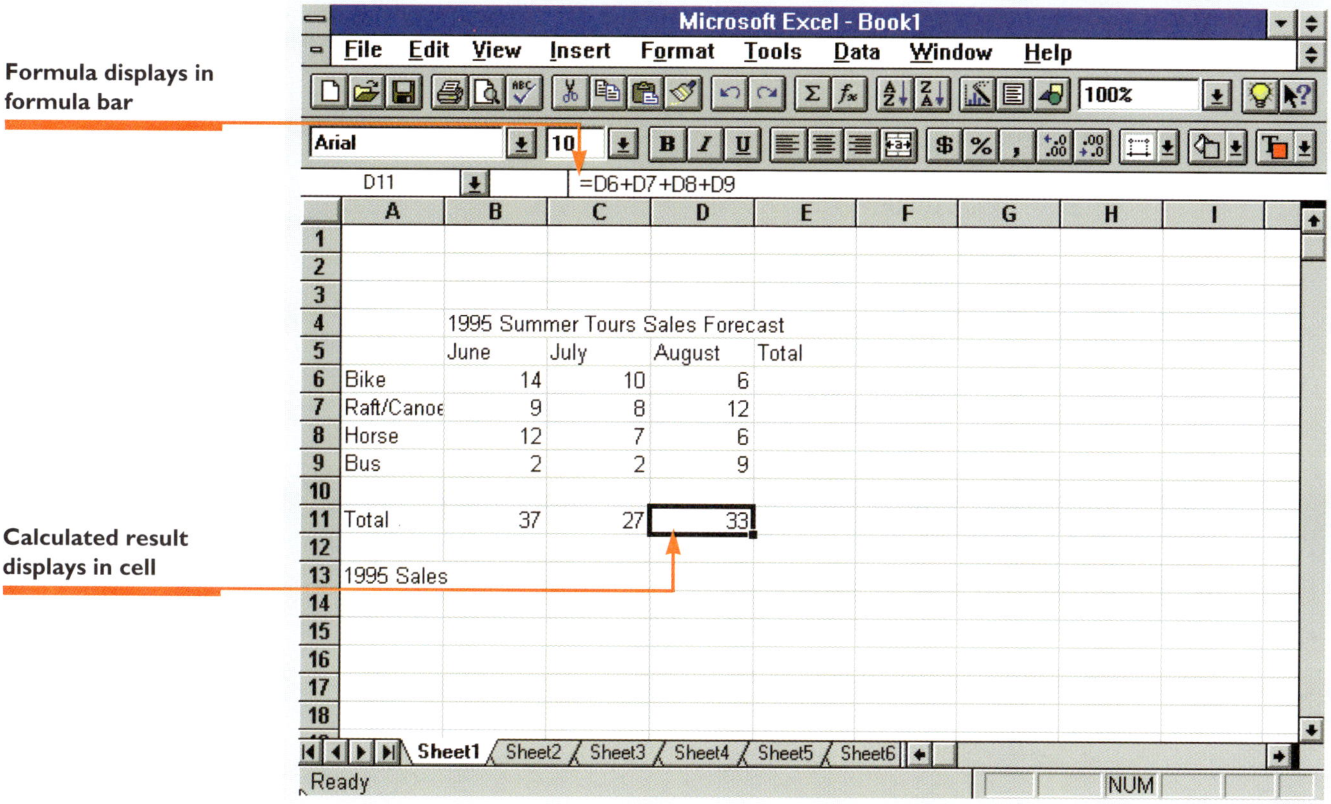

Formula displays in formula bar

Calculated result displays in cell

TABLE 2-3:
Excel arithmetic operators

OPERATOR	PURPOSE	EXAMPLE
+	Performs addition	=A5+A7
−	Performs subtraction	=A5-10
*	Performs multiplication	=A5*A7
/	Performs division	=A5/A7

TROUBLE?

If the formula instead of the result displays in the cell after you press [Enter], check that you began the formula with = (equal sign). ■

Entering formulas, continued

Now that Susie has calculated the monthly total tour sales for 1994, she can use these figures to calculate her forecast for 1995. She will use the multiplication symbol, * (the asterisk), to write the formula calculating a 20% increase of 1994 sales. This time you will click the cell address to be included in the formula rather than type it.

STEPS

6 Click cell **B13**, type **=**, click **B11**, type ***1.2**, then press **[Enter]**
   This formula calculates the result of multiplying the total monthly tour sales for June, cell B11, by 1.2. The result of 44.4 displays in cell B13. Now calculate the 20% increase for July and August.

7 Click cell **C13**, type **=**, click **C11**, type ***1.2**, then press **[Enter]**

8 Click cell **D13**, type **=**, click **D11**, type ***1.2**, then click the **Enter button**
   Compare your results with Figure 2-12.

FIGURE 2-12: Formula and result for 20% increase

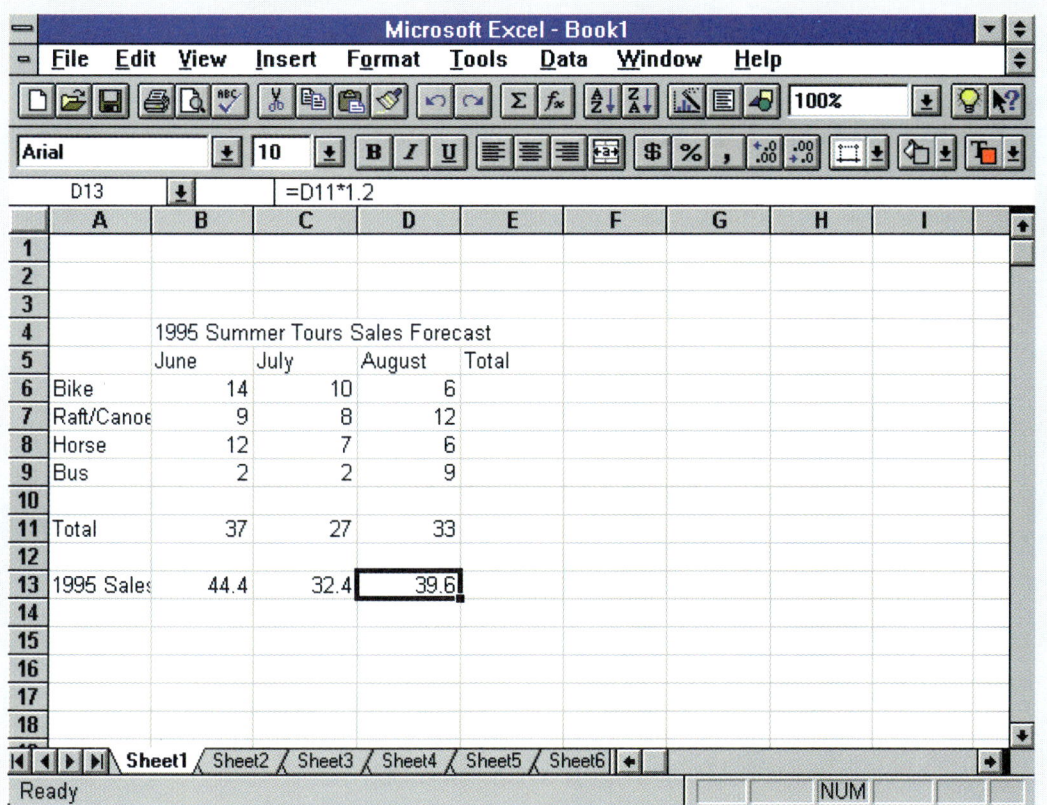

Order of precedence in Excel formulas

Each of the formulas for Susie's calculations involves only one arithmetic operator, but a formula can include several operations. When you work with formulas that have more than one operator, the order of operation is very important. If a formula contains two or more operators, such as 4 + .55/4000 * 25, the computer performs the calculations in a particular sequence, based on these rules:

Calculated 1st   Calculation of exponents
Calculated 2nd   Multiplication and division, left to right
Calculated 3rd   Addition and subtraction, left to right

In the example 4 + .55/4000 * 25, Excel performs the arithmetic operations in the following order. First, 4000 is divided into .55. Next Excel multiplies the result of .55/4000 by 25, then adds 4 to the result. You can change the order of calculations by using parentheses. Operations inside parentheses are calculated before any other operations.

Using Excel functions

Functions are predefined worksheet formulas designed to save you time and enable you to do complex calculations easily. Functions always begin with the formula prefix (=). ▶ Use the SUM function to calculate totals in Susie's worksheet.

STEPS

1. **Click cell E6**
   This is the cell where Susie wants to display the total of all bike tours for June, July, and August.

2. **Move the pointer over the AutoSum tool** Σ **on the Standard toolbar, as shown in Figure 2-13**
   The AutoSum tool sets up the SUM function to add the values in the cells above the cell pointer. If there are no values in the cells above the cell pointer, as in cell E6, it adds the values in the cells to the left of the cell pointer—in this case, the values in cells B6, C6, and D6.

3. **Click** Σ
   The formula =SUM(B6:D6) displays in the formula bar and in cell E6. The information inside the parentheses is the **argument**. An argument can be a value, a range of cells, text, or another function. After verifying that Excel has selected the correct range, in this case cells B6, C6, and D6, you need to confirm the entry.

4. **Click the Enter button** ✓ **or press [Enter] to calculate the result**
   The result of 30 appears in cell E6. Now calculate the three-month totals of Raft/Canoe tours.

5. **Click cell E7, click** Σ, **then click the Enter button** ✓ **or press [Enter]**

6. Use the same method to enter the SUM function in cells E8 (horse tour totals), E9 (bus tour totals), and E11 (1994 tour totals)

7. **Click cell E13, then click** Σ
   AutoSum sets up a function to add the values in the 1995 Sales row.

8. **Click** ✓ **to confirm the entry**
   See Figure 2-14.

FIGURE 2-13:
AutoSum ToolTip

AutoSum ToolTip ──▶

FIGURE 2-14:
Worksheet with all functions entered

SUM function entered in cell

Result of SUM function

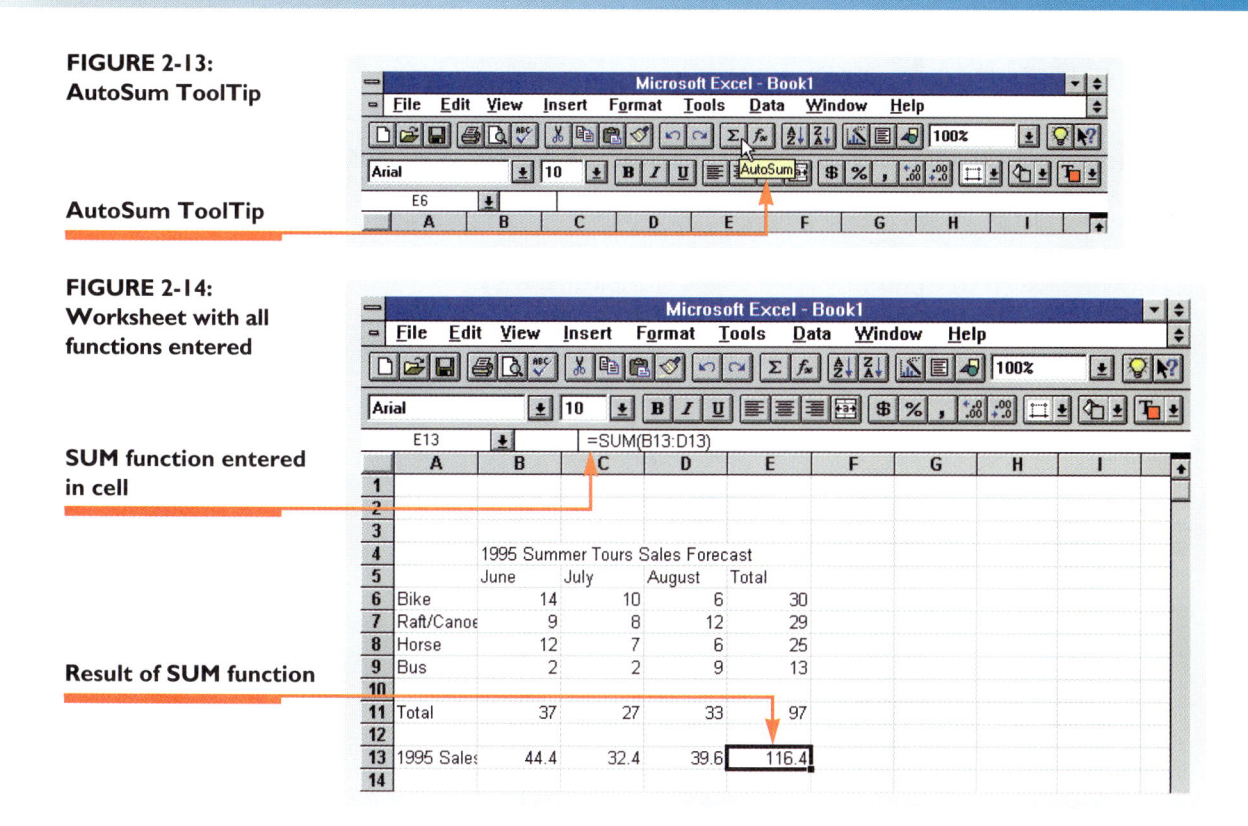

Using the Function Wizard

The Function Wizard tool, [fx], is located to the right of the AutoSum tool on the Standard toolbar and in the formula bar. To use the Function Wizard, click [fx], then click the category containing the function you want, and then click the desired function in the first Function Wizard dialog box. The function displays in the formula bar (Figure 2-15). Click Next to display the second Function Wizard dialog box then fill in values or cell addresses for the arguments.

Function Wizard tool

Function Wizard tool

Functions and arguments appear in formula bar

Description of selected function

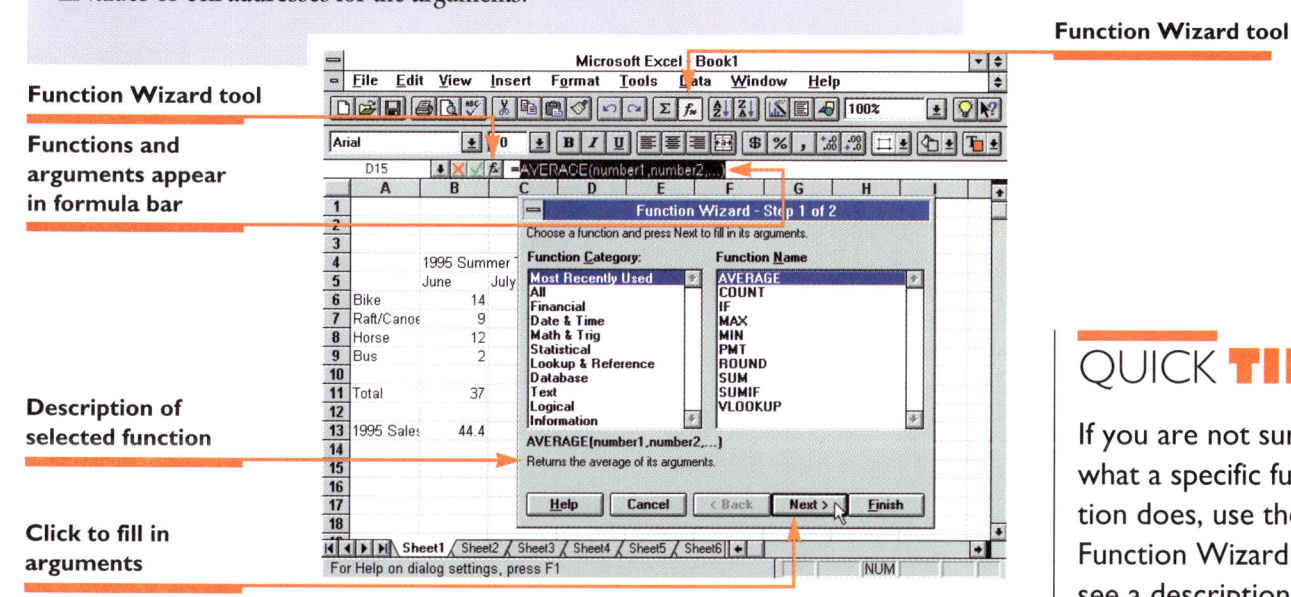

Click to fill in arguments

FIGURE 2-15: First Function Wizard dialog box

QUICK TIP

If you are not sure what a specific function does, use the Function Wizard to see a description of the function.

EXCEL 5 UNIT 2 BUILDING A WORKSHEET

Saving a workbook

As you learned in the Working with Windows section, to store a workbook permanently, you must save it to a file on a disk. You should save your work every 10 to 15 minutes, especially before and after making significant changes in a worksheet and before printing. You can save this file to the MY_FILES directory on your Student Disk. ▶ Name and save Susie's workbook to your Student Disk. For more information about your Student Disk, refer to "Read This Before You Begin" at the beginning of these units.

Steps

1 **Click File on the menu bar, then click Save As**
The Save As dialog box displays on the screen. See Figure 2-16.

2 **Double-click the text in the File Name text box to select the default name, then type tours**
Filenames can contain up to eight characters. These characters can be lower- or uppercase letters, numbers, or any symbols except for spaces, commas, or the following: \ / [ ] " ^ : , * ?. Excel automatically adds the .XLS extension to the filename.

3 **Click the Drives list arrow**

4 **Click a: to select drive A (or click b: if your Student Disk is in drive B)**
Do not save files on the internal hard disk, drive C, unless you are working on your own computer. If you didn't create a MY_FILES directory in the Working with Windows section, skip Step 5 and continue with Step 6.

5 **Double-click the MY_FILES directory, then click OK**
The Save As dialog box closes and the Summary Info dialog box displays. As you create more files with Excel, you will probably decide to use the Summary Info boxes to help you organize your files.

6 **Click OK**
The Summary Info dialog box closes, and the filename displays in the title bar at the top of the workbook. The workbook and all of the worksheets are saved to the MY_FILES directory on your Student Disk as a file named TOURS.XLS. Next, enter Susie's name at the top of the worksheet. It is good practice to enter the name of the person who developed the worksheet in case anyone has any questions about the worksheet.

7 **Click cell A2, type Susie Kwan, then press [Enter]**

8 **Click File on the menu bar, then click Save**
You could also click the Save tool 🖫 on the Standard toolbar or use the keyboard alternative [Ctrl][S] to choose the Save command. This saves the changes made to a file that already has been named. Save a file frequently while working in it to protect all data. Table 2-4 shows the difference between the Save and the Save As commands.

FIGURE 2-16: Save As dialog box

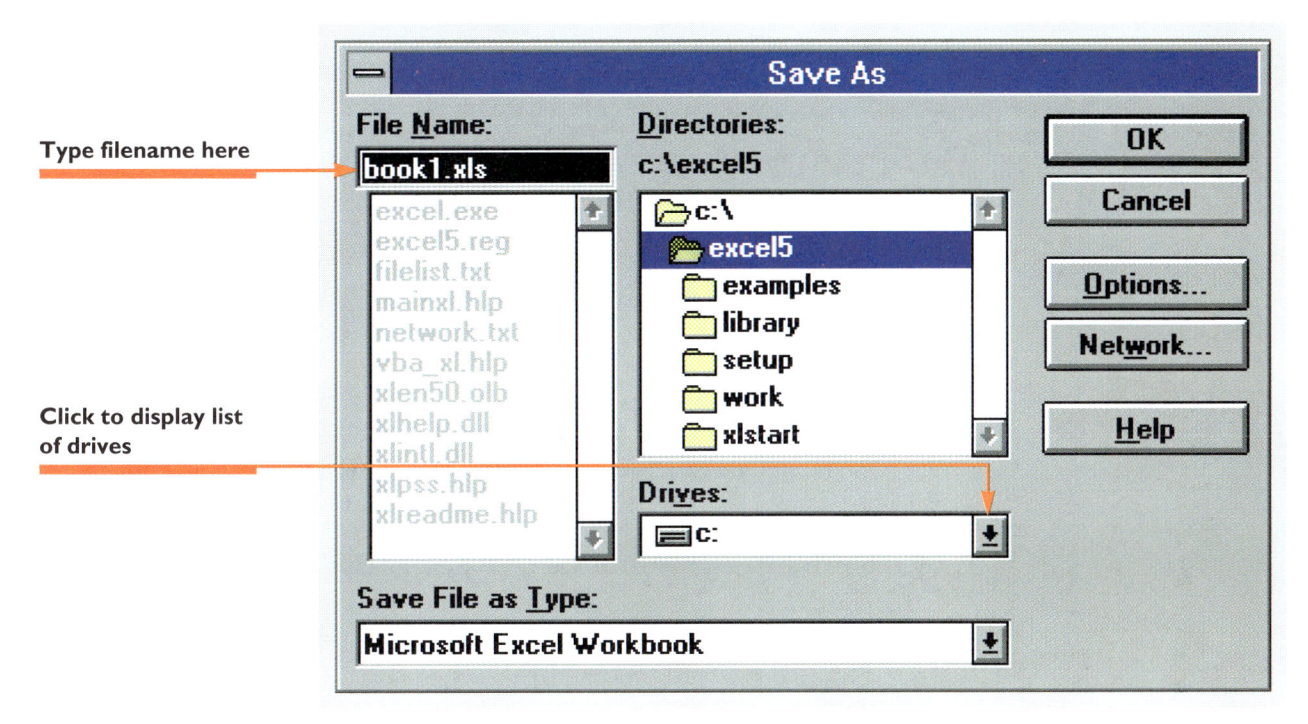

Type filename here →

Click to display list of drives →

[Save As dialog box showing File Name: book1.xls, Directories: c:\excel5, file list including excel.exe, excel5.reg, filelist.txt, mainxl.hlp, network.txt, vba_xl.hlp, xlen50.olb, xlhelp.dll, xlintl.dll, xlpss.hlp, xlreadme.hlp; directory tree with c:\, excel5, examples, library, setup, work, xlstart; Drives: c:; Save File as Type: Microsoft Excel Workbook; buttons: OK, Cancel, Options..., Network..., Help]

Creating backup files

It's good practice to back up your files in case something happens to your disk. To create a backup copy of a file, save the file again to a second disk or with another file extension such as .BAK.

TROUBLE?

If you save a file to the wrong disk or directory, you can save it again to the correct disk using the Save As command. ■

TABLE 2-4:
The difference between the Save and Save As commands

COMMAND	DESCRIPTION	PURPOSE
Save As	Saves file, requires input name.	To save a file the first time, to change the filename, or to save the file for use in a different application. Useful for back-ups.
Save	Saves named file.	To save any changes to the original file. Fast and easy—do this often to protect your work.

EXCEL 5 UNIT 2 BUILDING A WORKSHEET

Previewing and printing a worksheet

You print a worksheet when it is completed to have a paper copy to reference, file, or send to others. You can also print a worksheet that is not complete to review or work on when you are not at a computer. Before you print a worksheet, you should preview it. When you preview a worksheet, you see a copy of the worksheet exactly as it will appear on paper. You preview the worksheet to make sure that it will fit on a page before you print it. Table 2-5 provides printing tips. ▶ Print a copy of Susie's worksheet.

Steps

1. **Make sure the printer is on and that it is on-line**
   If a file is sent to print and the printer is off, an error message results. Next, preview the worksheet.

2. **Click the Print Preview tool on the Standard toolbar**
   You could also click File on the menu bar and then click Print Preview. A miniature version of the worksheet appears on the screen, as shown in Figure 2-17. Look at this image to see if the worksheet fits on the page or pages planned. If there were more than one page, you could click the Next and Previous buttons to move between pages. After verifying that the preview image is correct, print the worksheet.

3. **Click Print**
   The Print dialog box displays, as shown in Figure 2-18.

4. **Make sure that the Selected Sheet(s) radio button is selected and that 1 appears in the Copies text box**
   Now you are ready to print the worksheet.

5. **Click OK**
   The Printing dialog box displays on the screen while the file is sent to the printer. Notice that the Printing dialog box contains a Cancel button, which you can use to cancel the print job.

6. **Click File, then click Close to close the workbook**

TABLE 2-5:
Worksheet printing guidelines

BEFORE YOU PRINT	COMMENT
Check the printer	Make sure the printer is on and on-line, has paper, and there are no error messages or warning signals.
Check the printer selection	Use the Printer Setup command in the Print dialog box to verify the correct printer is selected.
Preview the worksheet	Take a quick look at the formatted image to check page breaks and page setup (vertical or horizontal).

FIGURE 2-17:
Print Preview screen

Move to another page

Enlarge the screen image

Print the worksheet

Return to worksheet

Mouse pointer

Change print options

FIGURE 2-18:
Print dialog box

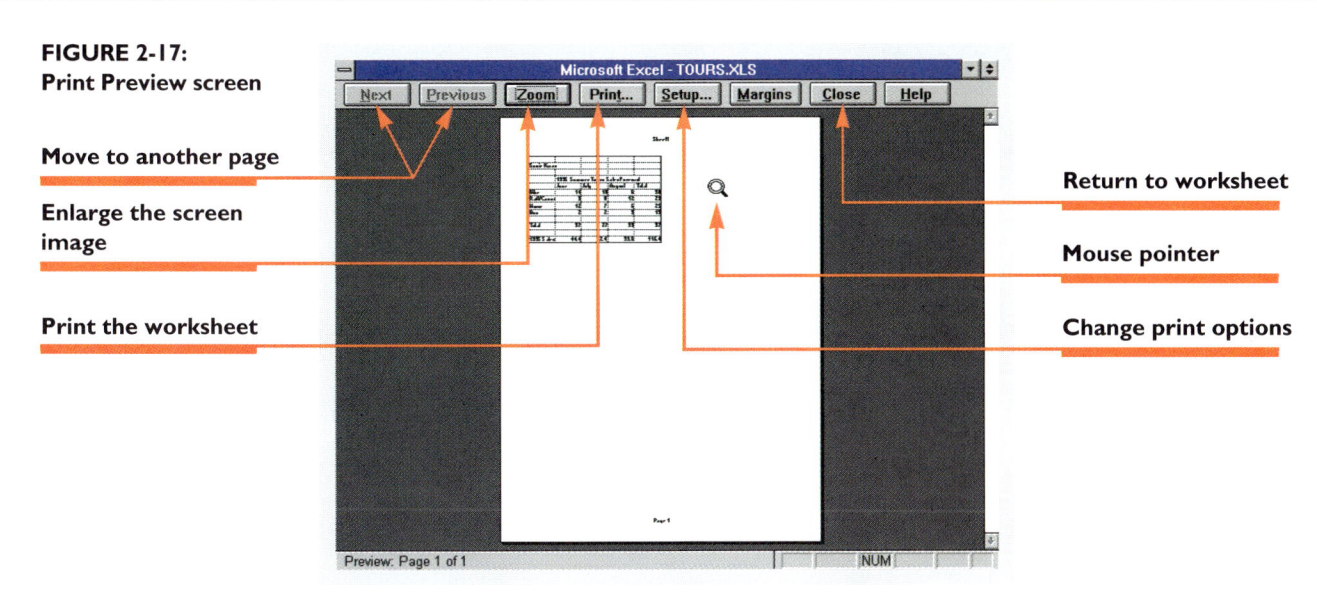

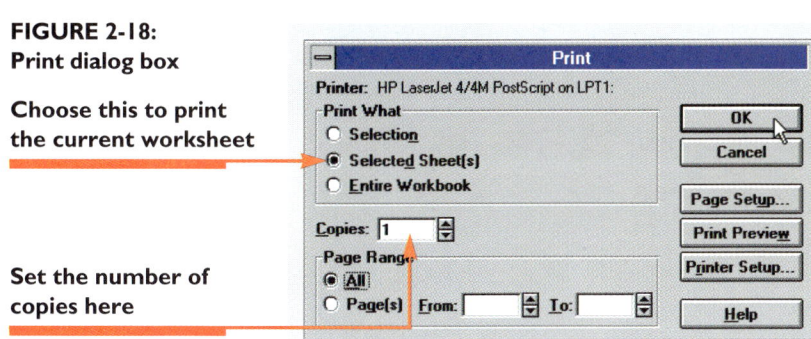

Choose this to print the current worksheet

Set the number of copies here

Using Zoom in print preview

When you are in the Print Preview window, you can make the image of the page larger by clicking the Zoom button. You can also position the mouse pointer over a specific part of the worksheet page, then click it to view that section of the page (Figure 2-19). While the image is zoomed in, use the scroll bars to view different sections of the page.

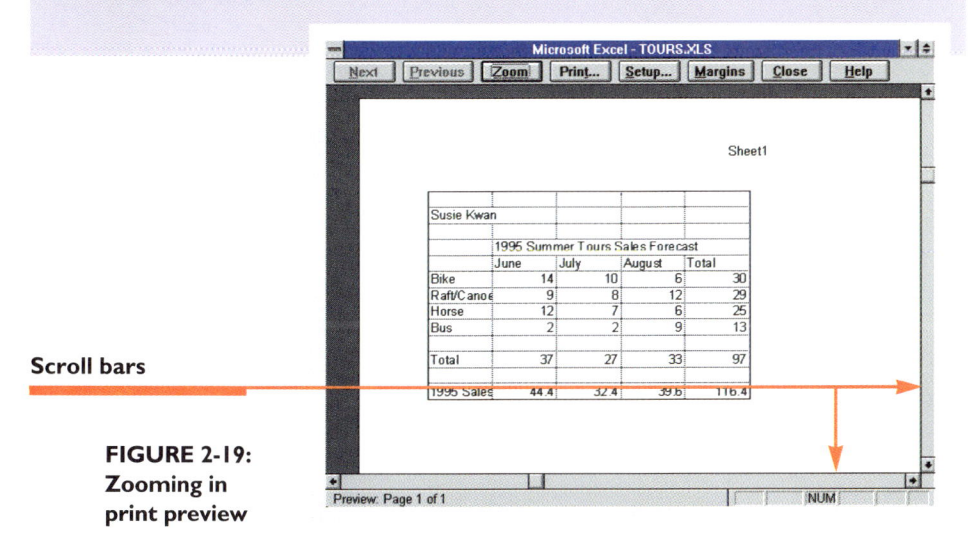

Scroll bars

FIGURE 2-19:
Zooming in print preview

QUICK TIP

It's a good idea to save prior to printing. That way, if anything happens to the file while being sent to the printer, you have a clean copy saved to your disk.

EXCEL 5 UNIT 2 **BUILDING** A WORKSHEET

CONCEPTS REVIEW

Label each of the elements of the Excel screen shown in Figure 2-20.

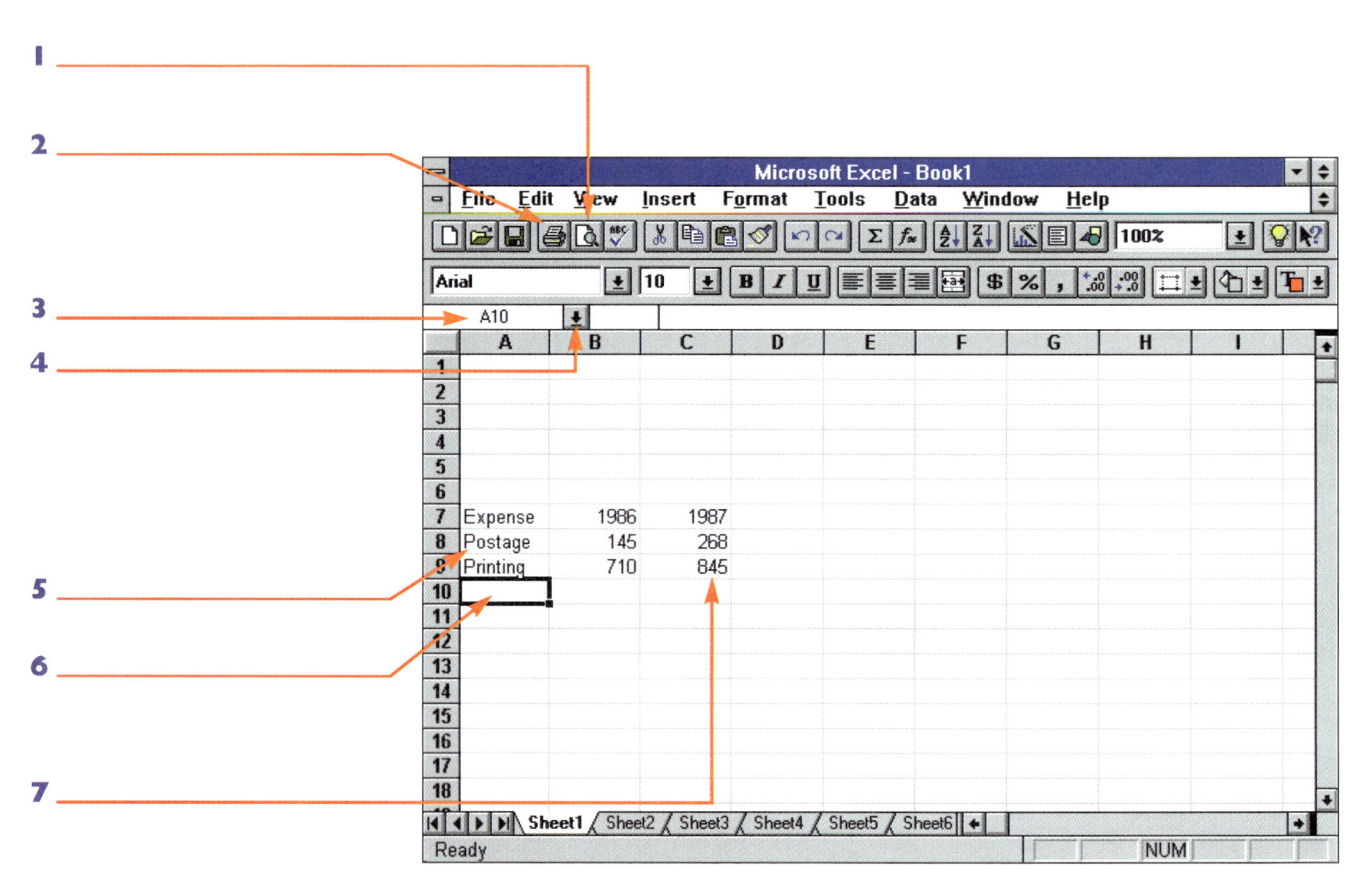

FIGURE 2-20

Match each of the terms with the statement that describes its function.

8 A special predefined formula that provides a shortcut for commonly used calculations

9 A cell entry that performs a calculation in an Excel worksheet.

10 A specified group of cells, which can include the entire worksheet

11 The location of a particular cell in a worksheet, identified by a column letter and row number

12 The character that identifies a value as a label

a. Range
b. Function
c. Cell address
d. Apostrophe
e. Formula

Select the best answer from the list of choices.

13 All of the following confirm an entry in a cell *except*:
 a. Cancel button
 b. Enter button
 c. Pressing [Enter]
 d. Pressing [↓]

14 The first character in any Excel formula is:
 a. *
 b. /
 c. =
 d. @

APPLICATIONS REVIEW

Enter your name and the date on all worksheets.

1. Enter data in a worksheet.
   a. Click the New Workbook tool to open a new workbook.
   b. Rename the Sheet1 tab as Funds.
   c. Save the workbook as FUNDS.XLS.
   d. Click cell B1, then type "Shares."
   e. Click the Enter button to enter Shares in cell B1.
   f. Press [→] to move to cell C1, then type "Price."
   g. Press [Tab] to move to cell D1.
   h. Type "Sold" then press [Esc]. Note that the entry disappears from the cell. Leave cell D1 blank.
   i. Type "Total" in cell D7, then press [Enter].
   j. Compare your worksheet to Figure 2-21.
   k. Save your work and print the worksheet.

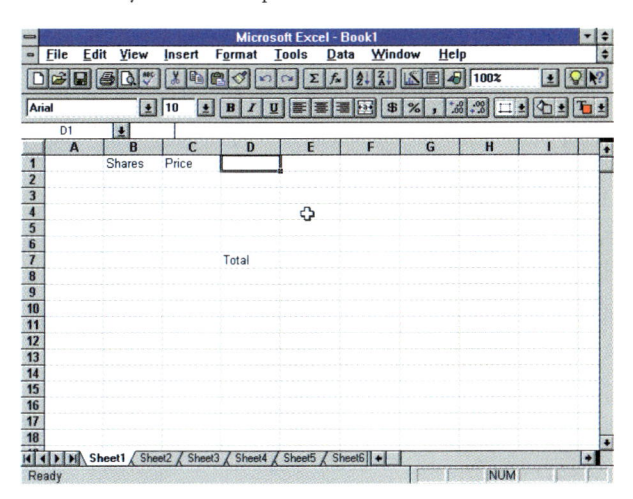

FIGURE 2-21

2. Add data to the existing worksheet and use named ranges.
   a. Enter the four mutual funds labels and values from Table 2-6 into the range A2:C5 in the Funds worksheet.

TABLE 2-6

	SHARES	PRICE
Arch	210	10.01
RST	50	18.45
United	100	34.50
Vista	65	11.15

   b. Name the range B2:B5 Shares.
   c. Name the range C2:C5 Price.
   d. Save and print the worksheet.

3. Add formulas to the existing worksheet.
   a. In cell B6, enter a formula to calculate the total number of shares.
   b. Save your work and print the data in the Funds worksheet.

4. Use functions in the FUNDS worksheet.
   a. In cell C7, use the Average function to determine the average price of the mutual funds listed.
   b. Type "Average Price" in cell A7.
   c. Save your work and print this worksheet.

5. Build a simple check register to balance a checkbook. Set up a new worksheet using the data from Table 2-7 in a new workbook.

TABLE 2-7

Check No.	Date	Description	Amount
1601	June 17	Cleaning	12.65
1602	June 29	Tickets	38.02
1603	July 18	Cable	14.50
1604	July 25	Food	47.98

   a. Rename the Sheet1 tab Checkbook.
   b. Type "Check Register" in cell A1.
   c. Enter the column labels in range A3:D3.
   d. Enter all four check numbers, with the corresponding dates, descriptions, and amounts in range A4:A7.
   e. Generate a total of the check amounts you have entered. Use the SUM function to display the total in cell D12.
   f. Save the workbook as CHECK.XLS, then print the worksheet.

6. Edit cell entries and preview the worksheet.
   a. The description for check 1601 should be Laundry.
   b. Edit the amount for check 1602 to 43.62.
   c. Edit the amount for check 1603 to 23.22.
   d. Save your work, then preview and print the worksheet.

7. Develop a worksheet that calculates the weekly payroll for Suncoast Security Systems. Open a new workbook and set up the worksheet using the data from Table 2-8.

TABLE 2-8

EMPLOYEE	HOURS WORKED	HOURLY WAGE	GROSS PAY
D. Hillman	32	9	
S. Lipski	25	12	
L. Skillings	40	7	

a. Enter the column labels, beginning in cell A3.

b. Enter the employee names, hours worked, and wage information.

c. Use a formula to calculate the total number of employee hours worked this week. Enter this total in the appropriate cell.

d. Rename the Sheet1 tab as Suncoast.

e. Save the workbook as SUNSEC.XLS and then print the worksheet

8 Enter formulas and use functions in the Suncoast worksheet.

a. In range D4:D6, enter formulas that calculate the gross pay for each employee.

b. Calculate the total amount of wages that Suncoast will pay out this week. Enter this total in the cell adjacent to the total hourly wage.

c. Type "Total" in cell E8.

d. Using the AVG function in cell C11, determine the average hourly wage paid to employees at Suncoast.

e. Type "Average Wage" in cell A11.

f. Save your work, then print the worksheet.

g. Close the workbook.

INDEPENDENT CHALLENGES

You are the box office manager for Lightwell Players, a regional theater company. Your responsibilities include tracking seasonal ticket sales for the company's main stage productions and anticipating ticket sales for the next season. Lightwell Players sell four types of tickets: reserved seating, general admission, senior citizen tickets, and student tickets. The 1993-94 season included productions of *Hamlet, The Cherry Orchard, Fires in the Mirror, The Shadow Box,* and *Heartbreak House.*

Open a new workbook and save it as THEATER.XLS. Plan and build a worksheet that tracks the sales of each of the four ticket types for all five of the plays. Calculate the total ticket sales for each play, the total sales for each of the four ticket types, and the total sales for all ticket types. Enter your own sales data, but assume the following: the Lightwell Players sold 800 tickets during the season; reserved seating was the most popular ticket type for all of the shows, except for *The Shadow Box*; and no play sold more than 10 student tickets. Plan and build a second worksheet in the workbook that reflects a 5% increase in all ticket types.

To complete this independent challenge:

1 Think about the results you want to see, the information you need to build these worksheets, and the calculations that must be performed.

2 Sketch sample worksheets on a piece of paper, indicating how the information should be laid out. What information should go in the columns? In the rows?

3 Build the worksheets by entering a title, the row labels, the column titles, and the formulas. Use named ranges to make the worksheet easier to read, and rename the sheet tabs to easily identify the contents of each worksheet. (Hint: If your columns are too narrow, try making them wider by clicking Format on the menu bar, then Column, and then Width.)

4 Use separate worksheets for the ticket sales and projected sales showing the 5% increase.

5 Save your work, then preview and print the worksheets.

You have been promoted to Computer Lab Manager at your school, and it is your responsibility to make sure there are enough computers for students during scheduled classes. Currently, you have four classrooms: three with IBM PCs and one with Macintoshes. Classes are scheduled Monday, Wednesday, and Friday in two-hour increments from 9:00 a.m. to 5:00 p.m. (the lab closes at 7:00 p.m.) and each room can currently accomodate 20 computers.

Open a new workbook and save it as LABMNGR.XLS. Plan and build a worksheet that tracks the number of students who can currently use available computers per two-hour class. Create your enrollment data, but assume that current enrollment averages at 85% of each room's daily capacity. Using an additional worksheet, show the impact of an enrollment increase of 25%. To complete this independent challenge:

1 Think about how to construct these worksheets to create the desired output.

2 Sketch a sample worksheet on a piece of papaer, indicating how the information should be laid out.

3 Build the worksheets by entering a title, the row labels, the column titles, and the formulas. Use named ranges to make the worksheet easier to read.

4 Use separate sheets for actual enrollment and projected changes.

5 Save your work, then preview and print the worksheets.

UNIT 3

OBJECTIVES

▶ Open an existing worksheet

▶ Insert and delete rows and columns

▶ Copy and move cell entries

▶ Copy and move formulas

▶ Copy formulas with absolute references

▶ Adjust column widths

▶ Check spelling

Revising
A WORKSHEET

Building on your ability to create a worksheet and enter data into it, you will now learn how to insert and delete columns and rows, move and copy cell contents, and resize columns. ▶ The managers at Nationwide Travel told Susie Kwan that it would be helpful to have forecasts for the entire year, so Susie prepared a worksheet containing the Spring and Fall Tours Sales Forecast, and another worksheet with the Winter Tours Sales Forecast. She created these new worksheets as Sheet2 and Sheet3 in the workbook containing the 1995 Summer Tours Sales Forecast. Having three related worksheets in one workbook makes it easy for Susie to compare them. ▶

Opening an existing worksheet

Sometimes it's useful to create a new worksheet by modifying one that already exists. This saves you from having to retype information. Throughout this book, you will be instructed to open a file from your Student Disk, use the Save As command to create a copy of the file with a new name, and then modify the new file by following the lesson steps. Saving the files with a new name keeps your original Student Disk files intact in case you have to start the lesson over again or you wish to repeat an exercise. ▶ Open Susie's 1995 Tours Forecast workbook, then use the Save As command to create a copy with a new name.

STEPS

1 Start Excel then click the **Open tool** on the Standard toolbar
The Open File dialog box displays. See Figure 3-1. Notice that it is very similar to the Save As dialog box you saw in Unit 2.

2 Click the **Drives list arrow**
A list of the available drives displays. Locate the drive that contains your Student Disk. In this text, we assume your Student Disk is in drive A.

3 Click **a:** to select drive A (or click **b:** if your Student Disk is in drive B)
A list of the files on your Student Disk displays in the File Name list box.

4 In the File Name list, click **unit3.xls**
The selected filename replaces the default filename placeholder in the File Name text box.

5 Click **OK**
The file UNIT3.XLS opens. You could also double-click the filename in the File Name list to open the file. To create and save a copy of this file with a new name, use the Save As command.

6 Click **File** on the menu bar, then click **Save As**
The Save As dialog box displays, as shown in Figure 3-2.

7 Make sure the Drives list box displays the drive that contains your Student Disk and double-click the **MY_FILES directory**
You should save all your files to your MY_FILES directory on your Student Disk, unless instructed otherwise. If you did not create a MY_FILES directory in "Working with Windows," continue with Step 8 to save your files to the root directory on your Student Disk.

8 In the File Name text box, select the file unit3.xls (if it is not selected already), then type **tourinfo**

9 Click **OK** to close the Save As dialog box, then click **OK** again to close the Summary Info dialog box
The file UNIT3.XLS closes and a duplicate file named TOURINFO.XLS is now open.

FIGURE 3-1: Open File dialog box

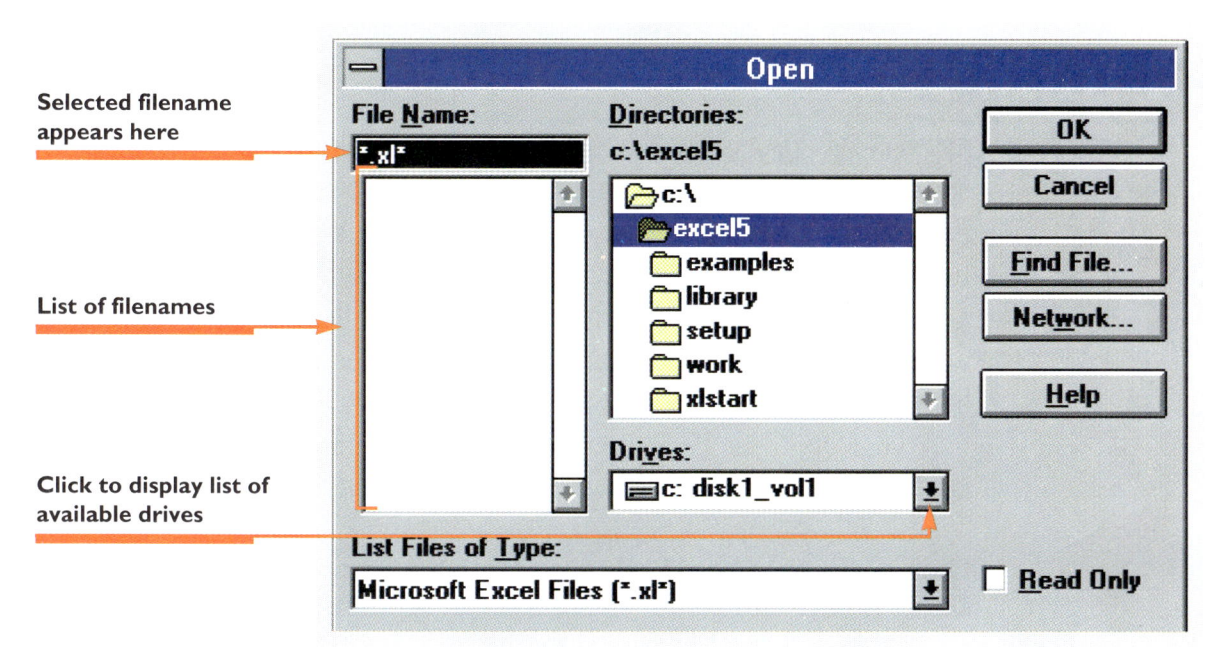

Selected filename appears here →

List of filenames →

Click to display list of available drives →

FIGURE 3-2: Save As dialog box

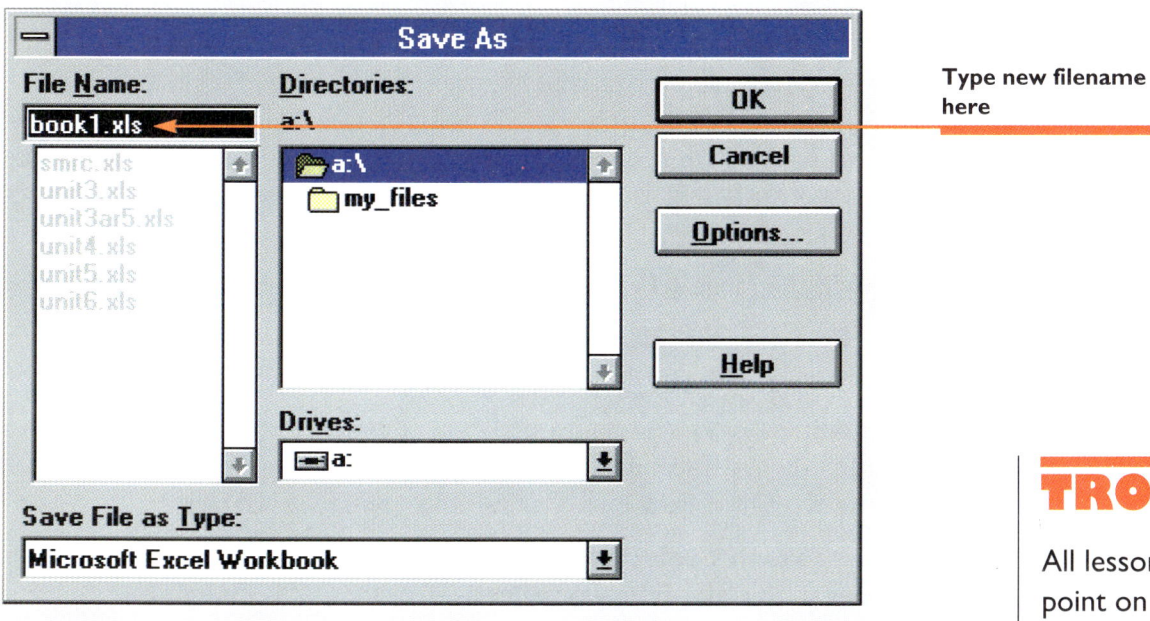

Type new filename here →

TROUBLE?

All lessons from this point on assume you have Excel running. If you need help, refer to the lesson called "Starting Microsoft Excel 5.0 for Windows" in Unit 1.■

EXCEL 5 UNIT 3 **REVISING** A WORKSHEET

Inserting and deleting rows and columns

As you modify a worksheet, you might find it necessary to insert or delete rows and columns. For example, you might need to insert rows to accommodate new inventory products or remove a column of yearly totals that are no longer current. Inserting or deleting rows or columns can also help to make your worksheet more attractive and readable. ▶ Susie has already improved the appearance of her worksheet by boldfacing the column headings. Next, she decides to insert a row between her worksheet title and the column labels. Also, Susie decides to discontinue bus tours for the 1995 summer season because of slow sales in 1994, so she needs to delete the row containing bus tour information.

1. **Double-click the Sheet1 tab, then rename it Summer**
   This will identify this sheet of the workbook.

2. **Click cell A5, click Insert on the menu bar, then click Cells**
   The Insert dialog box displays. See Figure 3-3. You can choose to insert a column or a row, or you can shift the cell contents in the active column right or active row down. Susie wants to insert a row to add some space between the title and column headings.

3. **Click the Entire Row radio button, then click OK**
   A blank row is inserted between the title and the month labels. When you insert a new row, the contents of the worksheet shifts down from the newly inserted row. When you insert a new column, the contents of the worksheet shifts to the right from the point of the new column. Now Susie wants to delete the row containing information about bus sales. Because the formulas in row 12 use ranges whose **anchors** (cells used in the range address) are in row 10, she can't delete row 10 without having to change the formulas. To get around this problem, she will clear the data from row 10, then she will delete the blank row 11 so the worksheet doesn't have two blank rows together.

4. **Highlight the range A10:E10 to select the Bus tour information**

5. **Click Edit then click Clear**
   The Clear cascading menu displays.

6. **Click All**
   The data in the range A10:E10 disappears. Notice that the formula results in rows 12 and 14 are adjusted because of the deletion of bus tour sales. Now delete a blank row.

7. **Click the row 11 selector button** (the gray box containing the row number to the left of the worksheet)
   This selects all of row 11. See Figure 3-4.

8. **Click Edit on the menu bar, then click Delete**
   Excel deletes row 11, and all rows below this shift up one row. Susie is satisfied with the appearance of her worksheet and decides to save the changes.

9. **Click the Save tool on the Standard toolbar to save your changes**

EXCEL 5 UNIT 3 **REVISING A WORKSHEET**

FIGURE 3-3:
Insert dialog box

Choose to insert row

FIGURE 3-4:
Worksheet with row 11 selected

Inserted row

Row 11 selector button

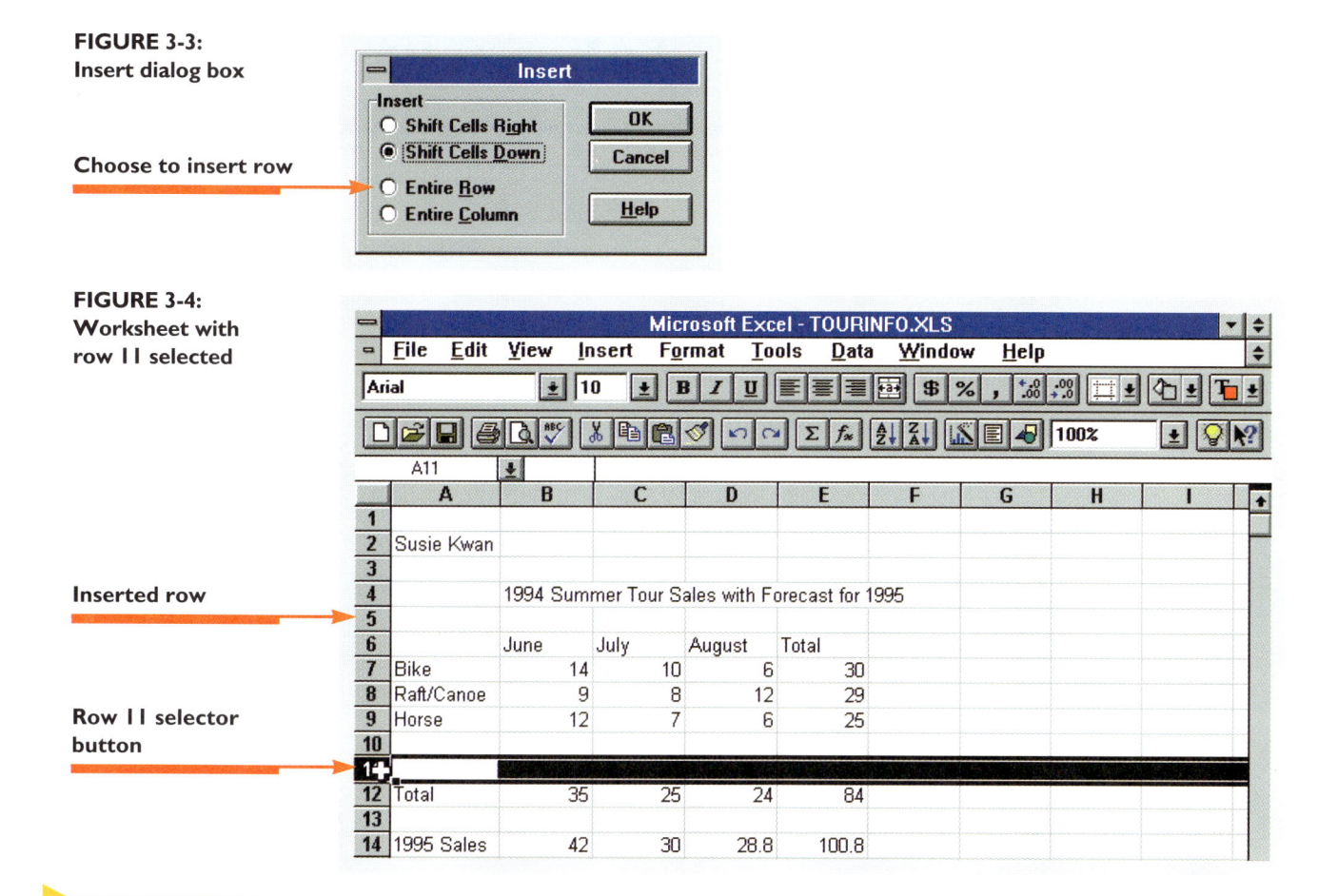

Using dummy columns and rows

When you use a range in a formula and you add or delete columns and rows within that range, Excel automatically adjusts the formula to include the new information. When you need to add a column or row at the end of a range, the formula must be modified to include the new data. A **dummy column** or **dummy row** is a blank column or row that is included at the end of a range, as shown in Figure 3-5. Then, if you add another column or row, the formula will be modified to include the new data.

Rows included in formula

Formula with dummy row

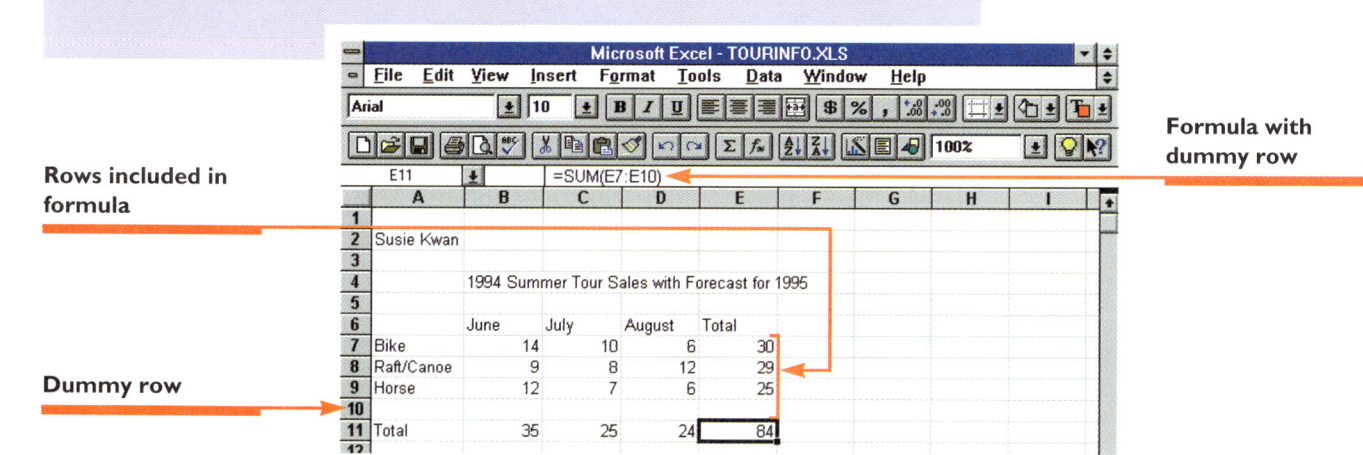

Dummy row

FIGURE 3-5: Formula with dummy row

Copying and moving cell entries

Using the Cut, Copy, and Paste tools or Excel's drag and drop feature, you can copy or move information from one cell or range in your worksheet to another. ▶ Susie decided to include the 1995 forecast for Spring and Fall Tours Sales in her TOURINFO workbook. She has already entered the Spring report in Sheet2 and is ready to finish entering the labels and data for the Fall report. Use the Copy and Paste tools and drag and drop to copy information from the Spring report to the Fall report.

1 Double-click the **Sheet2 tab**, then rename it **Spring-Fall**
Don't worry if you see any misspellings, they will be corrected later. First, Susie wants to copy the labels identifying the types of tours from the Spring report to the Fall report.

2 Select the range A4:A9, then click the **Copy tool** on the Standard toolbar
This copies the selected range (A4:A9) and places the copied information on the Clipboard. The **Clipboard** is a temporary storage file that holds all the selected information you copy or cut. The Cut tool would remove the selected information from the sheet and place it on the Clipboard. To copy the contents of the Clipboard to a new location, you click a new cell and then use the Paste command.

3 Click cell **A13**, then click the **Paste tool**
The contents of the Clipboard are copied into range A13:A18. When pasting the contents of the Clipboard into the worksheet, you need to specify only the first cell of the range where you want the copied selection to go. Susie decides to use drag and drop to copy the Total label.

4 Click cell **E3** to select it, then move the mouse pointer to any edge of the cell until the pointer changes to

5 While the pointer is , press and hold **[Ctrl]**
The pointer changes to .

6 While still pressing [Ctrl], press and hold the left mouse button, then drag the cell contents to E12
As you drag, an outline of the cell moves with the pointer, as shown in Figure 3-6. When you release the mouse button, the Total label appears in cell E12. Susie now decides to move the worksheet title to cell A1. You do not need to press [Ctrl] when you move data to a new cell.

7 Click cell **C1**, move the mouse pointer to the edge of the cell until it changes to , and then drag the cell contents to A1
Susie now needs to enter Fall sales data into the range B13:D16, as shown in Figure 3-7.

8 Referring to Figure 3-7, enter the sales data for the fall tours into the range B13:D16
Compare your worksheet to Figure 3-7, then continue to the next lesson.

FIGURE 3-6: Using drag and drop to copy information

- Paste tool
- Copy tool
- Cut tool
- Copied cell
- Outline of copied cell
- Drag and drop pointer to copy data

FIGURE 3-7: Worksheet with fall tours data entered

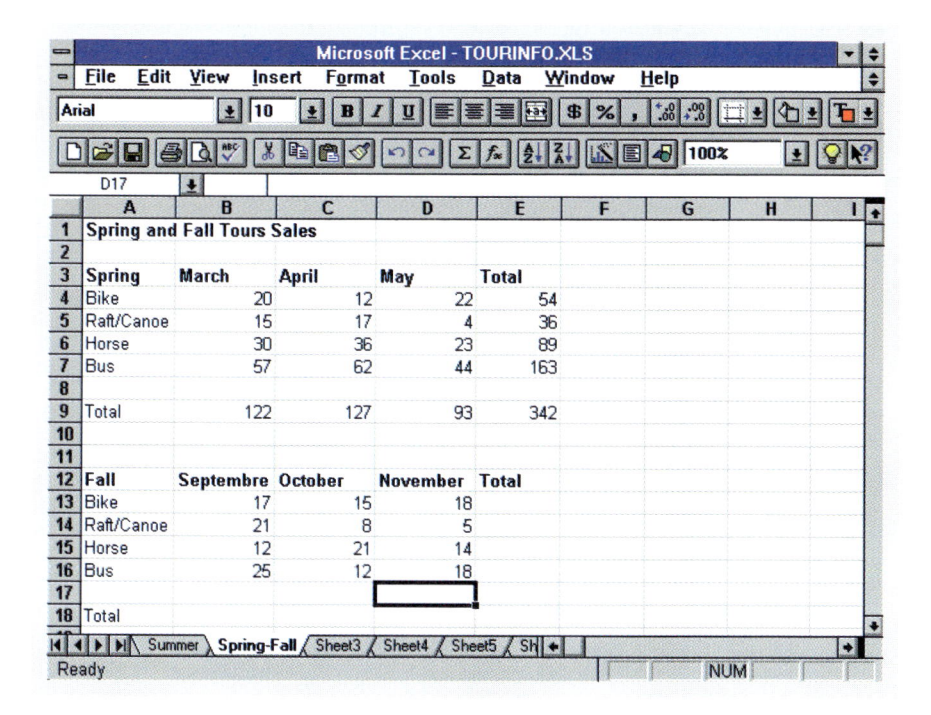

Adding and deleting worksheets

You can add or delete worksheets as necessary. To add a worksheet, click Insert in the menu bar and then click Worksheet. A new worksheet is added immediately before the active worksheet. To delete a worksheet, click Edit in the menu bar and then click Delete Sheet. The active worksheet is deleted, and the worksheet immediately after becomes the active worksheet.

TROUBLE?

When you drag and drop data into occupied cells, you will be asked if you want to replace the existing cells. Click OK to replace the contents with the cell you are moving.

EXCEL 5 UNIT 3 REVISING A WORKSHEET

Copying and moving formulas

Copying and pasting formulas allows you to reuse formulas you've already created. Copying formulas, rather than retyping them, helps prevent new typing errors. ▶ Susie wants to copy the formulas that total the types of tours and that add the tours per month from the Spring Tours report to the Fall Tours report.

STEPS

1. **Click E4 then click the Copy tool on the Standard toolbar**
   This copies the formula for calculating the total number of spring bike tours to the Clipboard. Notice that this formula is displayed in the formula bar as =SUM(B4:D4).

2. **Click cell E13 then click the Paste tool**
   The formula from cell E4 is copied into cell E13. A new result of 50 displays in cell E13. Notice in the formula bar that the cell references have changed so that the range B13:D13 appears in the formula. Formulas in Excel contain relative cell references. A **relative cell reference** tells Excel to copy the formula to a new cell, but to substitute new cell references that are in the same relative position to the new formula location. In this case, Excel inserted cells D13, C13 and B13, the three cell references immediately to the left of E13. Notice that the lower-right corner of the active cell contains a small square. This is the **fill handle**. Susie will now use the fill handle to copy the formula in cell E13 to cells E14, E15, and E16.

3. **Move the pointer over the fill handle until it changes to +**

4. **Drag the fill handle to select cells E13 through E16**
   See Figure 3-8. Once you release the mouse button, the fill handle copies the formula from the active cell (E13) and pastes it into each cell of the selected range. Again, because the formula uses relative cell references, cells E14 through E16 correctly display the totals for Raft/Canoe, Horse and Bus tours.

FIGURE 3-8: Selected range using the fill handle

Formula in E13 will be copied to E14:E16

Mouse pointer

Filling ranges with series of labels

You can fill cells with a series of labels using the fill handle. You can fill cells with sequential months, days of the week, years, and text plus a number (Quarter 1, Quarter 2,...). Figure 3-9 shows a series of months being created with the fill handle. As you drag the fill handle, the contents of the last filled cell displays in the name box. You can also use the Fill Series command on the Edit menu.

Mouse pointer

Last filled cell

Contents of active cell

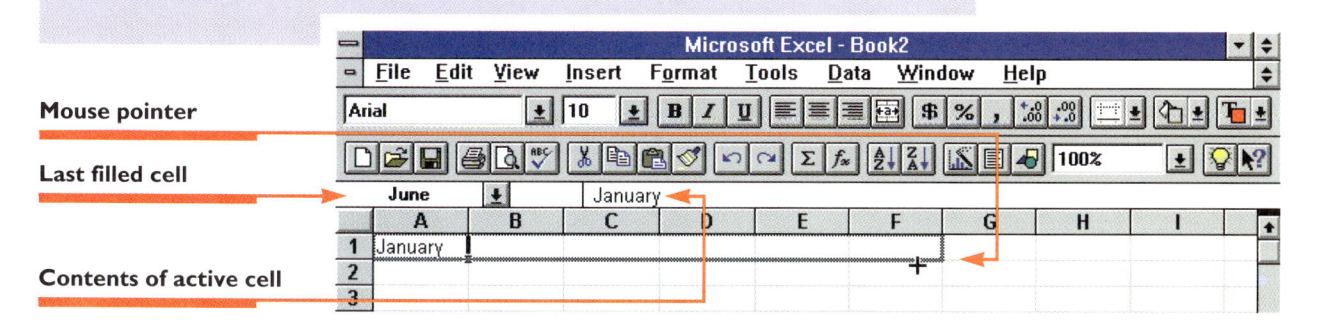

FIGURE 3-9: Using the fill handles to create a label series

QUICK TIP

Use the Fill Series command to examine all of Excel's available fill series options.

Copying and moving formulas, continued

To complete the Fall Tours part of her worksheet, Susie now must copy the formulas from the range B9:E9 to the range B18:E18. To do this, she'll use the Copy and Paste commands and the Fill Right command.

STEPS

5 Click cell **B9**, click **Edit** on the menu bar, then click **Copy**
The Copy command has the same effect as clicking the Copy tool. See Table 3-1 for Cut, Copy, Paste, and Undo shortcuts.

6 Click cell **B18**, click **Edit**, then click **Paste**
See Figure 3-10. The formula for calculating the September tours sales displays in the formula bar. You can also cut, copy, and paste between all the sheets in a workbook. Now Susie will use the Fill Right command to copy the formula from cell B18 to cells C18, D18 and E18.

7 Select the range **B18:E18**

8 Click **Edit**, click **Fill**, then click **Right**
The rest of the totals are filled in correctly. Compare your worksheet to Figure 3-11. Susie is done with this worksheet so she decides to save it.

9 Click the **Save tool** on the Standard toolbar

TABLE 3-1:
Cut, Copy, Paste, and Undo shortcuts

TOOL	KEYBOARD	MENU/COMMANDS	DESCRIPTION
	[Ctrl][X]	Edit, Cut	Deletes the selection from the cell or range and places it in Clipboard
	[Ctrl][C]	Edit, Copy	Copies the selection to the Clipboard
	[Ctrl][V]	Edit, Paste	Pastes the contents of the Clipboard in the active cell or range
	[Ctrl][Z]	Edit, Undo	Undoes the last editing action

FIGURE 3-10:
Worksheet with copied formula

Copied formula cell references

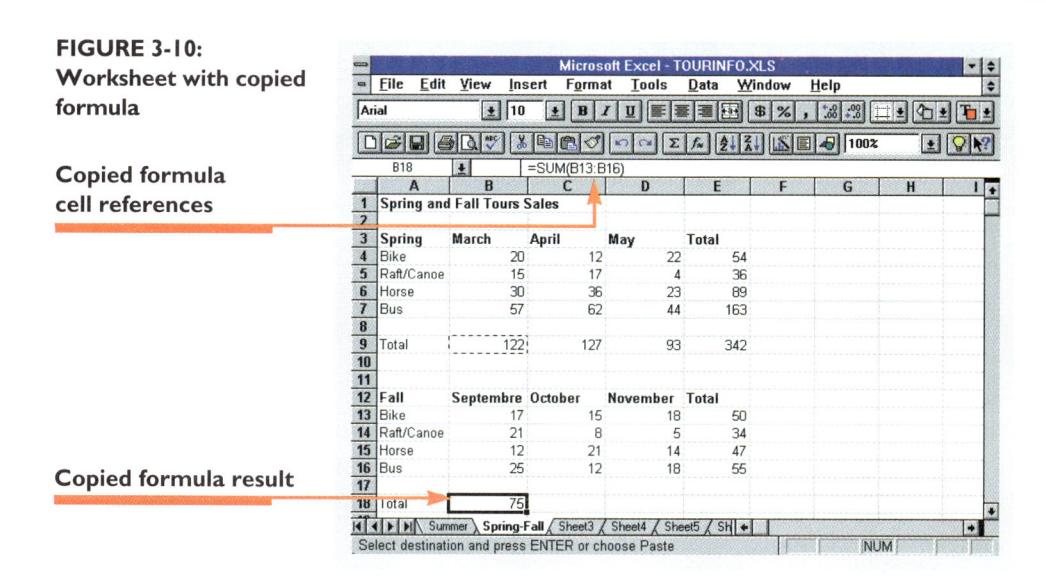

Copied formula result

FIGURE 3-11:
Completed worksheet with all formulas copied

Using Find & Replace to edit a worksheet

If the worksheet is large and you need to make repeated changes to a worksheet's labels or formulas, use the Replace command on the Edit menu to locate the data you want to change and change it. The Replace dialog box is shown in Figure 3-12. Enter the text, values, or formulas you want to change, called the **search criteria**, in the Find What text box. In the Replace with text box, enter the text, values, or formulas you want to replace the search criteria. Click Find Next to find the next occurrence of the search criteria and then click Replace to replace it with the replacement data, or click Replace All to replace all the instances of the search criteria in the workbook with the replacement data.

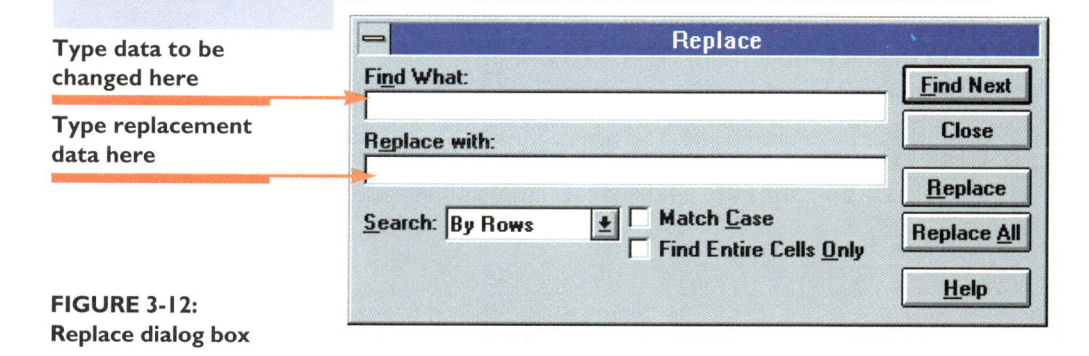

Type data to be changed here

Type replacement data here

FIGURE 3-12:
Replace dialog box

EXCEL 5 UNIT 3 REVISING A WORKSHEET

Copying formulas with absolute cell references

Sometimes you might want a cell reference to always refer to a particular cell address. In such an instance, you would use an absolute cell reference. An **absolute cell reference** always refers to a specific cell address, even if you move the formula to a new location. You identify an absolute reference by placing a dollar sign ($) before the row letter and column number of the cell address (for example $A$1). ▶ Susie decides to add a column that calculates a possible increase in the number of Spring tours in 1996. She wants to do a what-if analysis and recalculate the spreadsheet changing the percentage that the tours might increase.

Steps

1. Click **G1**, type **Change**, then press **[→]**
   Susie will store her increase factor, which will be used in the what-if analysis, in cell H1.

2. Click **H1**, type **1.1**, then press **[Enter]**

3. Click **F3**, type **1996?**, then press **[Enter]**
   Now, she will create a formula that refers to her increase factor in cell H1.

4. In cell **F4**, type **=E4*H1**, then click the **Enter button**
   The result, 59.4, appears in cell F4. Susie now uses the fill handle to copy the formula in cell F4 to F5:F7.

5. Drag the fill handle to select cells F4 through F7
   The resulting values in range F5:F7 are all zeros. When Susie looks at the formula in cell F5, which is =E5*H2, she realizes she needs to use an absolute reference to cell H1. Susie can correct this error by editing cell F4 using [F4], a shortcut key, to change the relative cell reference to an absolute cell reference.

6. Click cell **F4**, press **[F2]** to change to edit mode, then press **[F4]**
   Dollar signs appear making the H1 reference absolute. See Figure 3-13.

7. Click the **Enter button**
   Now that the formula correctly contains an absolute cell reference, Susie uses the fill handle again to copy the formula in cell F4 to the range F5:F7.

8. Drag the fill handle from cell F4 to cell F7
   Now Susie completes her what-if analysis by changing the value in cell H1 from 1.1 to 2.5.

9. Click **H1**, type **2.5**, then click the **Enter button**
   The values in the range F4:F7 all change. Compare your worksheet to Figure 3-14.

FIGURE 3-13: Worksheet with absolute cell reference in cell F4

Absolute cell reference in formula

Incorrect values due to relative references

FIGURE 3-14: Worksheet recalculated with new value in cell H1

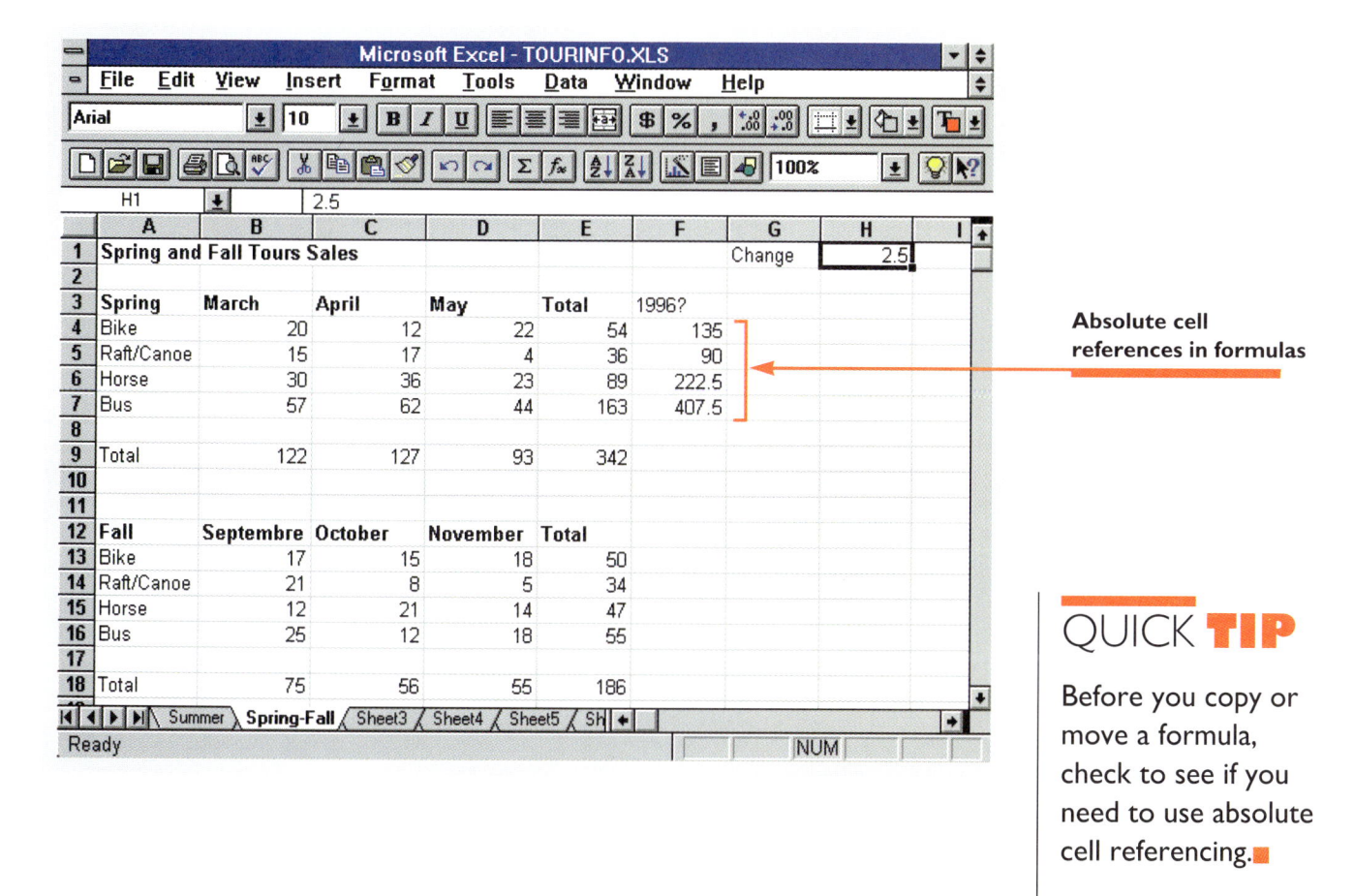

Absolute cell references in formulas

QUICK TIP

Before you copy or move a formula, check to see if you need to use absolute cell referencing.

EXCEL 5 UNIT 3 REVISING A WORKSHEET

Adjusting column widths

As you work with a worksheet, you might need to adjust the width of the columns to make your worksheet more usable. The default column width is 8.43 characters wide, a little less than one inch. With Excel, you can adjust the column width for one or more columns using the mouse or the Column command on the Format menu. Table 3-2 describes the commands available on the Format Column menu. ▶ As Susie looks over the worksheet, she notices that the columns containing the labels and data for the spring tour sales are much wider that they need to be. She decides to adjust these column widths.

Steps

1. **Move the mouse pointer to the column line between columns B and C**
   The mouse pointer changes to ✥, as shown in Figure 3-15. You can now make the column wider or narrower.

2. **Drag the column line to the left until column B is just wide enough to accommodate the March heading**
   Susie notices now that "Septembre" is not completely visible and this must be corrected.

3. **Move the mouse pointer to the column line between columns B and C until it changes to ✥, then double-click the left mouse button**
   The width of column B is automatically resized to fit the widest entry. This feature is called AutoFit. Next, Susie decides to make columns C, D, and E the same width as column B. Use the Column Width command on the Format menu to adjust several columns to the same width.

4. **Select the C, D, and E column selector buttons** (the gray boxes containing the column letters just above the worksheet)

5. **Click Format on the menu bar, click Column, then click Width**
   The Column Width dialog box displays. See Figure 3-16. Move the dialog box, if necessary, by dragging its title bar so you can see the contents of the worksheet.

6. **Type 10 in the Column Width text box, then click OK**
   The column widths change to reflect the new settings. Susie is satisfied and decides to save her worksheet.

7. **Click the Save tool on the Standard toolbar**

TABLE 3-2: Format Column commands

COMMAND	DESCRIPTION
Width	Set the width to a specific number of characters
AutoFit Selection	Fit the widest entry
Hide	Hide
Unhide	Unhide column(s)
Standard Width	Reset to default widths

FIGURE 3-15: Preparing to change the column width

Mouse pointer between columns B & C

FIGURE 3-16: Worksheet with Column Width dialog box

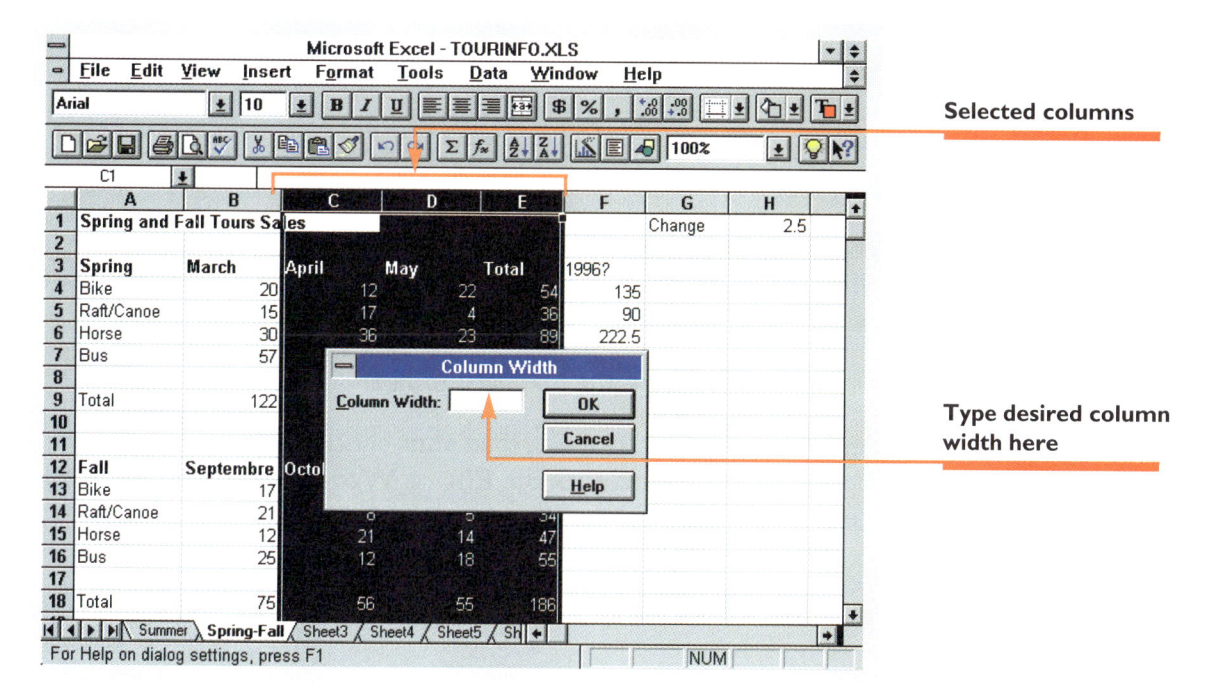

Selected columns

Type desired column width here

Specifying row height

The Row Height command on the Format menu allows you to customize row height to improve readability. Row height is calculated in **points**, units of measure also used for fonts. One inch equals 72 points. The row height must exceed the size of the font you are using. For example, if you are using a 12-point font, the row height must be more than 12 points. Normally, you don't need to adjust row heights manually. If you format something in a row to be a larger point size, Excel will adjust the row to fit the largest point size in the row.

QUICK TIP

To reset columns to the default width, select the range of cells and then use the Column Standard Width command on the Format menu. Click OK in the dialog box to accept the default width. ■

EXCEL 5 UNIT 3 REVISING A WORKSHEET

Checking spelling

It's important that your data be accurate as well as attractive. Just as you would use a spell checker in any business document, it's vital that you show the same attention to detail in your worksheets. Excel's built-in dictionary allows you to check a single word or an entire worksheet. ▶ Susie's forecast will be circulated among the managers at Nationwide Travel so she decides to check the spelling before the worksheet is printed.

Steps

1. **Click cell A1 or press [Ctrl][Home]**
   Excel begins spell-checking at the active cell and continues spell-checking to the end of the worksheet.

2. **Click the Spell Check tool on the Standard toolbar**
   You could also click Tools on the menu bar, then click Spelling. The Spelling dialog box displays, indicating the first word the dictionary does not recognize is "Septembre". See Figure 3-17. The dialog box provides suggestions for replacing the unrecognized word.

3. **Click Change in the Change To text box, to accept the suggested spelling**
   Excel tells you when it has finished checking the spelling of the active worksheet. See Figure 3-18.

4. **Click OK**
   Susie is satisfied that her worksheet is correct. She decides to save her changes and then preview and print the workbook.

5. **Click the Save tool on the Standard toolbar**

6. **Click the Print Preview tool, then after checking the appearance of the worksheets, click Print, click the Entire Workbook radio button, then click OK**

7. **After the worksheets have printed, click File on the menu bar, then click Close**

FIGURE 3-17: Spelling dialog box

Click to ignore suggested change

Error will be changed to selection

Click to accept suggested change

Spelling error

FIGURE 3-18: Finished spell checking dialog box

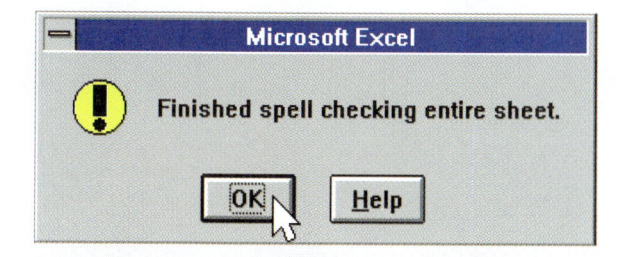

Modifying the dictionary

Excel's dictionary can be modified to include words you use frequently, such as proper nouns. To add a word to the dictionary, click Add in the Spelling dialog box when the desired word appears in the Not in Dictionary area. To neither correct nor add a highlighted word, click Ignore in the dialog box. If you are working with networked computers, however, you might not be able to modify the dictionary.

EXCEL 5 UNIT 3 REVISING A WORKSHEET

CONCEPTSREVIEW

Label each of the elements of the Excel screen shown in Figure 3-19.

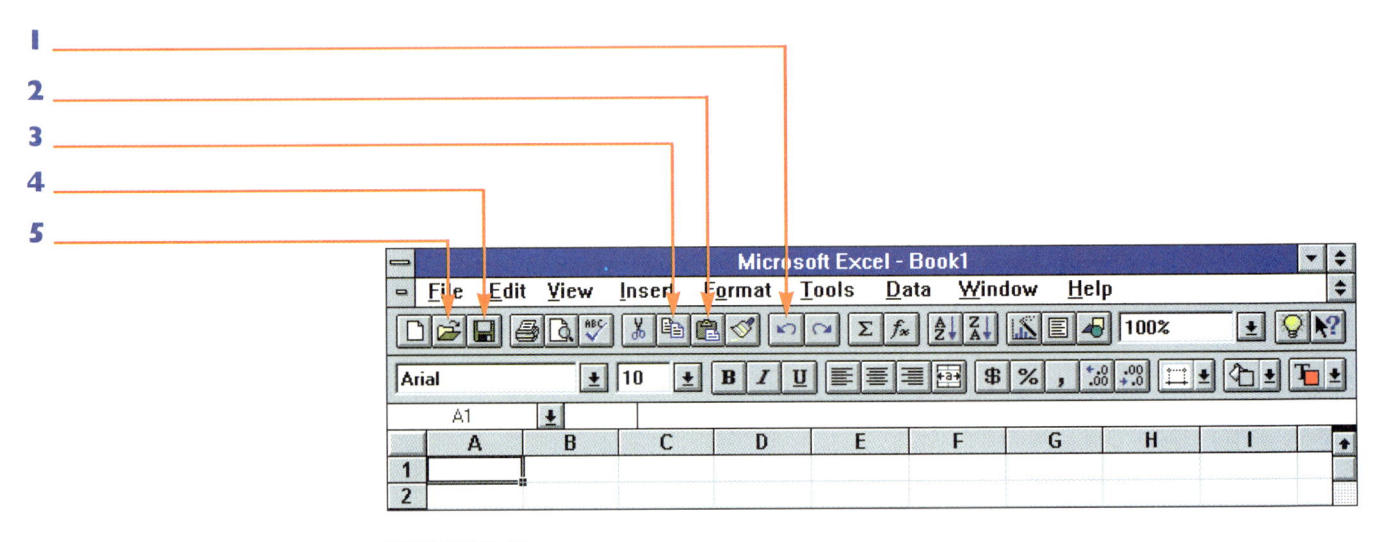

1 _____
2 _____
3 _____
4 _____
5 _____

FIGURE 3-19

Match each of the statements to the command it describes.

6 Adds a new row or column in the active worksheet

7 Erases the contents of a cell or range of cells

8 Duplicates the contents of a cell

9 Reverses your most recent action or command

10 Pastes the contents of the Clipboard in the active cell

a. Undo tool
b. Edit Delete
c. Insert Row/Column
d. [Ctrl][V]
e. Copy tool

Select the best answer from the list of choices.

11 When you copy data using the Copy tool, Excel places the selected data on the:
   a. Border
   b. Menu
   c. Clipboard
   d. Range

12 A cell address which changes when copied into a new location is called a(n)
   a. absolute reference
   b. relative reference
   c. mixed reference
   d. combined reference

13 Cell D4 contains the formula =A4+B4+C4. If you copy this formula to cell D5, what will the formula be in cell D5?
   a. =$A$4+$B$4+$C$4
   b. =A4+B4+C4-D4
   c. =D5-D4
   d. =A5+B5+C5

APPLICATIONS REVIEW

1. Create a workbook in which you will enter and correct cell data.

   a. Open a new workbook and rename the Sheet1 tab as MUSIC.
   b. Save the workbook as SHARP.XLS.
   c. Enter the title B. SHARP INSTRUMENTS, INC. in cell A1.
   d. Enter the column headings in cells B3, C3, and D3 using the data from Table 3-3.

   TABLE 3-3
   B. SHARP INSTRUMENTS, INC.

	Oct. 1995	Nov. 1995	Dec. 1995
Cellos			
Guitars			
Pianos			
Tubas			

   e. Enter the four instruments down the left side of the worksheet in the range A4:A7. The labels Cellos, Guitars, Pianos, and Tubas display in the range.
   f. Adjust the column widths to the widest entry in each column.
   g. Use the Clear command to remove the contents of cell A7. Only three instruments are now listed on the worksheet.
   h. Click cell B4, enter the number 40, then press [Enter]. The value displays in cell B4.
   i. Click the Undo tool to undo your last action. Cell B4 is now empty.
   j. Click the Save File tool to save your work.

2. Copy and paste values in the existing worksheet.

   a. Enter the value 50 in cell B4, then press [Enter].
   b. Click cell B4, click Edit on the menu bar, then click Copy.
   c. Select the range B4:C6 then press [Ctrl][V].
   d. Enter the value 60 in cell D4, then press [Enter].
   e. Use the Copy tool and the Paste tool to copy the contents of cell D4 to range D5:D6.
   f. Save your workbook.

3. Use the Fill Down shortcut to copy formulas in the existing worksheet.

   a. Enter a formula in cell E4 to calculate the total cello sales during the three-month period. Use cell references, not actual numbers, to build this formula.
   b. Position the cell pointer in cell E4, then select the range E4:E6.
   c. Click Edit on the menu bar, then click Fill Down. Excel copies the formula from cell E4 to the selected range.
   d. Click cell E5 and notice the formula in the formula bar. Excel automatically adjusted the formula so that it calculated the guitar data in row 5.

4. Use an absolute cell reference to calculate sales tax.

   a. Click cell C10, then type .075.
   b. Type "Sales Tax Rate" in cell A10.
   c. Type "Sales Tax" in cell F3.
   d. Enter a formula in cell F4 that calculates the total sales tax for each cellos. Use an absolute cell reference, not actual numbers, to build this formula.
   e. Use the fill handle to copy the formula from cell F4 to range F5:F6.
   f. Save your workbook.
   g. Print a copy of the worksheet, then close the file.

5. Modify a payroll worksheet.

   a. Open the file UNIT3AR5.XLS on your Student Disk.
   b. Save this workbook as SUNCOAST.
   c. Adjust all column widths using the AutoFit feature.
   d. Click the row 5 selector button, click Insert, then click Rows. A new, blank row displays between S. Lipski and L. Skillings.
   e. Enter the new employee, F. Monticello.
   f. Enter 40 for Monticello's hours worked, then 11 for his hourly wage.
   g. Copy the appropriate formula to calculate Monticello's gross pay.
   h. Delete the row containing payroll information for S. Lipski, using the Delete command.
   i. Add the first names of all employees to the Employee column. These are Daniel Hillman, Frank Monticello, and Laurie Skillings.
   j. Save your work.

6 Adjust column widths in the SUNCOAST workbook.

   a. Use the AutoFit feature to make the employee column adjust to the widest entry.

   b. When you are satisfied with the revised worksheet, save your workbook.

   c. Save your work and use print preview to examine the worksheet.

7 Use the drag and drop method to move data in the SUNCOAST workbook.

   a. Select the range of cells containing the entire payroll.

   b. Drag the range down three rows so that you can add some titles to the worksheet.

   c. Enter the company's name, Suncoast, in cell A1, then enter the label Weekly Payroll in cell A2.

   d. Use drag and drop to move the contents of cell A2 to cell C1.

   e. Save your work, then print the worksheet.

   f. Close the workbook.

INDEPENDENT CHALLENGES

As a sales representative for Jason Pharmaceuticals Corporation, you attend many medical conferences all over the country. You have a budgeted expense account for this travel. At the end of each month, you are required to submit an expense report to your Accounting Department. This report shows how your actual expenses compare with your budgeted expenses.

Plan and build a worksheet that itemizes your monthly expenses and shows the difference between the budgeted and actual expenses. Include a separate section that shows the total budgeted amount, the total amount spent, and the percentage of budget used.

Your monthly travel budget is as follows: $3,000 for airline tickets, $1,500 for lodging, $750 for automobile rental, and $1,100 for meals.

Enter your own data for the actual expenses. You can assume that you did not use all of your allotted budget, except for the car rental, which was $200 over budget.

To complete this independent challenge:

1. Sketch a sample worksheet on a piece of paper, indicating how the information should be organized. How will you calculate the differences between budgeted and actual expenses? What formulas can you copy to save time and keystrokes? Which cell contents can you refer to in order to calculate the budget totals and the percentage of budget used?

2. In a new workbook, build a worksheet named EXPENSE by entering a title, row labels, column titles, and formulas. Remember to use the budgeted amounts listed above, but enter your own actual amounts.

3. Save this workbook as BUDGET1.XLS.

4. Before printing, preview the file so you know what the worksheet will look like. Adjust any items as needed, then print the worksheet.

5. A new company-wide policy allows you to submit up to $100 in miscellaneous travel expenses (parking, dry cleaning, and so on). This expense must appear in the row after the lodging entry on your report. Revise the worksheet to insert the new data regarding miscellaneous expenses. Make sure your totals and percentages reflect the new data entry. Save your changes, then print the revised worksheet.

Using the monthly budget of $3,000 for air travel, $1,500 for lodging, $750 for automobile rental, and $1,100 for meals, plan and build a worksheet that projects the economic effect of a 5% increase in all travel expenses. Include additional projections that show the effect of a 10%, 20%, and 30% increase, as well as a 5% and 10% decrease in expenses.

To complete this independent challenge:

1. Sketch a sample worksheet on a piece of paper, indicating how the information should be organized. How will you show projected increases and decreases in expenses? What type of cell references will you use?

2. In a new workbook, build a worksheet named PROJECTIONS by entering a title, row labels, column titles, and formulas. Use the expense amounts listed above.

3. Save this workbook as BUDGET2.XLS.

4. Before printing, preview the file so you know what the worksheet will look like. Adjust any items as needed, then print the worksheet.

5. In addition to the travel expenses already budgeted, the company has decided to add $45 per diem to the expense list. Please include this new item to the list, and revise any formulas to reflect this new entry. Save your changes, then print the revised worksheet.

UNIT 4

OBJECTIVES

▶ Format values

▶ Format cell data with fonts and point sizes

▶ Format cell data with attributes and alignment

▶ Customize the toolbar

▶ Use colors, patterns, and borders

▶ Use AutoFormat

▶ Freeze rows and columns

Enhancing A WORKSHEET

You already know how to create a worksheet, how to add and delete information in cells, and how to insert and delete rows and columns. In this unit, you will learn how to use tools and menu commands to change fonts, and add colors and borders to create attractive and effective worksheets. You will also learn how to use numeric formatting to display values as dates, percentages, and currency. ▶ Steven McCann works in the Marketing Department of the Nationwide Travel Company. Steven needs to improve the appearance of worksheets he creates to make them more attractive and easier to read and use. ▶

Formatting values

Formatting is how information displays in cells; it does not alter your data in any way. To format a cell, you must first select it and then apply formatting you want. You can also format a range of cells; this is called **range formatting**. Cells and ranges can be formatted before or after data is entered. Values can be formatted in several ways. Sometimes when you enter values in a cell, the cell might appear to display incorrect information. This is because you've used the wrong number format. ▶ Steven looks at his worksheet that tracks marketing expenditures and due dates for invoices. He has already formatted some of the values in the worksheet and he wants to finish.

STEPS

1 Open the worksheet UNIT4.XLS, then save it as MARKETNG
Refer to the lesson "Opening an existing worksheet" in Unit 3 if you need help. First, Steven wants to format the Cost ea. data so it displays with a dollar sign.

2 Select the range **E4:E32**, then click the **Currency tool** 💲 on the Formatting toolbar
Excel adds dollar signs and two decimal places to the Cost ea. data. Columns G, H, and I contain dollar values also, but Steven doesn't want to repeat the dollar sign.

3 Select the range **G4:I32**, then click the **Comma tool** on the Formatting toolbar
Column J contains percentages.

4 Select the range **J4:J32**, click the **Percentage tool** %, then click the **Increase Decimal tool** to show 1 decimal place
Data in the % of Total column displays as percentages. Now Steven wants to reformat the invoice dates.

5 Select the range **B4:B31**, click **Format**, then click **Cells**
The Format Cells dialog box displays, as shown in Figure 4-1. You can also use this dialog box to format ranges with currency, comma, and percentages.

6 Select the format d-mmm-yy in the Format Codes list box, then click **OK**
Notice that the selected dates change appearance. Steven doesn't need the year to appear in the Inv Due column.

7 Select the range **C4:C31**, click **Format**, click **Cells**, click **d-mmm**, then click **OK**
Compare your worksheet to Figure 4-2. Now save the workbook.

8 Click the **Save tool** on the Standard toolbar

FIGURE 4-1:
Number Format dialog box

Select a category

Sample of selected format

Select a format code

FIGURE 4-2:
Worksheet with formatted values

Modified date format

Decrease decimal tool

Increase decimal tool

Comma tool

Percentage tool

Currency tool

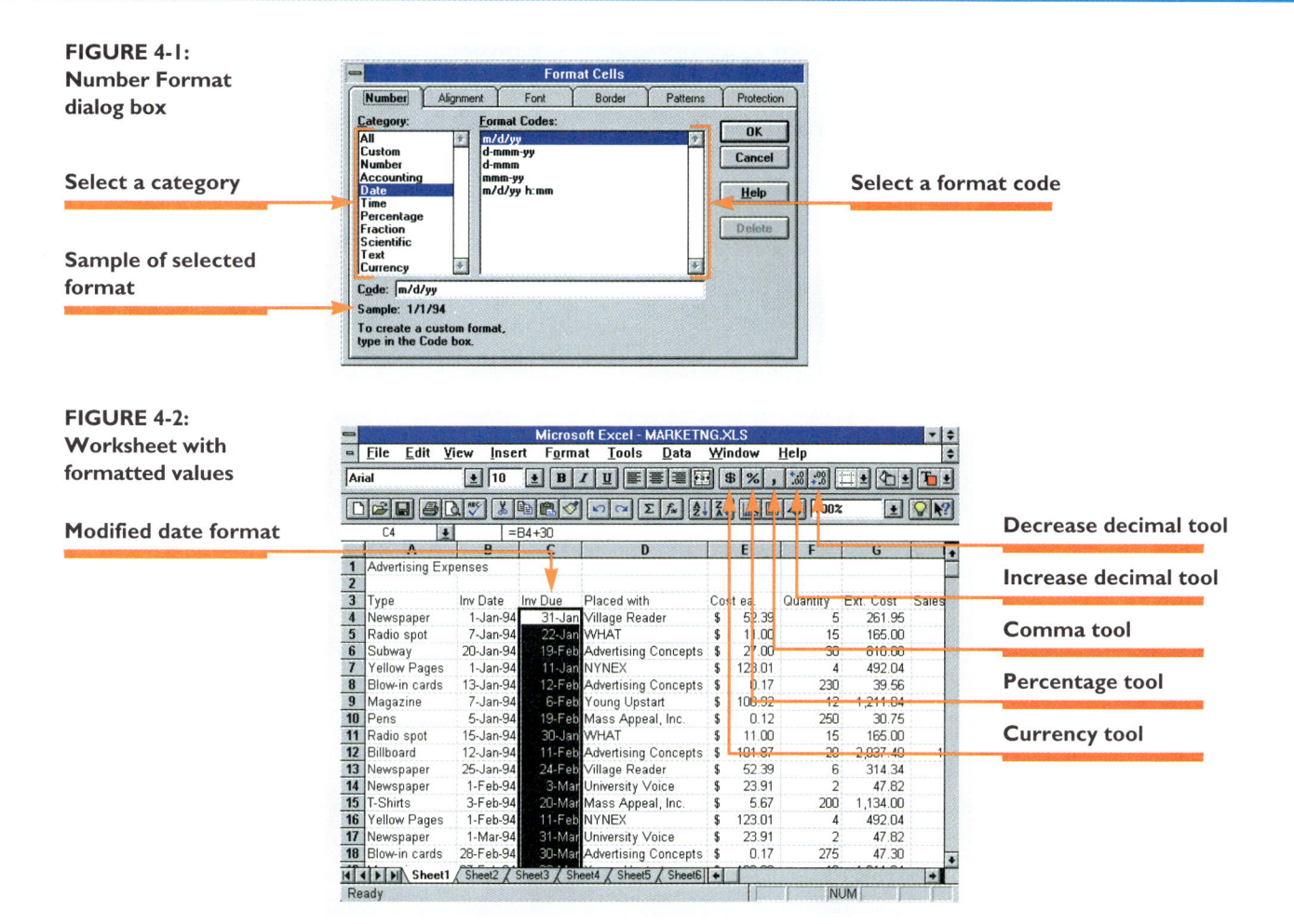

Using the Format Painter tool

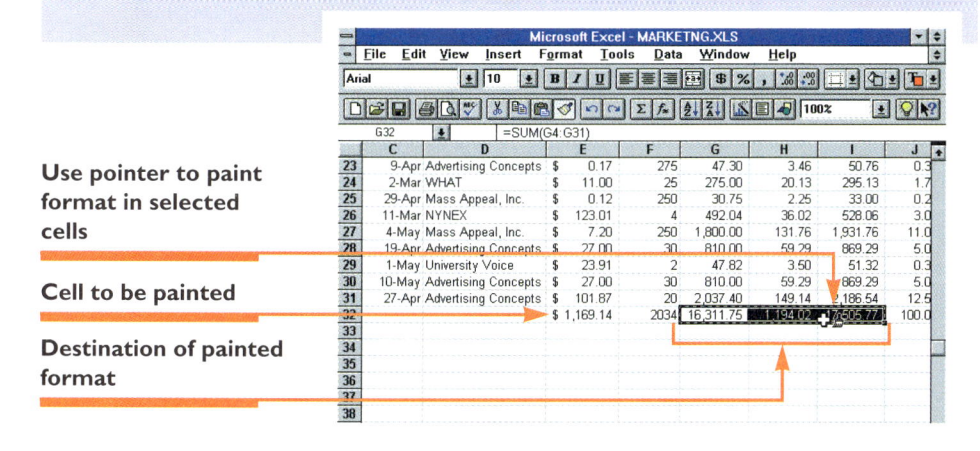

A cell's format can be "painted" into other cells using the Format Painter tool. This is similar to using drag and drop to copy information, but instead of copying cell contents, you only copy the cell format such as alignment and boldface. Select the cell containing the desired format and then click. The pointer changes to, as shown in Figure 4-3. Use this pointer to select the cell or range you want to contain the painted format.

Use pointer to paint format in selected cells

Cell to be painted

Destination of painted format

FIGURE 4-3: Using the Format painter

QUICK TIP

Pick which cells will contain dollar signs and decimal places carefully: both take up additional space and might not be necessary.■

EXCEL 5 UNIT 4 **ENHANCING** A WORKSHEET

71

Formatting cell data with fonts and point sizes

The **font** is the style and size of type used to display information in cells. The default font in Excel is 10-point Arial. A **point** is a measure of the size of a font. You can change the font, the size, or both of any entry or section in a worksheet. Table 4-1 shows several fonts in different sizes. ▶ Steven decides to improve the appearance of the worksheet. He wants to make the title and labels stand out. He'll do this by changing the size and font of these labels.

STEPS

1. Press **[Ctrl][Home]** to move to cell A1

2. Click **Format**, click **Cells**, then click the **Font tab**
   See Figure 4-4. Steven decides to change the title from Arial, the default font, to Times New Roman, and he will increase the font size to 24.

3. Click **Times New Roman** in the font list box, then click **24** in the size list box, then click **OK**
   If you don't have Times New Roman in your list of fonts, choose another font. The title font displays in 24-point Times New Roman, and the formula bar displays the new font and size information. Steven decides to make the column headings bigger, too.

4. Select the range **A3:J3**, click **Format**, then click **Cells**
   The Font tab should still be the front-most tab.

5. Click **Times New Roman** in the font list box, click **14** in the Size list box, then click **OK**

6. Resize the column widths in columns A through J so the larger labels fit in their cells, then click cell **A3**
   When you are done, compare your worksheet to Figure 4-5.

7. Click the **Save tool** 💾 to save your formatting changes

TABLE 4-1: Types of formatting

FONT	12 POINT	24 POINT
Arial	Excel	Excel
Helvetica	Excel	Excel
Palatino	Excel	Excel
Times	Excel	Excel

FIGURE 4-4: Font tab of the Format Cells dialog box

- Current font
- Available font
- Click to select effects 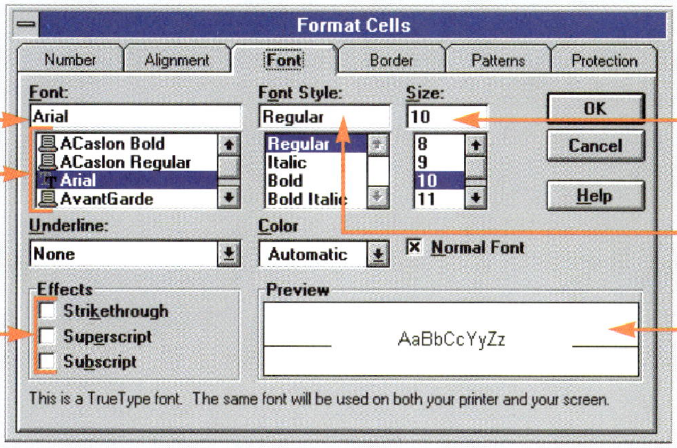
- Type a custom size or select a size from the list
- Select a formatting attribute
- Sample of selected font

FIGURE 4-5: Worksheet with newly formatted title and column headings

- Point size of current cell
- Title after changing to 24-point Times New Roman
- Column heading now 14-point Times New Roman

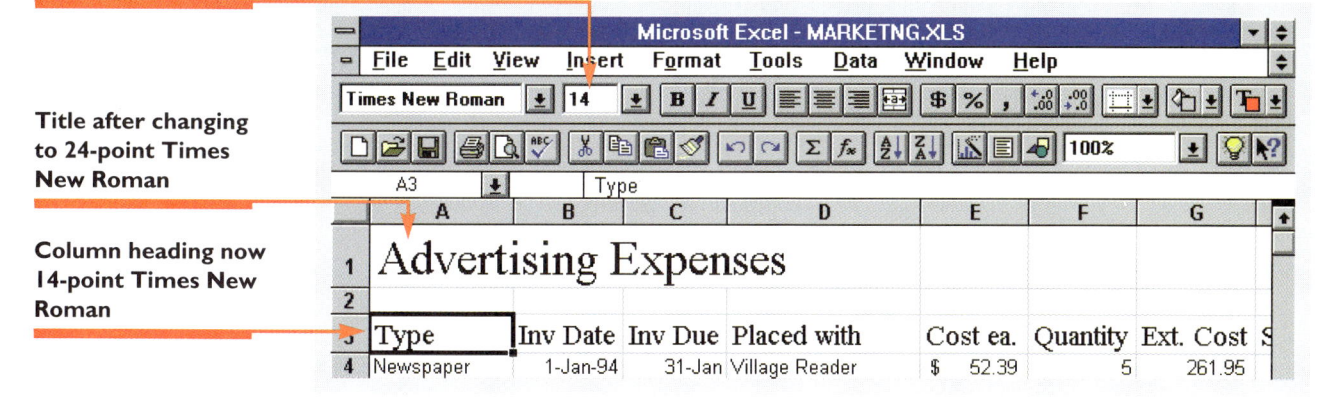

Using the Formatting toolbar to change fonts and sizes

The font and size of the active cell appear on the Formatting toolbar. Click the Font list box, as shown in Figure 4-6, to see a list of available fonts. If you want to change the font, first select the text, then click the Font list arrow and choose the font you want. You can change the size of selected text in the same way, but click the Size list arrow to display a list of available point sizes.

Available fonts will depend on your selected printer

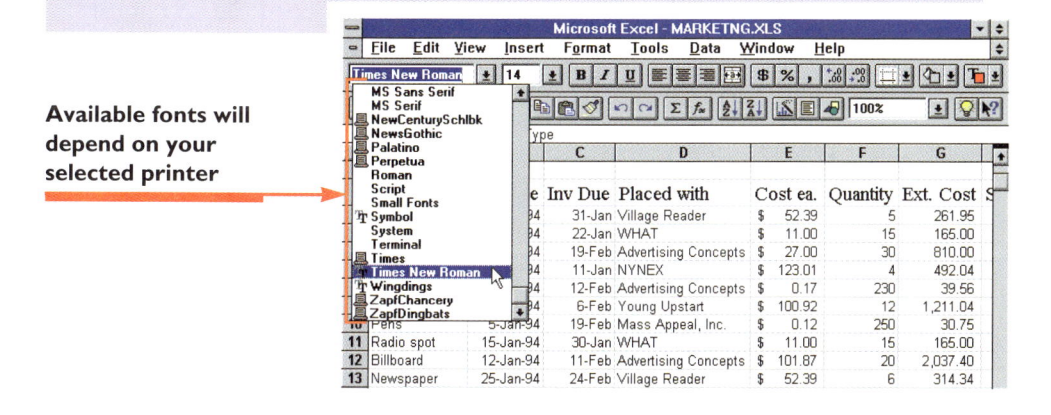

FIGURE 4-6: Available fonts on the Formatting toolbar

QUICK TIP

The Format Cells dialog box displays a sample of the selected font. Use the Format Cells command if you're unsure of the style of a font. ■

EXCEL 5 UNIT 4 ENHANCING A WORKSHEET

73

Formatting cell data with attributes and alignment

Attributes are styling features such as bold, italics, and underlining. You can apply bold, italics, and underlining from the Formatting toolbar or from the Font tab of the Format Cells dialog box. You can also change the alignment of text in cells. Left, right, or center alignment can be applied from the Formatting toolbar, or from the Alignment tab of the Format Cells dialog box. See Table 4-2 for a description of the available formatting tools. ▶ Steven wants to further refine his worksheet by boldfacing, underlining, and centering some of the labels.

STEPS

1. Click cell **A1** to select the title Advertising Expenses, then click the **Bold tool**
   The title Advertising Expenses appears in bold.

2. Select the range **A3:J3**, then click the **Underline tool**
   Excel underlines the column headings in the selected range.

3. Click cell **A3**, click the **Italics tool**, then click the **Bold tool**
   The word "Type" appears in boldface italic type. Notice that the Bold, Italics, and Underline tools are selected. Steven decides he doesn't like the italic formatting. He will remove it by clicking again.

4. Click
   Excel removes italics from cell A3.

5. Continue adding bold formatting to the rest of the column headings in the range B3:J3
   Steven wants to center the title over the data.

6. Use any method to widen the columns in the range B3:J3

7. Select the range **A1:F1**, then click the **Center Across Columns tool**
   The title Advertising Expenses is centered across six columns. Now Steven decides to center the column headings in their cells.

8. Select the range **A3:J3**, then click the **Align Center tool** to center the text in each cell of the range
   Steven is happy with the formatting on this worksheet and decides to save his changes.

9. Click the **Save tool**
   Compare your results with those shown in Figure 4-7. Highlighting information on a worksheet can be very useful, but overuse of any attribute can make a document less readable and distracting. Be consistent, adding emphasis the same way throughout a workbook or set of documents.

EXCEL 5 UNIT 4 **ENHANCING** A WORKSHEET

Align Center tool

Tools depressed

FIGURE 4-7: Worksheet with formatting attributes applied

Title centered across columns

Column headings centered, bold, and underlined

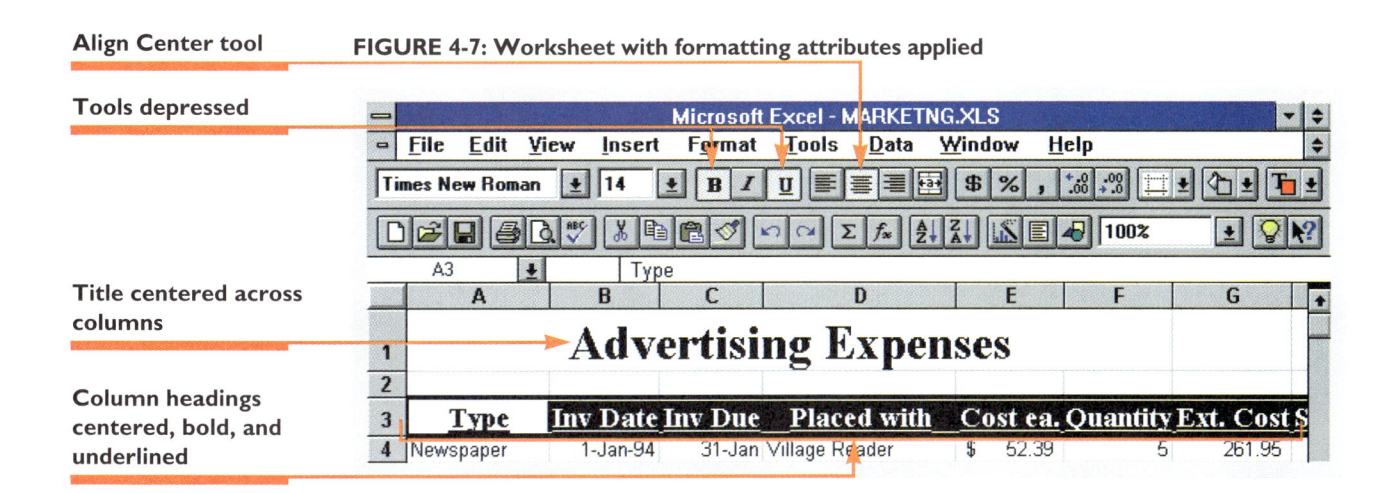

Formatting non-contiguous ranges

You can format non-contiguous (cells not touching one another) by selecting the first range, then holding down [Ctrl] while selecting each subsequent range. Once all the desired ranges are selected, apply the formatting attributes as you normally would. Figure 4-8 shows the selection of multiple ranges. To deselect the ranges, click anywhere within the worksheet.

Range

Ranges

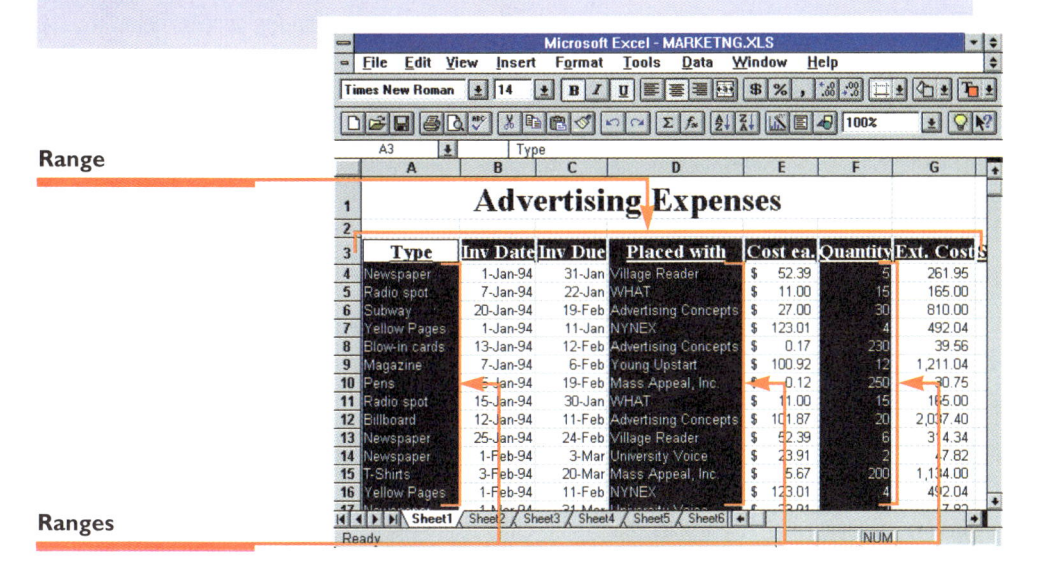

FIGURE 4-8: Multiple ranges selected

TABLE 4-2: Formatting tools

ICON	DESCRIPTION	ICON	DESCRIPTION
B	Adds boldface	≡	Aligns left
I	Italicizes	≡	Aligns right
U	Underlines	≡	Centers
▦	Adds lines or borders	▦	Centers across columns

QUICK **TIP**

Use the GoTo (F5) key or the name list box as a way of quickly selecting a range to be formatted.∎

Customizing the toolbar

To enable you to work as efficiently as possible, Excel has provided toolbars from which you can directly carry out most commonly performed tasks. You can further customize your environment by adding tools not present on a toolbar or by deleting those tools you rarely use. You can also create your own toolbars and display them as you see fit. ▶ Steven realizes that he spends a lot of time making his worksheets look attractive for presentations. He decides to create his own toolbar, and add formatting tools not currently displayed on the Standard or Formatting toolbars.

STEPS

1 Click **View** then click **Toolbars**
The Toolbars dialog box displays, as shown in Figure 4-9.

2 Double-click **Standard** in the Toolbar Name text box at the bottom of the dialog box, type **Steven's**, then click **OK**
This creates a new floating toolbar called "Steven's" in the worksheet window. The Customize dialog box, from which you will drag tools to the new toolbar displays.

3 Click **Formatting** in the Categories list box, then click the **Dark Shading tool**
Notice that when you click a tool, sometimes called a button, a description appears below the Categories list box. See Figure 4-10.

4 Drag to Steven's toolbar
The new tool appears in the toolbar, and the toolbar expands to accommodate it.

5 Click **Text Formatting** in the Categories list box, then click the **Double Underlining tool**, then drag it to Steven's toolbar

6 Click **Drawing** in the Categories list box, then drag the Pattern tool to Steven's toolbar

7 Click **Edit** in the Categories list box, then drag the Delete Row tool, Delete Column tool, Insert Row tool, and Insert Column tool to Steven's toolbar
Steven is satisfied with his new toolbar and decides to close the Customize dialog box.

8 Click **Close** in the Customize dialog box
Compare your results with Steven's toolbar shown in Figure 4-11. Your toolbar might look slightly different. You can add and delete tools from existing toolbars by using the arrow keys to select the name of the toolbar in the Tools dialog box, then clicking Customize.

FIGURE 4-9: Toolbars dialog box

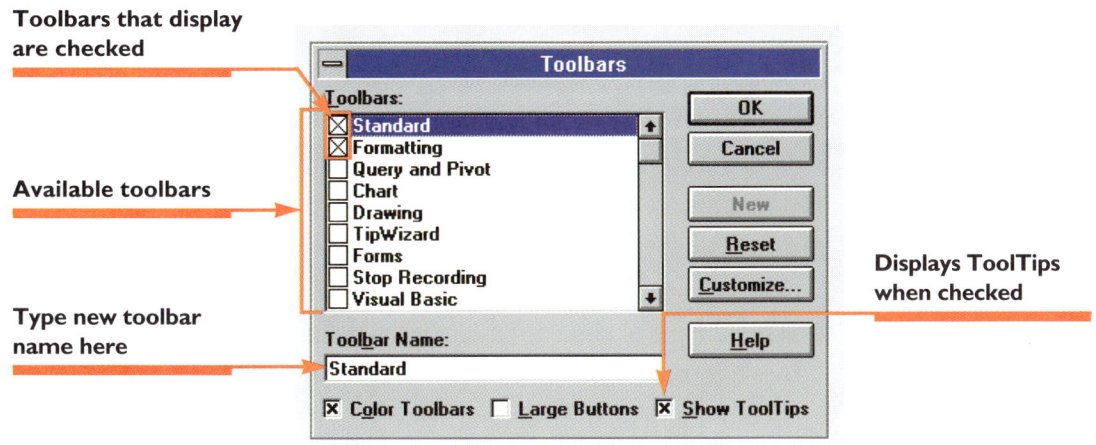

- Toolbars that display are checked
- Available toolbars
- Type new toolbar name here
- Displays ToolTips when checked

FIGURE 4-10: Customize dialog box

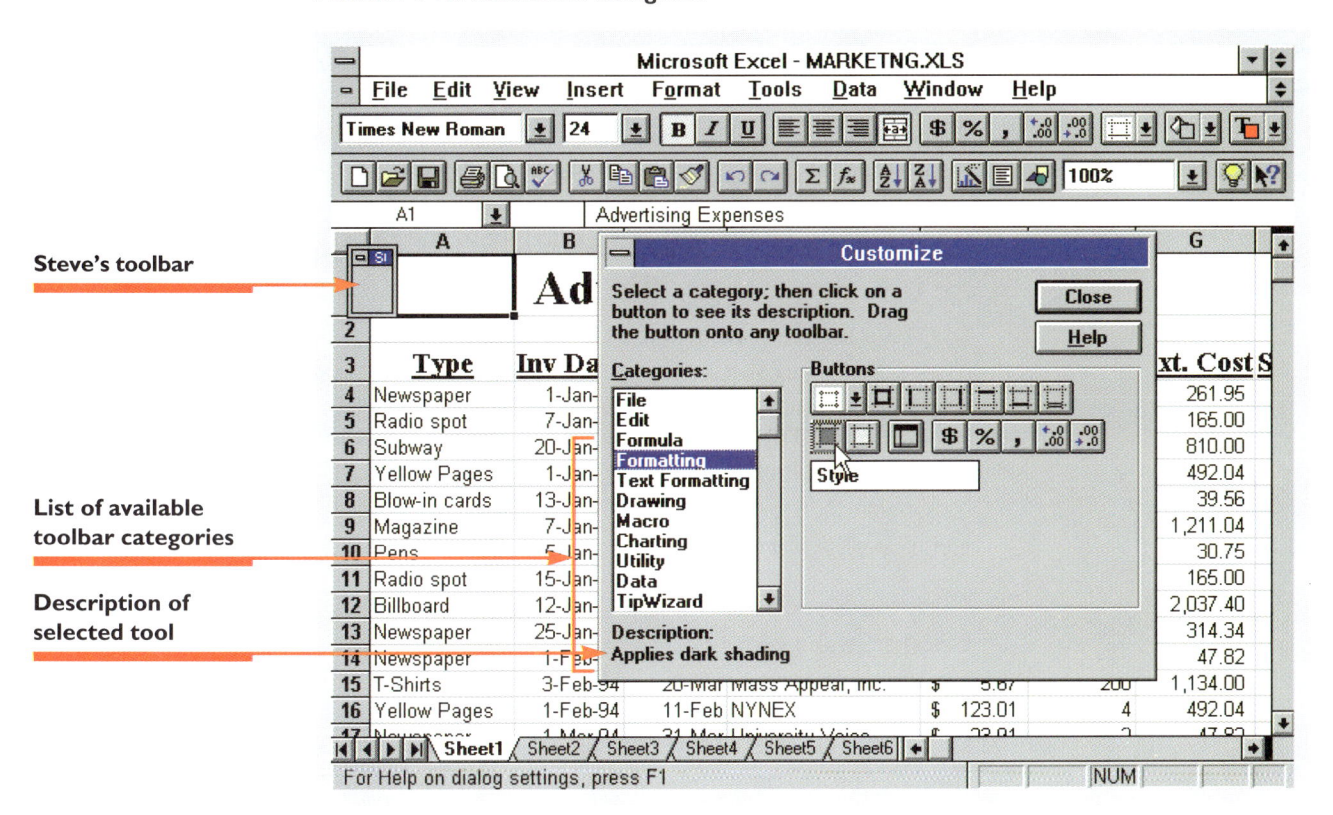

- Steve's toolbar
- List of available toolbar categories
- Description of selected tool

FIGURE 4-11: Steven's toolbar

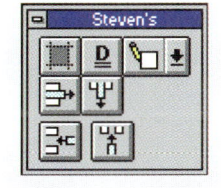

TROUBLE?

If you are working on a network, your new toolbars and/or changes might not be saved.

EXCEL 5 UNIT 4 ENHANCING A WORKSHEET

77

Using colors, patterns, and borders

You can use colors, patterns, and borders to enhance the overall appearance of a worksheet and to improve its readability. You can add these enhancements using the Patterns tab in the Format Cells dialog box or by using the Borders and Color tools on the Formatting toolbar and the Pattern tool on Steven's toolbar. When you use the Format Cells dialog box, you can see what your enhanced text will look like in the Sample box. ▶ Borders can be applied to all the cells in a worksheet or only to selected cells. Types of border tools are listed in Table 4-3. Color can be applied to the background of a cell or range or to cell contents. If your computer does not have a color monitor, the color palette will appear in shades of gray. Patterns can be applied to the background of a cell or range. ▶ Steven has decided to add a border, color, and a pattern to the title of the worksheet.

1 Select the range **B1:E1** where the title, Advertising Expenses, is located, then click the **Color tool** list arrow on the Formatting toolbar
The color palette appears. See Figure 4-12. When applying a background color, make sure that you have first selected the entire range in which the label or value displays on the screen.

2 Click **Yellow** (in the first row, third from the right)

3 Click the **Pattern tool** list arrow on Steven's toolbar
A palette of available patterns displays. Choose a pattern that will not obscure your text. Steven chooses the diamond pattern.

4 Click the **diamond pattern** (the last pattern in the third row)
When choosing a background pattern, consider that the more cell contents contrast with their background, the more readable the contents will be. Steven chooses a light pattern for his background. Next, Steven will add a border.

5 Click the **Borders tool** list arrow, then click the **heavy bottom border** (the second choice in the second row)
Next, he decides to change the font color.

6 Click cell **A1**, click the **Font Color tool** list arrow, then click **Blue** (fourth color from the right in the first row)
The text changes to color. Steven's final title is shown in Figure 4-13. Satisfied with his formatting enhancements, Steven decides to save his changes.

7 Click the **Save tool**

FIGURE 4-12: Color palette on the toolbar

Color tool

Color palette

FIGURE 4-13: Worksheet with borders and color formatting

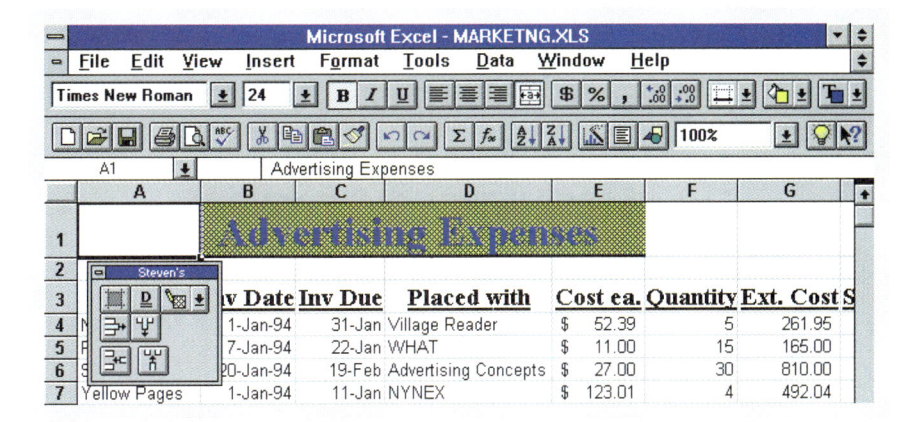

Using color to organize a worksheet

Use color to give a distinctive look to each part of a worksheet. For example, you might want to apply a light blue to all the rows containing the subway data and a light green to all the rows containing the newspaper data. Be consistent throughout a group of worksheets, and try to avoid colors that are too bright and distracting.

TABLE 4-3: Border Tools

TOOL	DESCRIPTION	TOOL	DESCRIPTION
	No border		Thin border around range
	Single underline		Left border
	Double underline		Right border
	Thick bottom, thin top border		Double bottom, single top
	Outline all in range		Thick bottom border
	Thick border around range		

QUICK TIP

Colors should be used sparingly. Excessive use can divert the reader's attention.

EXCEL 5 UNIT 4 **ENHANCING** A WORKSHEET

Using AutoFormat

Using colors within your worksheet is good way to enhance data; however, it would be tedious to format a large worksheet in this manner. Excel provides 16 preset formats called **AutoFormats**, which allows instant formatting of large amounts of data. AutoFormats include colors and cell attributes such as numeric formatting, borders, fonts, patterns, alignment, column width, and row height. AutoFormats are designed for worksheets with labels in the left column and top rows and totals in the bottom row or right column. ▶ Steven decides to use the AutoFormat feature to make his analysis of the advertising expenses data look more professional.

Steps

1 Click the **Sheet2 tab**
Move Steven's toolbar out of the way, if necessary.

2 Select the range **A4:D15**
Before choosing an AutoFormat, you must select the range to be formatted.

3 Click **Format** then click **AutoFormat**
The AutoFormat dialog box appears. When choosing an AutoFormat, consider how the data will be viewed. Steven wants to be able to reproduce two versions of his data for a quarterly marketing report: one will be black and white for an overhead transparency, the other will be in color.

4 Click **Colorful 1** in the Table Format list box
The Sample box previews your selection, as shown in Figure 4-14.

5 Click **OK** then click anywhere in the worksheet to deselect the range
The worksheet is now formatted using Colorful 1. Steven likes Colorful 1. Now he wants to find a suitable black and white format. Again, select the range first.

6 Click **Format** then click **AutoFormat**

7 Click **3D Effects 2,** click **OK**, then click anywhere in the worksheet to deselect the range
Compare your results to Figure 4-15. Steven is satisfied with this formatting and decides to save his changes.

8 Click the **Save tool**

FIGURE 4-14:
AutoFormat dialog box

AutoFormat list

Sample of selected AutoFormat

FIGURE 4-15:
3D Effects 2 AutoFormat

Formatted data for black and white overhead transparencies

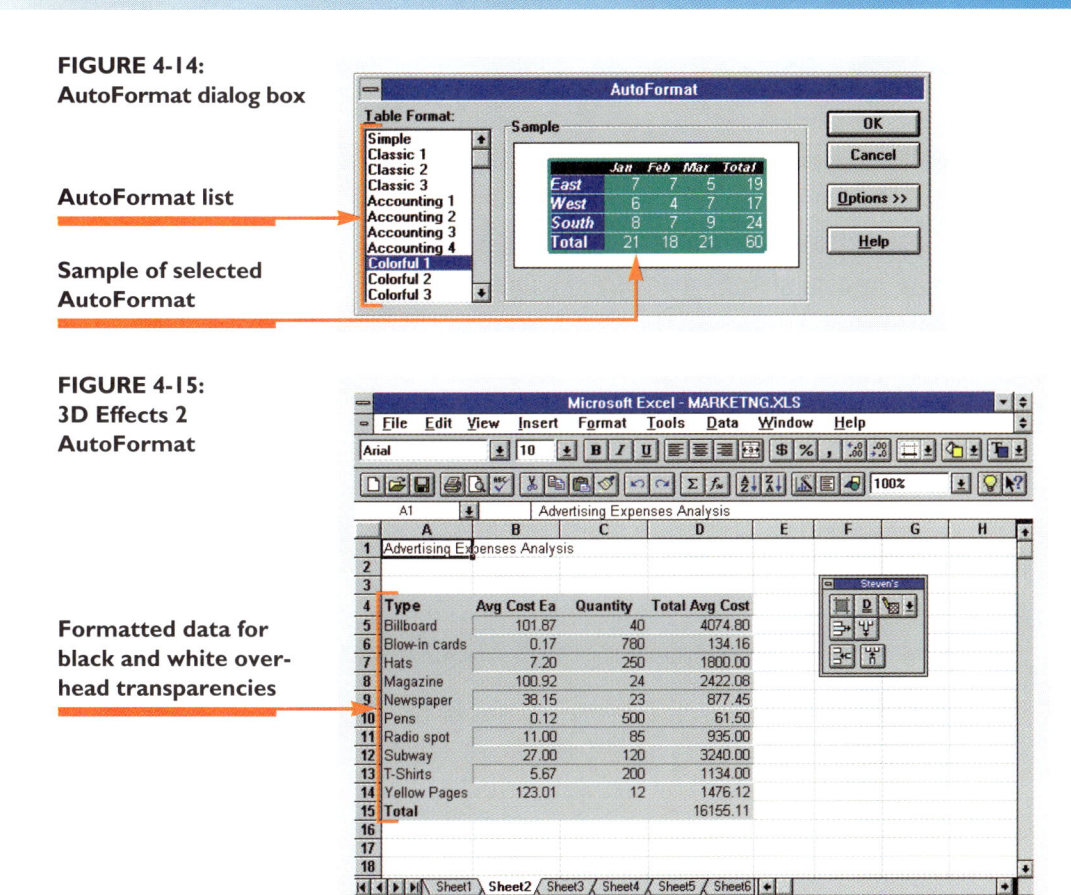

Integrating graphic images

You can integrate graphics files in a variety of formats in Excel spreadsheets. Place the cell pointer at the beginning of a range of blank rows where you will paste the graphic image. Click Insert on the menu bar and then click Picture. Select a graphic filename from the File name list box. To see a small, thumbnail sketch of the image, click the Preview Picture checkbox. Click OK to bring the graphic file into your worksheet. The image appears in the worksheet with small boxes called **handles** on each edge and corner. Click and drag the handles until the image is the size you want. See Figure 4-16.

Resizing pointer

Handles

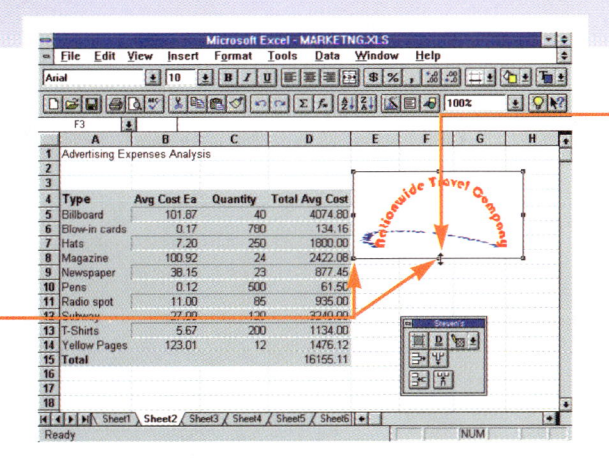

FIGURE 4-16: Worksheet with graphic image pasted in it

QUICK TIP

When selecting a large, unnamed range, select the upper left-most cell in the range, press and hold [Shift], then click the lower right-most cell in the range.

EXCEL 5 UNIT 4 ENHANCING A WORKSHEET

Freezing rows and columns

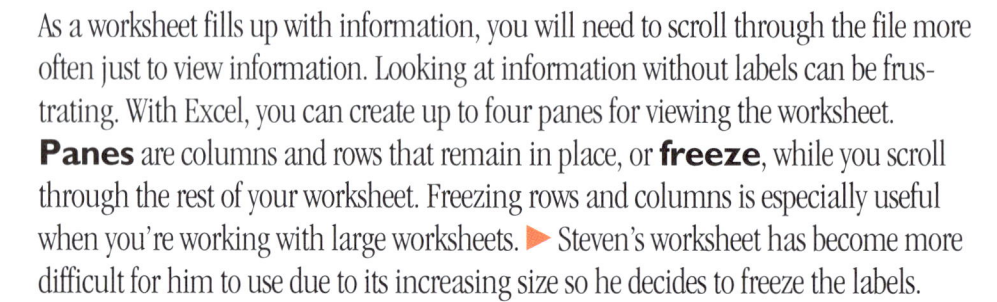

As a worksheet fills up with information, you will need to scroll through the file more often just to view information. Looking at information without labels can be frustrating. With Excel, you can create up to four panes for viewing the worksheet. **Panes** are columns and rows that remain in place, or **freeze**, while you scroll through the rest of your worksheet. Freezing rows and columns is especially useful when you're working with large worksheets. ▶ Steven's worksheet has become more difficult for him to use due to its increasing size so he decides to freeze the labels.

1 Click the **Sheet1 tab**

2 Press **[Ctrl][Home]** to move the cell pointer to A1, then click cell **B4**
Steven wants to be able to read the types of ads and view the information in the Total column at the same time. To do this, he will have to freeze column A. He also wants to be able to scroll down the worksheet and still read the column headings, so he will have to freeze the labels in row 3.

3 Click **Window**, then click **Freeze Panes**
Everything to the left and above the active cell is frozen. A thin line appears along the right side of the column to the left of the active cell and another line appears below the row above the active cell. See Figure 4-17.

4 Scroll down the worksheet using any method with which you're comfortable

5 Scroll the worksheet to the right
Notice that the information in column A and the information in rows 1-3 stayed on the screen. See Figure 4-18.

6 Press **[Ctrl][Home]**
The cell pointer moves to cell B4, not A1. You can click in the frozen area of the worksheet and edit the contents of the cells there. Steven is satisfied with his worksheet. He decides to save and print it.

7 Click the **Save tool**
Before printing his worksheet, Steven wants to preview it.

8 Click the **Print Preview tool**
Notice that this worksheet will print sideways on the paper, known as **landscape mode**.

9 Click **Print** then click **OK**

FIGURE 4-17:
Worksheet with frozen columns and rows

Frozen panes

Lines separating frozen & unfrozen panes

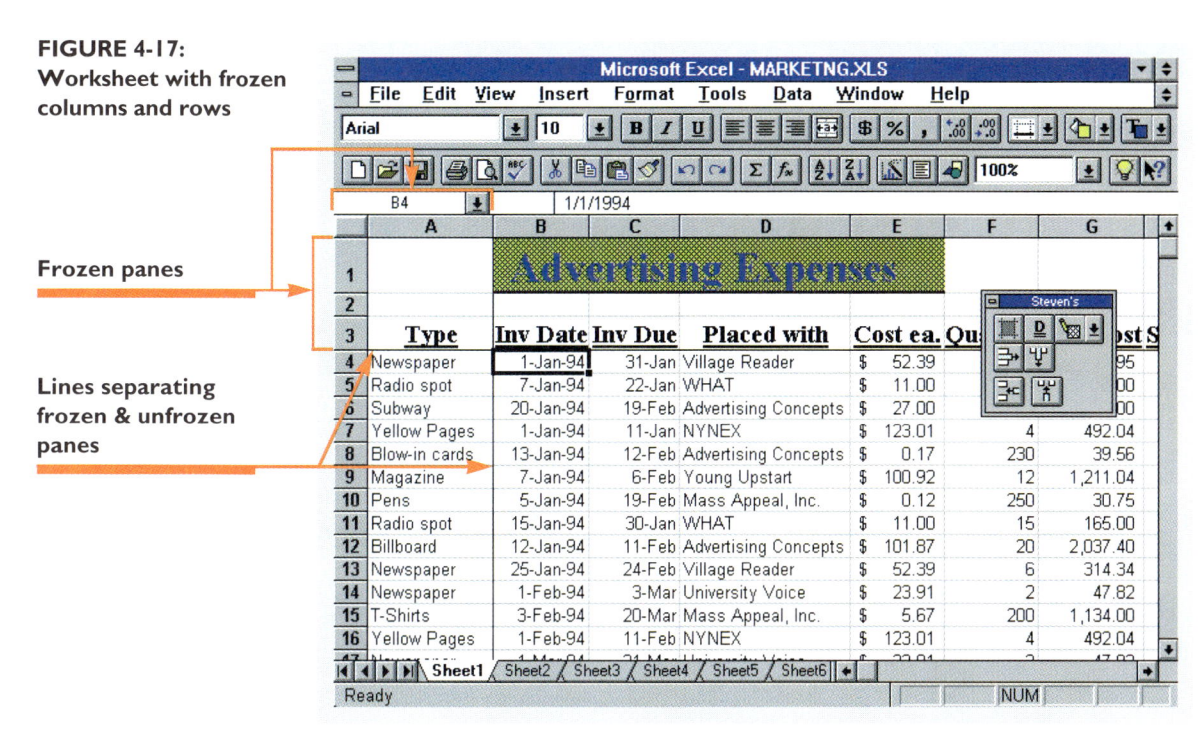

FIGURE 4-18:
Worksheet scrolled with labels frozen

Columns scrolled right

Rows scrolled down

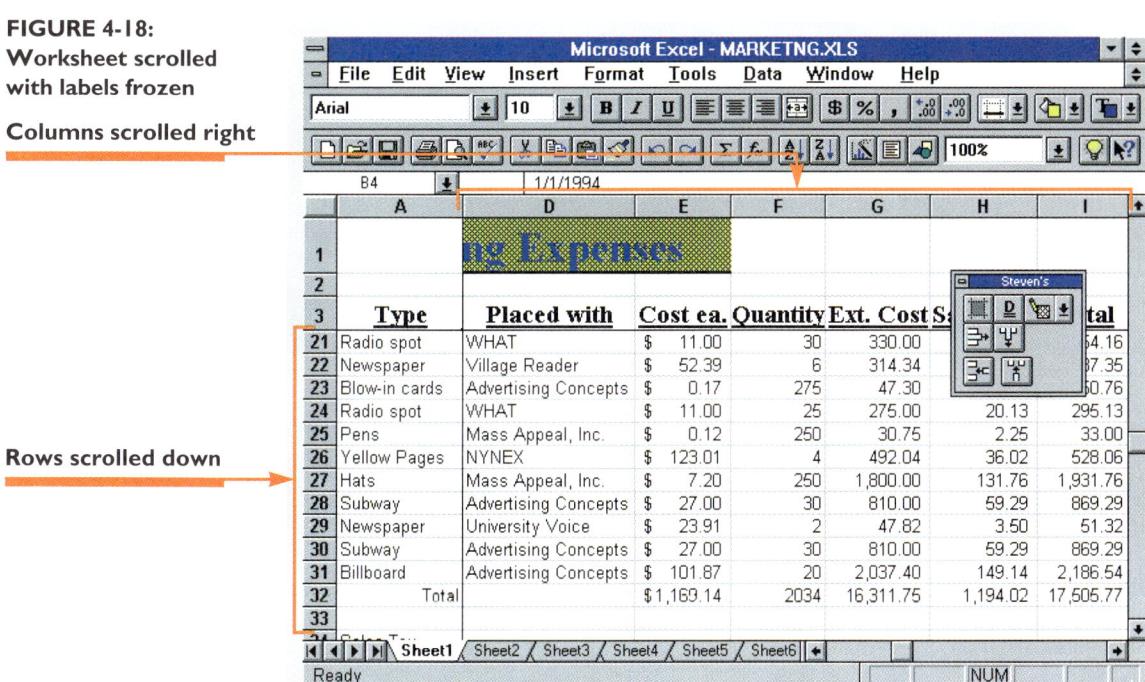

EXCEL 5 UNIT 4 **ENHANCING** A WORKSHEET

QUICK TIP

You may want to add the Freeze Panes tool ⊞ (found in the Utility category) to your toolbar.∎

CONCEPTSREVIEW

Label each of the elements of the Excel screen shown in Figure 4-19.

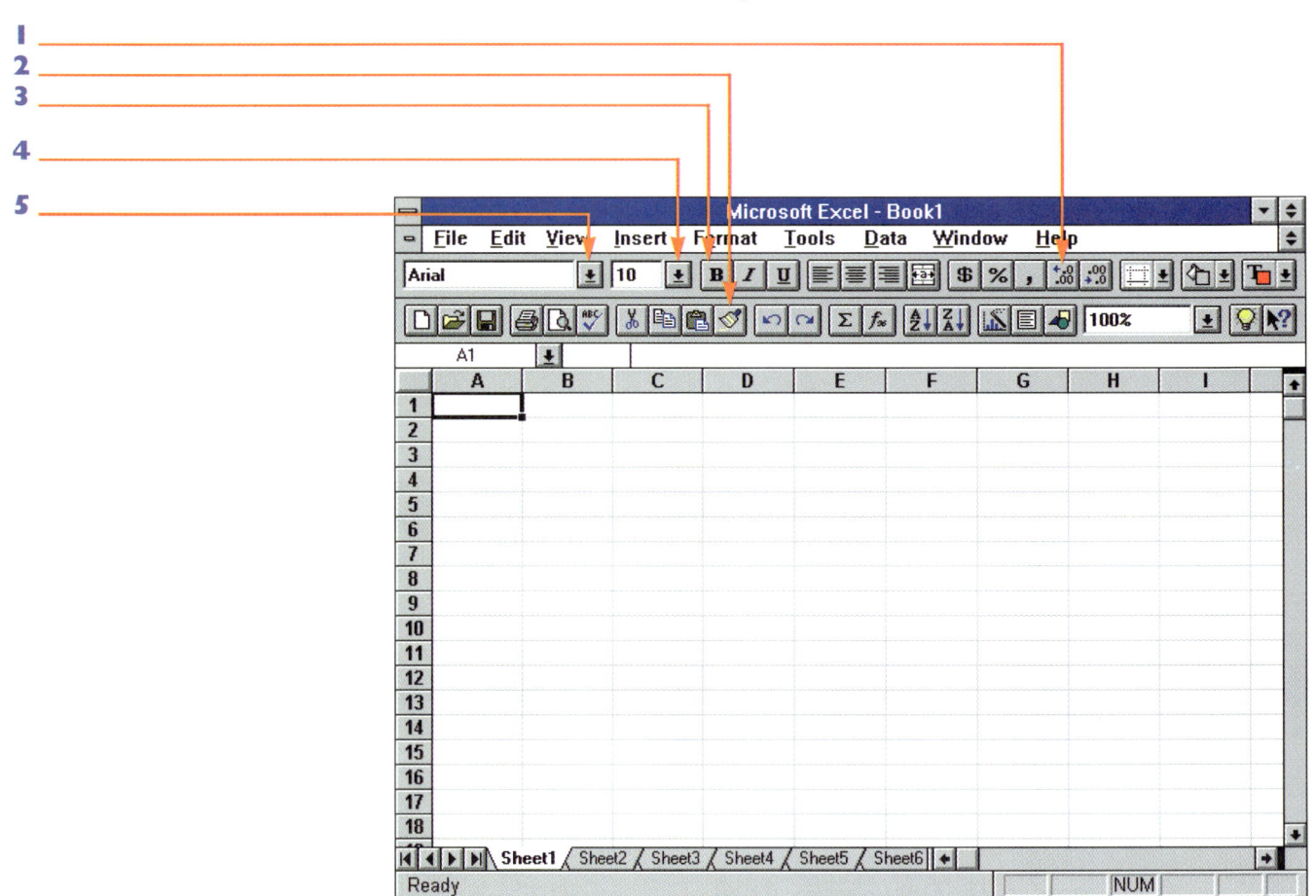

1 _____
2 _____
3 _____
4 _____
5 _____

FIGURE 4-19

Match each of the statements with the tool it describes.

6 Centers selected cells across columns

7 Adds thick outline border to selected cells

8 Increases number of decimals in a value

9 Decreases number of decimals in a value

10 Changes the display format of a values to Currency

a. [+.0/.00]
b. [$]
c. [↔]
d. [▢]
e. [.00/+.0]

Select the best answer from the list of choices.

11 The number 5707 formatted with Currency displays as:
   a. $5707
   b. $5707.00
   c. $57.07
   d. $5,707.00

12 When you apply a pattern, it affects:
   a. The worksheet page
   b. The active row
   c. The active column
   d. Selected cells

13 Which of the following is *not* true of AutoFormat?
   a. It is applied with the Format Painter tool.
   b. It works only with named ranges.
   c. It is designed for data having totals in the bottom row.
   d. It instantly formats large amounts of data.

14 Freeze columns or rows to:
   a. Protect data from alteration
   b. Hide cells from others
   c. See many worksheets at once
   d. Always see columns or rows

APPLICATIONS REVIEW

1. Build an inventory report.
   a. Open a new workbook.
   b. Enter the information from Table 4-4 in your worksheet.
   c. Save this workbook as CHAIRS to your Student Disk.

   TABLE 4-4
   Country Oak Chairs, Inc.
   Quarterly Sales Sheet

Description	Price	Sold
Rocker	1299	1104
Recliner	800	1805
Bar stool	159	1098
Dinette	369	1254

2. Format dollar amounts in the existing worksheet.
   a. Select the range of values in the Price column.
   b. Click the Currency tool.
   c. Save your workbook.

3. Use the Comma format in the existing worksheet.
   a. Select the range of values in the Sold column.
   b. Format the range using the Comma format with no decimal places.
   c. Enter a formula in the appropriate cell to calculate the total number of chairs sold. Adjust the number formatting, as needed.
   d. Enter the label Total in the cell next to the formula.
   e. Save your workbook.

4. Format labels in the existing worksheet.
   a. Select the worksheet title Country Oak Chairs, Inc.
   b. Click the Bold tool to apply boldface to the worksheet title.
   c. Select the label Quarterly Sales Sheet.
   d. Click the Underline tool to apply underlining to the label.
   e. Select the range of cells containing the column headings.
   f. Click the Align Center tool to center the column headings.
   g. Resize the column widths as necessary to fit the data.
   h. Save your work.

5. Use patterns, color, and borders in the existing worksheet.
   a. Select the cell containing the total number of chairs sold.
   b. Use the Outline Border tool to add a border having an appropriate line style.
   c. Select the worksheet title Country Oak Chairs, Inc., then click Format, click Cells on the menu bar, then click Patterns.
   d. Use the Font Color tool to select a font color.
   e. Apply background color to the worksheet column titles and the row labels.
   f. Save your work.

6. Freeze a row in the existing worksheet.
   a. Enter the names of chairs down the left side of the worksheet, directly under the Dinette entry. Continue entering names until you can no longer view the entire screen without scrolling.
   b. Place your cell pointer in column A just below the row containing the column headings (Description, Price, Sold).
   c. Click Window then click Freeze Panes.
   d. Scroll down the worksheet to check that the labels stay on the top of the screen.
   e. Save and close the workbook.

7. Create a new toolbar.
   a. Open a new workbook.
   b. Click View then click Toolbars.
   c. Double-click Standard, type your first and last name, then click OK.
   d. Click Text Formatting in the Categories list box, then click the Light Shading tool, then drag it to your toolbar.
   e. Enter your name in cell A3.
   f. Lightly shade your name using your toolbar.
   g. Add at least five more tools not seen on either the Standard or Formatting toolbars, which you feel would be helpful.

INDEPENDENT CHALLENGES

Write Brothers is a Houston-based company that manufactures high-quality pens and markers. As the finance manager, one of your responsibilities is to analyze the monthly reports from your five district sales offices. Your boss, Joanne Parker, has just told you to prepare a quarterly sales report for an upcoming meeting. Since several top executives will be attending this meeting, Joanne reminds you that the report must look professional. In particular, she asks you to emphasize the company's surge in profits during the last month and to highlight the fact that the Northeastern district continues to outpace the other districts.

Plan and build a worksheet that shows the company's sales during the last three months. Make sure you include:

- The number of pens sold (units sold) and the associated revenues (total sales) for each of the five district sales offices. The five Write Brothers sales districts include: Northeastern, Midwestern, Southeastern, Southern, and Western.
- Calculations that show month-by-month totals and a three-month cumulative total.
- Calculations that show each district's share of sales (percent of units sold).
- Formatting enhancements to emphasize the recent month's sales surge and the Northeast district's sales leadership.

To complete this independent challenge:

1 Prepare a worksheet plan that states your goal, lists the worksheet data you'll need, and identifies the formulas for the different calculations.

2 Sketch a sample worksheet on a piece of paper, indicating how the information should be formatted. How will you make the numbers easy to read? How will you show dollar amounts? What information should be shown in bold? What information will require a border around it? Do you need to use more than one font? More than one point size?

3 Build the worksheet with your own sales data. Enter the titles and labels first, then enter the numbers and formulas. Save the workbook as WRITE.XLS.

4 Make enhancements to the worksheet. Format labels and values, change attributes and alignment, and add borders. Remember to check your spelling.

5 Before printing, preview the file so you know what the worksheet will look like. Adjust any items as needed, and print a copy. Save your work before closing the file.

6 Submit your worksheet plan, preliminary sketches, and the final printout.

As the new computer lab manager of your class, you are responsible for all the computer equipment used in your classroom. In addition knowing the current hardware and software capabilities and approximate capital costs, you must also be concerned with the number of hours the equipment is used, whether or not you would like to make any upgrades prior to the next semester, and the approximate costs of those upgrades. Plan and build a workbook that details the hardware and software used in your classroom. Make sure you include:

- The number of units and number of hours used
- Calculations that show the approximate value of hardware by unit and within the room
- The installed software and its total calculated value
- A "wish list" of hardware and software upgrades and their respective costs
- Formatting enhancements that emphasize the items or highest priority

To complete this independent challenge:

1 Prepare a worksheet plan that states your goal, lists the worksheet data you'll need, and identifies the formulas for the different calculations.

2 Sketch a sample worksheet on a piece of paper, indicating how the information should be formatted. How will you make the numbers easy to read? How will you show dollar amounts? What information should be shown in bold? What information will require a border around it? Do you need to use more than one font? More than one point size?

3 Build the worksheet with the data you have gathered. Estimate the costs of hardware and software if you are unsure. Enter the titles and labels first, then enter the numbers and formulas. Save the workbook as LABCOSTS.XLS.

4 Make enhancements to the worksheet. Format labels and values, change attributes and alignment, and add borders. Remember to check your spelling.

5 Before printing, preview the file so you know what the worksheet will look like. Adjust any items as needed, and print a copy. Save your work before closing the file.

6 Submit your worksheet plan, preliminary sketches, and the final printout.

UNIT 5

OBJECTIVES

- Plan and design a chart
- Create a chart
- Edit a chart
- Move and resize a chart
- Change the appearance of a chart
- Enhance a chart
- Add text annotations to a chart
- Preview and print a chart

Working
WITH CHARTS

Worksheets provide an effective way to organize information, but are not always the best format for presenting the data to others. Information in a selected range or worksheet can be easily converted to the visual format of a chart. Charts quickly communicate the relationships of data in a worksheet. In this unit, you will learn how to create a chart, change chart types, add text and arrows, and print a chart. ▶ Andrea Milkowski is the assistant to Steven McCann in the Marketing Department at Nationwide Travel. Steven asked Andrea to plan and create a chart showing the six-month sales history of a new tour program. ▶

Planning and designing a chart

Before creating a chart, you need to plan what you want your chart to show and how you want it to look. Andrea wants to create a chart showing the spring and summer sales of a new five-tour series called "Active Adventure Series." The five tours include a parachute dive from a small-engine aircraft, a bungee jump off of a cliff, a flight on a hang glider into a canyon, a mountain bike adventure, and a long-distance touring bike trip. In early June, Steven and Andrea launched a radio advertising campaign promoting the Active Adventure Series, which resulted in increased sales for the summer months. Andrea wants her chart to illustrate this dramatic sales increase. Andrea uses the worksheet shown in Figure 5-1 and the following guidelines to plan her chart.

Steps

1. **Determine the purpose of the chart, and identify the data relationships you want to communicate visually.**
   Andrea wants to create a chart that shows sales of the Active Adventure Series in the spring and summer months (March through August). She particularly wants to highlight the increase in sales that occurred in the summer months as a result of the advertising campaign.

2. **Determine the results you want to see and decide which chart type is most appropriate to use. Table 5-1 describes several different types of charts.**
   Because Andrea wants to compare related data (sales of the Active Adventure Series) over a time period (the months March through August), she decides to use a column chart.

3. **Identify the worksheet data you want the chart to illustrate.**
   Andrea is using data from her worksheet titled "Active Adventure Series, Spring and Summer Sales," as shown in Figure 5-1. This worksheet contains the sales data for the five tours from March through August.

4. **Sketch the chart and then use this sketch to decide where the chart elements should be placed.**
   *Andrea sketches her chart, as shown in Figure 5-2. She puts the months on the horizontal axis (the **x-axis**) and the number of tours sold on the vertical axis (the **y-axis**). The **tick marks** on the y-axis create a scale of measure for each value. Each value in a cell she selects for her chart is a **data point**. In any chart, each data point is visually represented by a **data marker**, which in this case is a column. A collection of related data points is a **data series**. In Andrea's chart, there are five data series (bungee jumping, parachuting, hang gliding, mountain biking, and bike touring) so she has included a **legend** to identify them.*

FIGURE 5-1:
Worksheet containing sales data

FIGURE 5-2:
Andrea's sketch of the column chart

Legend

After radio spots

Data series

Data marker

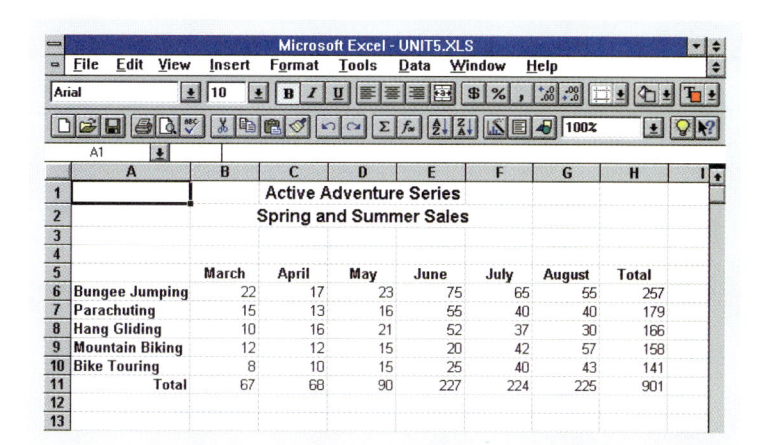

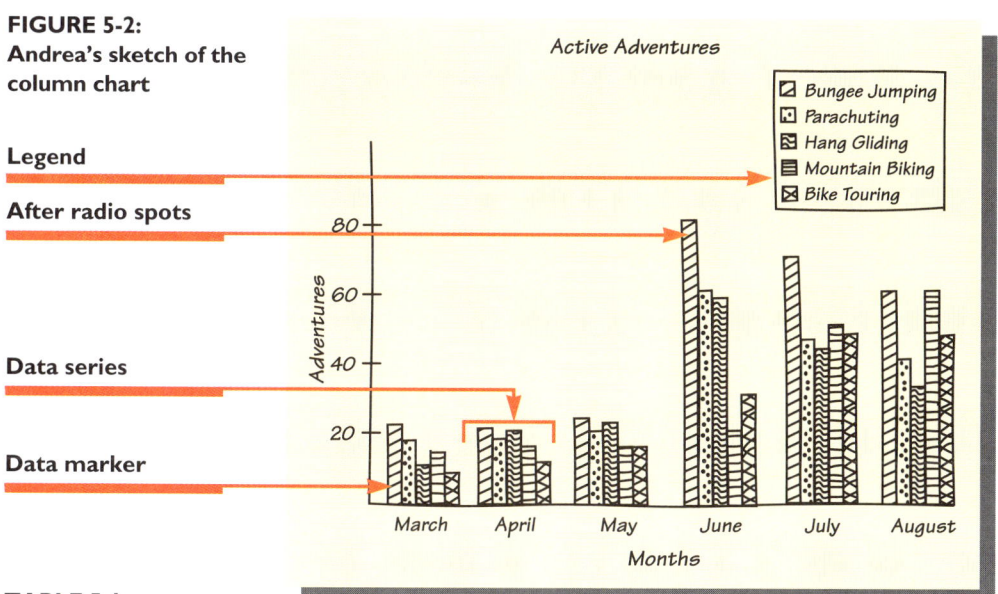

TABLE 5-1:
Commonly used chart types

TYPE	TOOL	DESCRIPTION
Area		Shows how volume changes over time.
Bar		Compares distinct, unrelated objects over time using a horizontal format. (Sometimes referred to as a horizontal bar chart in other spreadsheet programs.)
Column		Compares distinct, unrelated objects over time using a vertical format; the Excel default. (Sometimes referred to as a bar chart in other spreadsheet programs.)
Line		Compares trends over even time intervals; similar to an area chart.
Pie		Compares sizes of pieces as part of a whole; can have slices pulled away from the pie, or "exploded."
XY (scatter)		Compares trends over uneven time or measurement intervals; used in scientific and engineering fields for trend spotting and extrapolation.
Combination	N/A	Combines a column and line chart to compare data requiring different scales of measure.

EXCEL 5 UNIT 5 **WORKING** WITH CHARTS

Creating a chart

To create a chart in Excel, you first select the range containing the data you want to chart. Once you've selected a range, you can use Excel's ChartWizard to lead you through the chart creation process. ▶ Using the worksheet containing the spring and summer sales data for the Active Adventure series, Andrea will create a chart that shows the monthly sales of each type of Active Adventure from March through August.

STEPS

1. **Open the workbook UNIT5.XLS from your Student Disk, then save it as ACTIVE**
   First, Andrea needs to select the cells that include the monthly sales figures for each of the tour types, but not the totals. She also wants to include the cells containing the month and tour type labels.

2. **Select the range A5:G10, then click the ChartWizard tool on the Standard toolbar**
   When you click the ChartWizard tool, the mouse pointer changes to ⁺₁ₗ. See Figure 5-3. This pointer draws the border of the chart. Andrea decides to place the chart below the worksheet.

3. **Position ⁺₁ₗ with the cross at the top of cell A13, as shown in Figure 5-3, then drag the pointer to the lower-right corner of cell H24 to select the range A13:H24**
   The first dialog box displays which confirms the range of data to be charted.

4. **Make sure the range is the same as the one you selected, then click Next**
   The second ChartWizard dialog box lets you choose the type of chart you want to create.

5. **Click Next to accept the default chart type of Column**
   The third dialog box lets you choose the format of the chart. Andrea wants each type of adventure to have a different color bar so she again accepts the default choice.

6. **Click Next**
   The fourth ChartWizard dialog box shows a sample chart using the data you selected. Notice that the types of adventures (the *rows* in the selected range) are plotted according to the months (the *columns* in the selected range), and that the months are added as labels. You could switch this by clicking the Columns radio button below Data Series on the right side of the dialog box. Notice also that there is a legend showing each tour type data series and its corresponding color on the chart.

7. **Click Next**
   In the last ChartWizard dialog box you can make final adjustments to the chart. Andrea decides to add a title.

8. **Click the Chart Title text box, then type Active Adventures**
   After a moment, the title appears in the Sample Chart box. See Figure 5-4.

9. **Click Finish**
   The column chart displays in the defined plot area. See Figure 5-5. Your chart might look slightly different. Just as Andrea hoped, the chart shows the dramatic increase in sales between May and June. The **selection handles**, the small black squares at the corners and sides of the chart's border, indicate that the chart is selected. Anytime a chart is selected, the chart toolbar appears.

FIGURE 5-3:
Worksheet with selected range and ChartWizard pointer

ChartWizard tool depressed

Chart pointer

FIGURE 5-4:
Completed ChartWizard dialog box

Title added

Miniaturized Chart

Legend

Radio buttons for displaying legend

FIGURE 5-5:
Worksheet with column chart

Selection handles

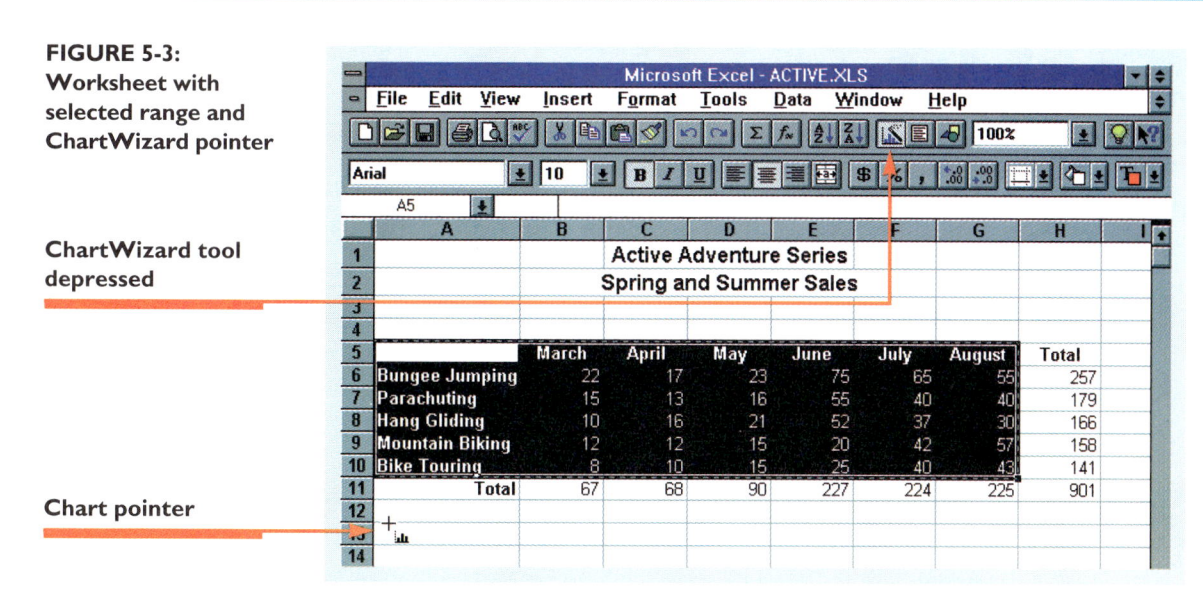

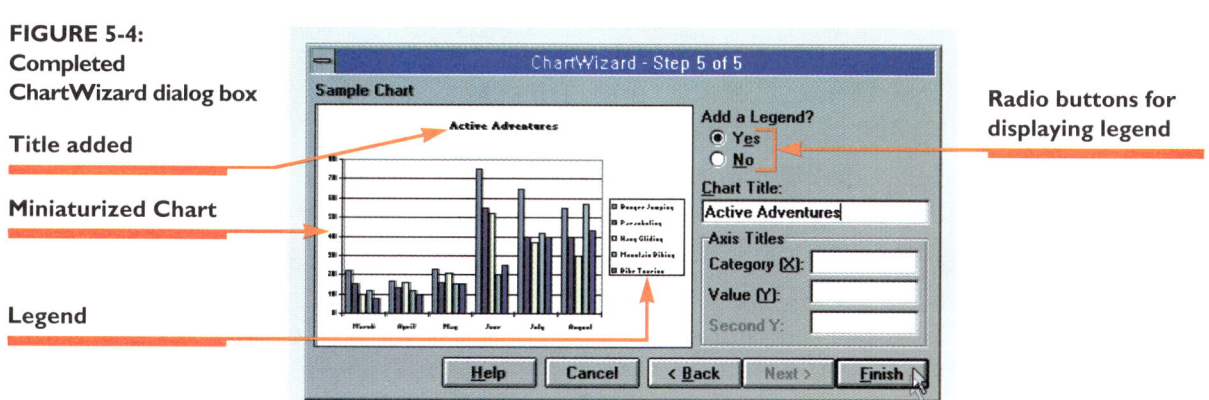

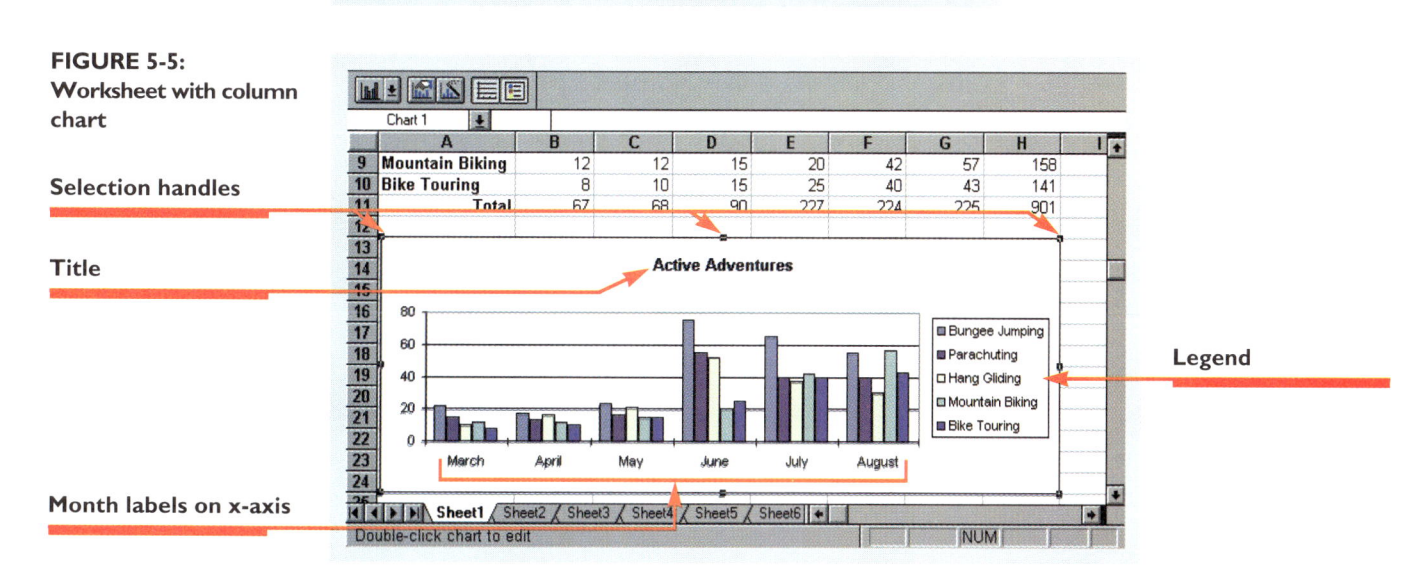

Title

Month labels on x-axis

Legend

TROUBLE?

If you want to delete a chart, select it and then press [Delete].■

EXCEL 5 UNIT 5 **WORKING** WITH CHARTS

91

Editing a chart

Once you've created a chart, it's easy to modify it. You can change data values in the worksheet, and the chart will automatically be updated to reflect the new data. You can also change chart types using the Chart tools on the Chart toolbar. Table 5-2 shows and describes the chart tools. ▶ Andrea looks over her worksheet and realizes she entered the wrong data for Hang Gliding tours in July and August. After she corrects this data, she wants to find out if another chart type will better demonstrate the data. She will convert the column chart to a line chart and a 3-D column chart to find this out.

STEPS

1. **Scroll the worksheet so that you can see both the chart and row 8, containing the Hang Gliding tour sales figures, at the same time**
   As you enter the correct values, watch the columns for July and August in the chart change to reflect the new data values.

2. **Click cell F8 and type 49 to correct the July sales figure, then press [→], type 45 in cell G8, then press [Enter]**
   The July and August hang gliding columns reflect the increased sales figures. See Figure 5-6.

3. **Select the chart by clicking anywhere within the chart border, then click the Chart Type tools list arrow on the Chart toolbar**
   The chart type tools display. See Figure 5-7.

4. **Click the 2-D Line Chart tool**
   The column chart changes to a line chart as shown in Figure 5-8. Andrea looks at the line chart and decides it is too cluttered for the months of March, April, and May. Next she'll see if the large increase in sales would be better presented with a three-dimensional column chart.

5. **Click, then click the 3-D Column Chart tool**
   A three-dimensional column chart displays. The three-dimensional column format is too crowded so Andrea switches back to the two-dimensional format. This format best represents the data.

6. **Click, then click the 2-D Column Chart tool**

7. **Click the Save tool**

TABLE 5-2:
Chart type tools

TOOL	DESCRIPTION	TOOL	DESCRIPTION
	Displays 2-D area chart		Displays 3-D area chart
	Displays 2-D bar chart		Displays 3-D bar chart
	Displays 2-D column chart		Displays 3-D column chart
	Displays 2-D line chart		Displays 3-D line chart
	Displays 2-D pie chart		Displays 3-D pie chart
	Displays 2-D scatter chart		Displays 3-D surface chart
	Displays 2-D doughnut chart		Displays radar chart

FIGURE 5-6:
Worksheet with new data entered for hang gliding

FIGURE 5-7:
Chart type tools list box

2-D Column Chart tool

2-D Pie Chart tool

3-D Column Chart tool

FIGURE 5-8:
Line chart

Too cluttered

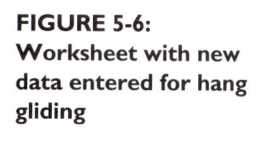

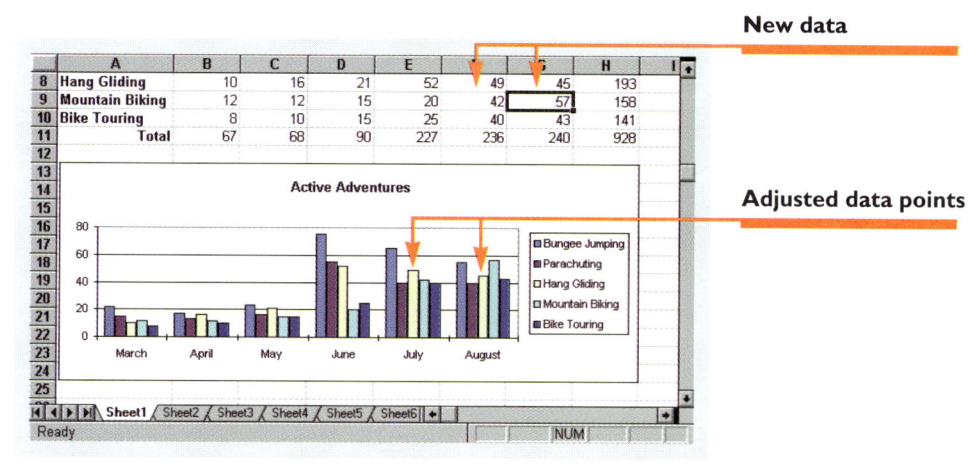

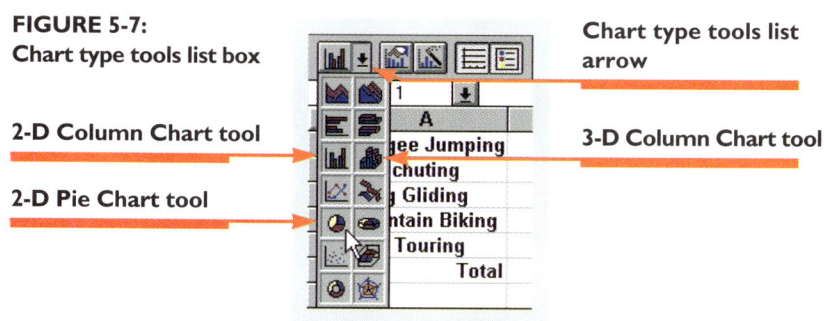

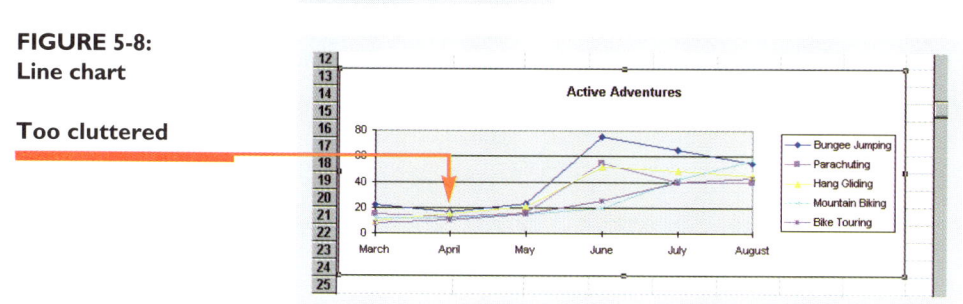

Rotating a chart

In a three-dimensional chart, columns or bars can sometimes be obscured by other data series within the same chart. You can rotate the chart until a better view is obtained. Double-click the chart, then click the tip of one of its axes and drag the handles until a more pleasing view of the data series appears. See Figure 5-9.

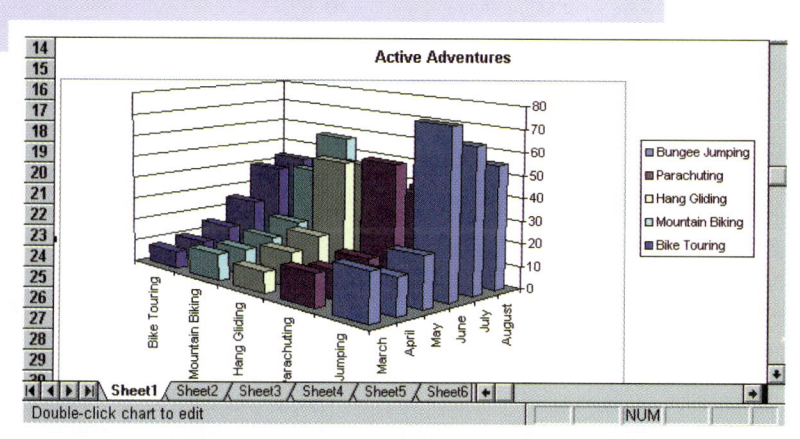

FIGURE 5-9:
3-D chart rotated with improved view of data series

EXCEL 5 UNIT 5 WORKING WITH CHARTS

93

Moving and resizing a chart

Charts are graphics, or drawn **objects**, and they have no specific cell or range address. You can move charts anywhere on a worksheet without affecting formulas or data in the worksheet. You can also easily resize a chart to improve its appearance by dragging the selection handles. Charts contain many elements, each a separate object that you can move and resize. To move an object, select it and then drag it or cut and copy it to a new location. To resize an object, use the selection handles. ▶ Andrea wants to increase the size of her chart and to center it on her worksheet. She also wants to move the legend up so that it is level with the title.

1. Click the chart to select it, scroll until row 31 is visible, then move the mouse pointer over the bottom center selection handle until the pointer changes to ↕

   The ↕ indicates that you can use a selection handle to resize the chart.

2. Hold down the mouse button and drag the lower edge of the chart to row 31, then release the mouse button

   As the chart is being resized, a dotted outline of the chart perimeter appears, and the mouse pointer changes to +. The chart length is increased.

3. Move the pointer over one of the selection handles on the right, then drag the chart about 1/2" to the right to the middle of column I

   See Figure 5-10. Andrea wants to move the legend up so that it is level with the chart title.

4. Double-click the **chart**

   The chart is now in Edit mode. **Edit mode** means that you can change elements within the chart border. When the chart is selected, you can move and resize the chart. In Edit mode, the border changes to a blue outline or the chart appears in its own window, and the menu bar changes to the Chart menu bar.

5. Click the **legend** to select it, then drag it to the upper-right corner of the chart until it is aligned with the chart title

   Selection handles display around the legend when you click it, and a dotted outline of the legend perimeter appears as you drag. See Figure 5-11.

6. Press **[Esc]** to deselect the legend

7. Click the **Save tool**

FIGURE 5-10:
Worksheet with resized and centered chart

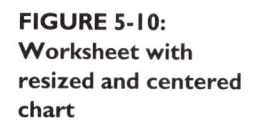

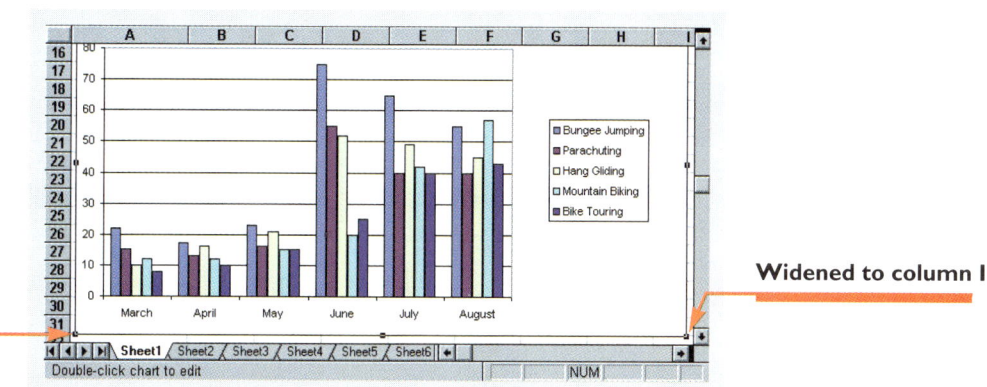

Lengthened to row 31

Widened to column I

FIGURE 5-11:
Worksheet with repositioned legend

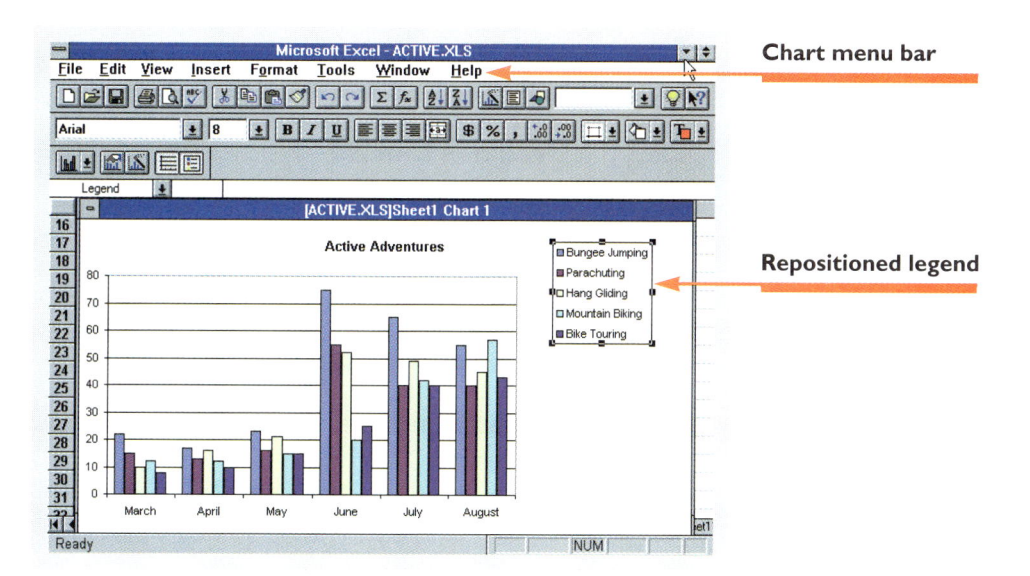

Chart menu bar

Repositioned legend

Viewing multiple worksheets

A workbook can be organized with a chart on one sheet, and the data on another sheet. With this organization, you can still see the data next to the chart by opening multiple windows of the same workbook. This allows you to see portions of multiple sheets at the same time. Click Window in the menu bar, then click New Window. A new window containing the current workbook opens. To see the windows next to each other, click Window in the menu bar, then click Arrange, then choose one of the options in the Arrange Windows dialog box. If you click Horizontal, the windows are arranged one on top of the other. You can open one worksheet in one window, and open a different worksheet in the second window. See Figure 5-12.

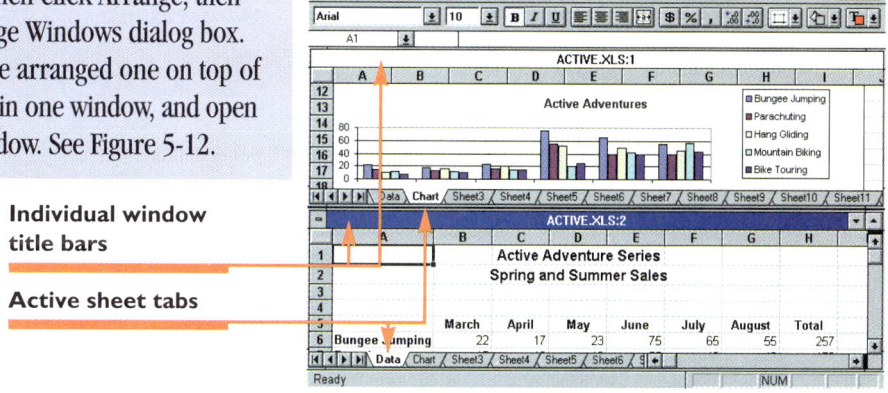

Individual window title bars

Active sheet tabs

FIGURE 5-12: Workbook with two worksheets displayed

EXCEL 5 UNIT 5 **WORKING** WITH CHARTS

Changing the appearance of a chart

After you've created a chart using the ChartWizard, you can use the Chart toolbar to change the colors of data series, add or eliminate a legend, and add or delete gridlines. **Gridlines** are the horizontal lines in the chart that enable the eye to follow the value on an axis. These tools are listed in Table 5-3. ▶ Andrea wants to make some changes in the appearance of her chart. She wants to see if the chart looks better without gridlines, and she wants to change the color of a data series.

STEPS

1 Make sure the chart is still in Edit mode with a blue border around it or in its own window

Andrea wants to see how the chart looks without gridlines. Currently gridlines display and the Gridlines tool on the Chart toolbar is depressed.

2 Click the **Gridlines tool**

The gridlines disappear from the chart and the tool is deselected. Andrea decides that the gridlines are necessary to the chart's readability.

3 Click again

The gridlines reappear. Andrea is not happy with the color of the columns for the Mountain Biking data series, and would like them to stand out more.

4 With the chart in Edit mode, double-click any column in the Mountain Biking data series

Handles appear on all the columns in the series, and the Format Data Series dialog box appears. See Figure 5-13. Make sure the Patterns tab is the front-most tab.

5 Click **yellow** (in the first row, the third from the right), then click **OK**

All the columns in the series are yellow. Compare the finished chart to Figure 5-14. Andrea is pleased with the change.

6 Click the **Save tool**

TABLE 5-3: Chart enhancement tools

TOOL	DESCRIPTION
	Adds/deletes gridlines
	Adds/deletes legend
	Returns to ChartWizard

FIGURE 5-13: Format Data Series dialog box

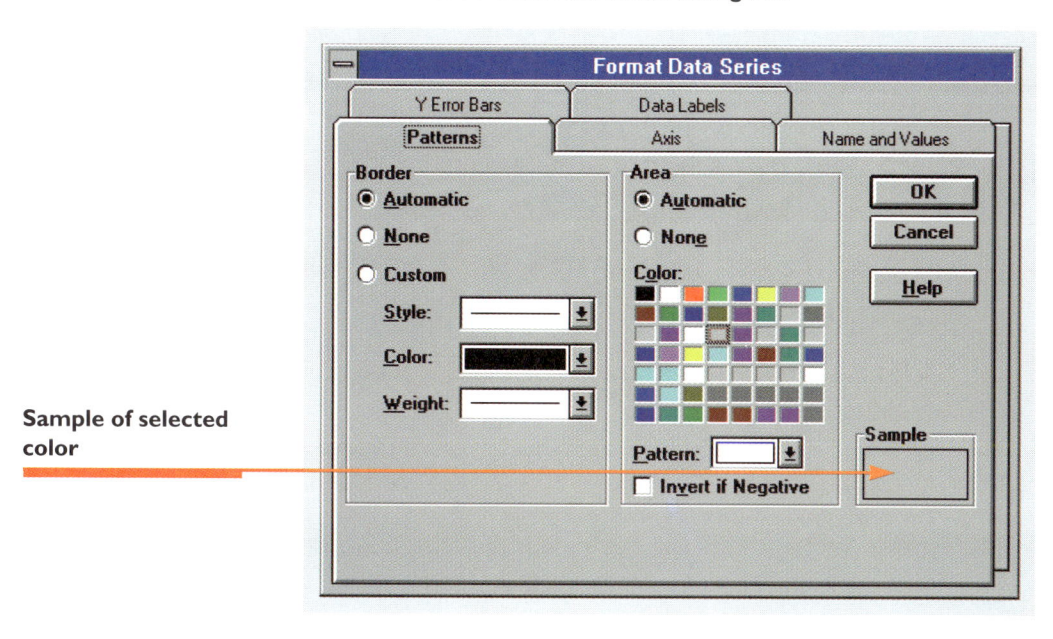

Sample of selected color

FIGURE 5-14: Chart with formatted data series

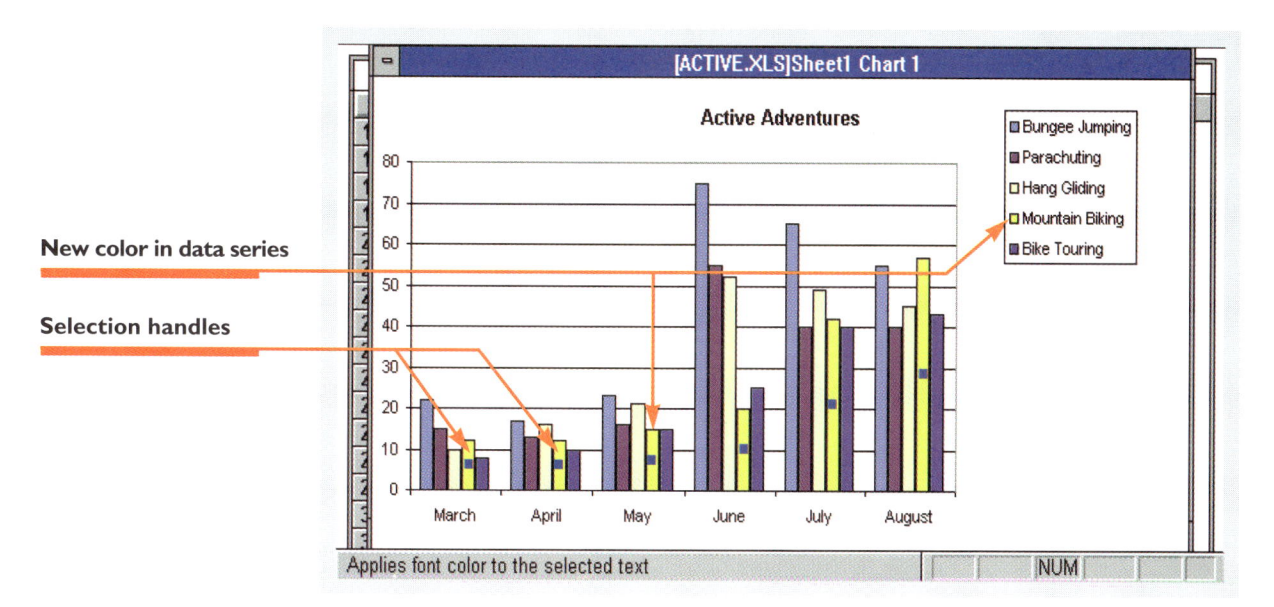

New color in data series

Selection handles

QUICK TIP

Experiment with different formats for your charts until you get just the right look. ■

97

EXCEL 5 UNIT 5 **WORKING** WITH CHARTS

Enhancing a chart

There are many ways to enhance a chart to make it easier to read and understand. You can create titles for the x-axis and y-axis, add graphics, or add background color. ▶ Andrea wants to improve the appearance of her chart by creating titles for the x-axis and y-axis. She also decides to add a drop shadow to the title.

STEPS

1. **Make sure the chart is in Edit mode**
   Andrea wants to add descriptive text to the x-axis.

2. **Click Insert on the Chart menu bar, click Titles, click Category (X) Axis, then click OK**
   A text box with selection handles around it and containing an X appears below the x-axis. See Figure 5-15.

3. **Type Months, then click the Enter button ✓ on the formula bar**
   The word "Months" displays below the month labels. If you wanted to move the axis title to a new position, you could click on an edge of the selection and drag it. If you wanted to edit the axis title, move the mouse pointer over the selected text box until it changes to I and click, then edit the text. Andrea now wants to add text to the y-axis.

4. **Click Insert on the Chart menu bar, click Titles, click Value (Y) Axis, then click OK**
   A selected text box containing a Y appears to the left of the y-axis.

5. **Type Adventures, press [Enter], then press [Esc] to deselect it**
   The word "Adventures" displays to the left of the tours. Next Andrea decides to add a drop shadow to the title.

6. **Click the title Active Adventures to select it**

7. **Click the Drawing tool 🖉 on the Standard toolbar**
   The Drawing toolbar displays.

8. **Click the Drop Shadow tool ▫ on the Drawing toolbar, then press [Esc] to deselect the title**
   A drop shadow appears around the title.

9. **Click the Drawing tool 🖉 on the Standard toolbar, then click the Save tool 💾**
   The Drawing toolbar disappears and the chart is saved. See Figure 5-16.

FIGURE 5-15:
Chart with selected text box

Text box

FIGURE 5-16:
Enhanced chart

Drop shadow added

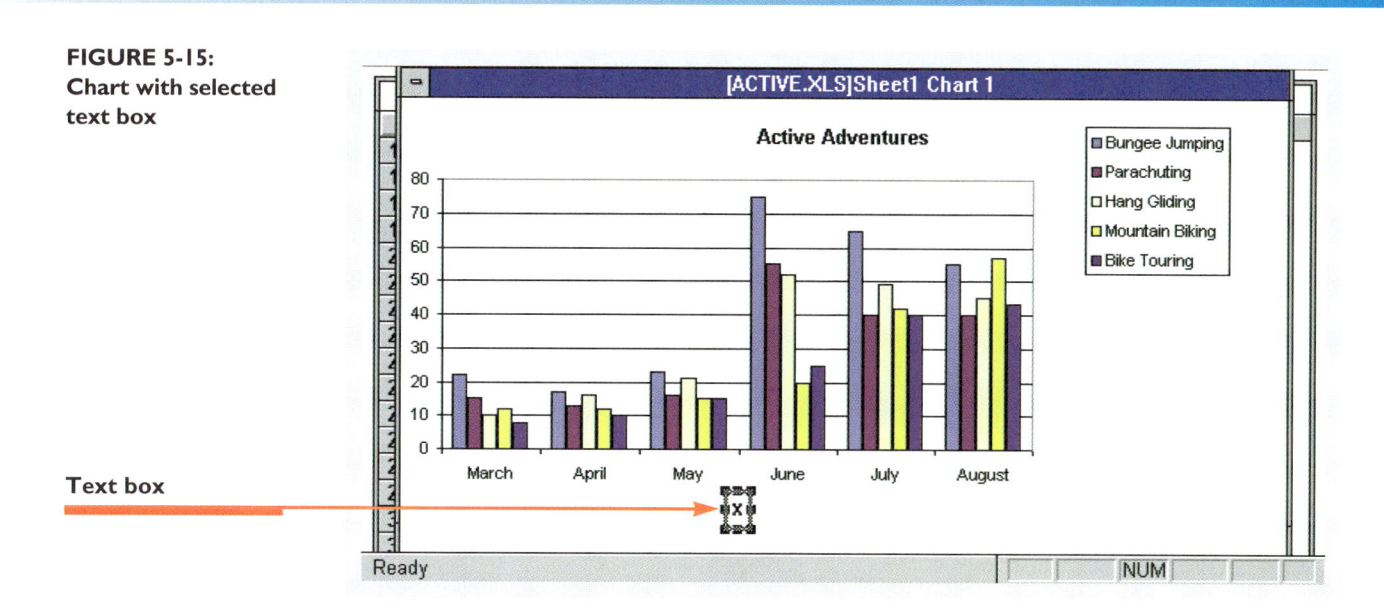

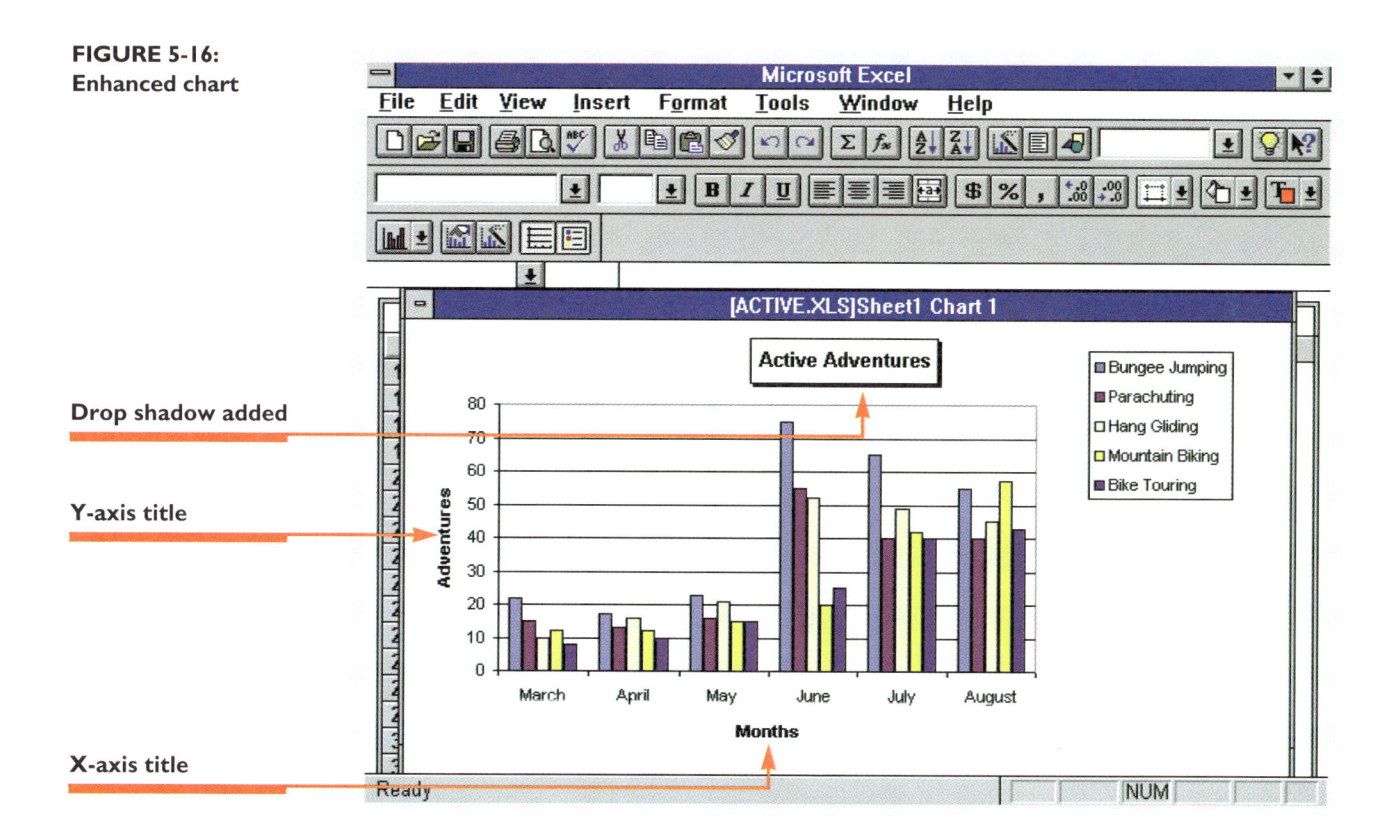

Y-axis title

X-axis title

Changing text font and alignment in charts

The font and the alignment of axis text can be modified to make it more readable or to better fit within the plot area. With a chart in Edit mode, double-click the text to be modified. The Format Axis dialog box displays. Click the Font or the Alignment tab, make the desired changes, then click OK.

Adding text annotations to a chart

You can add arrows and text annotations to highlight information in your charts. Text annotations are notes that you add to your charts to draw attention to a certain part of the chart. ▶ Andrea wants to add a text annotation and an arrow to highlight the June sales increase. She'll use the drawing tools to do this.

Steps

1 Make sure the chart is in Edit mode

Andrea wants to call attention to the June sales increase by drawing an arrow that points to the top of the June data series with text that says "After radio spots." To enter the text for an annotation, you simply start typing.

2 Type **After radio spots**, then click the **Enter button**

As you type, the text appears in the formula bar. After you confirm the entry, the text displays in a selected box within the chart window. See Figure 5-17. Your text box might be in a different spot on your screen.

3 Point to an edge of the text box, then press and hold the mouse button

The mouse pointer should remain ⇖ and the message in the status bar should say "Move selected objects." If the pointer changes to I or ↕, release the mouse button, click outside the text box area to deselect it, then select the text box again.

4 Drag the text box above the chart, as shown in Figure 5-18, then release the mouse button

Andrea is ready to add an arrow.

5 Click the **Drawing tool** on the Standard toolbar

The Drawing toolbar displays.

6 Click the **Arrow tool** on the Drawing toolbar

The mouse pointer changes to ✚.

7 Position ✚ under the word "spots" in the text box, click the mouse button, drag the line to the June sales, then release the mouse button

An arrowhead appears pointing to the June sales. Compare your finished chart to Figure 5-18.

8 Close the Drawing toolbar, then click the **Save tool**

FIGURE 5-17: Chart with new text box

- Drawing tool
- Move text box here
- Selected text box floating

FIGURE 5-18: Completed chart with text annotation and arrow

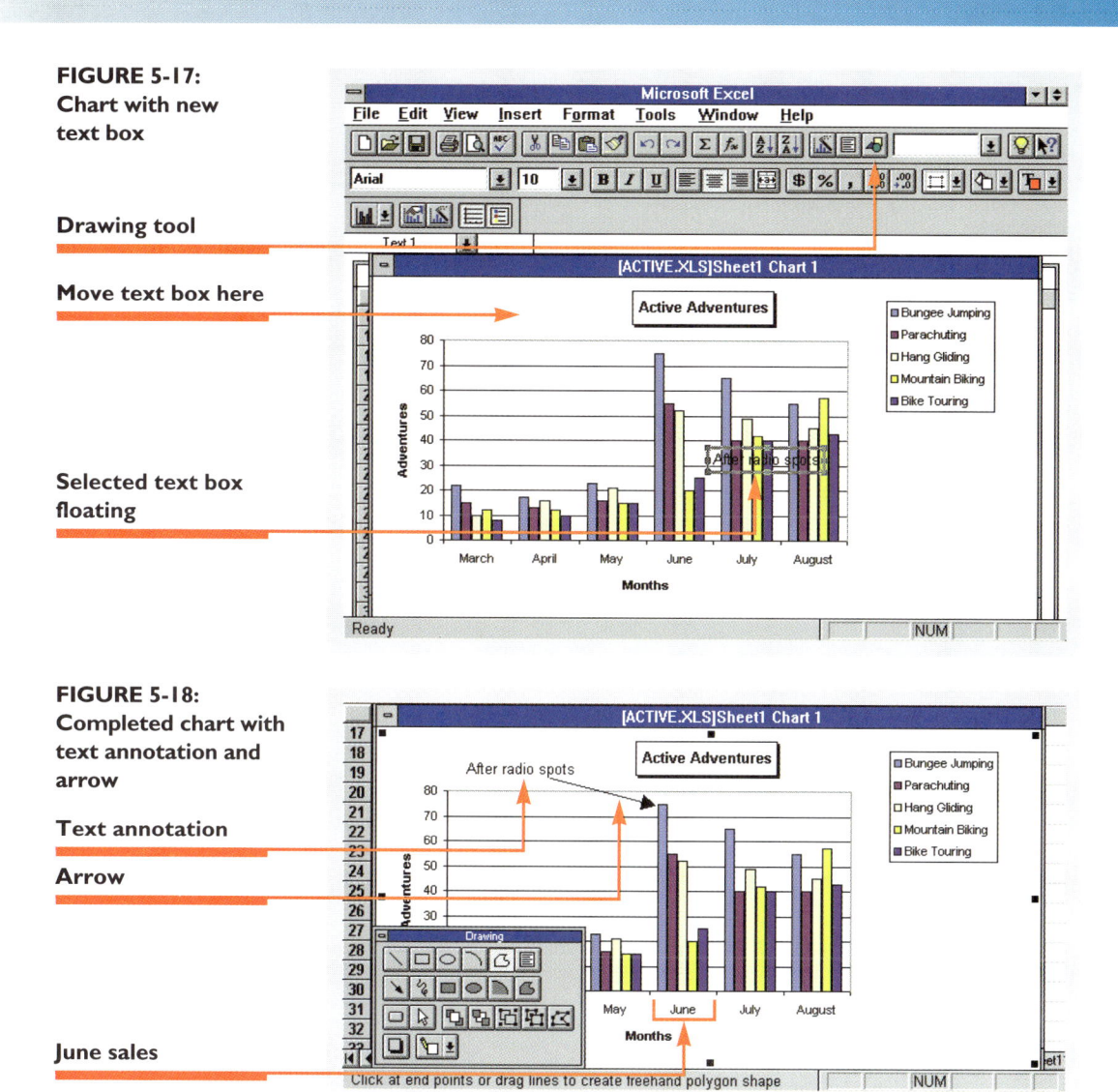

- Text annotation
- Arrow
- June sales

Pulling out a pie slice

Just as an arrow can call attention to a data series, you can emphasize a pie slice by exploding or pulling it away from the pie chart. Once the chart is in Edit mode, click the desired slice, then drag the slice away from the pie, as shown in Figure 5-19.

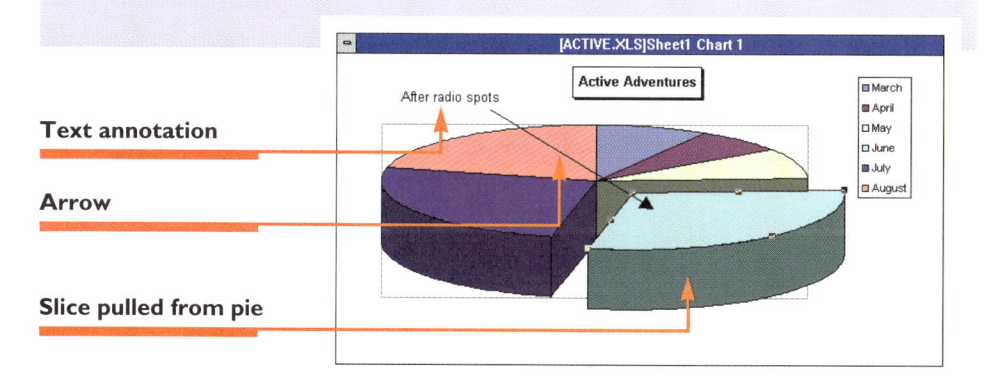

- Text annotation
- Arrow
- Slice pulled from pie

FIGURE 5-19: Exploded pie slice

QUICK TIP

You can insert text and an arrow in the data section of a worksheet by clicking the Text Box tool on the Standard toolbar, drawing a text box, then typing the text and adding the arrow.

EXCEL 5 UNIT 5 WORKING WITH CHARTS

101

Previewing and printing charts

After you complete a chart to your satisfaction, you will need to print it. You can print a chart by itself, or as part of the worksheet. ▶ Andrea is satisfied with her chart and wants to print it for the upcoming sales meeting. She will print the worksheet and the chart together, so that the sales force will see the actual sales numbers for each tour type.

STEPS

1. **Click any cell outside the chart to deselect the chart**
   If you only wanted to print the chart without the data, you would leave the chart selected.

2. **Click the Print Preview tool on the Standard toolbar**
   The Print Preview window opens. Andrea decides that the chart and data would look better if they were printed in **landscape** orientation, that is, with the page turned sideways. To change the orientation of the page, you must alter the page setup.

3. **Click Setup to display the Page Setup dialog box, then click the Page tab**

4. **Click the Landscape radio button**
   See Figure 5-20. Andrea would also like to eliminate the gridlines, which appear with the data.

5. **Click the Sheet tab, then click the Gridlines check box to deselect it**
   The chart and data will print too far over to the left of the page. You change this using the Margins tab.

6. **Click the Margins tab, double-click the Left text box, type 2.25, then click OK**
   The print preview of the worksheet displays again. The data and chart are centered on the page which is turned sideways, and no gridlines appear. See Figure 5-21. Andrea is satisfied with the way it looks and prints it.

7. **Click Print to display the Print dialog box, then click OK**
   Your printed report should look like the image displayed in the Print Preview window.

8. **Click the Save tool, click File on the menu bar, then click Close**
   Your workbook and chart close.

103

EXCEL 5 UNIT 5 **WORKING** WITH CHARTS

FIGURE 5-20: Page tab of the Page Setup dialog box

Landscape radio button

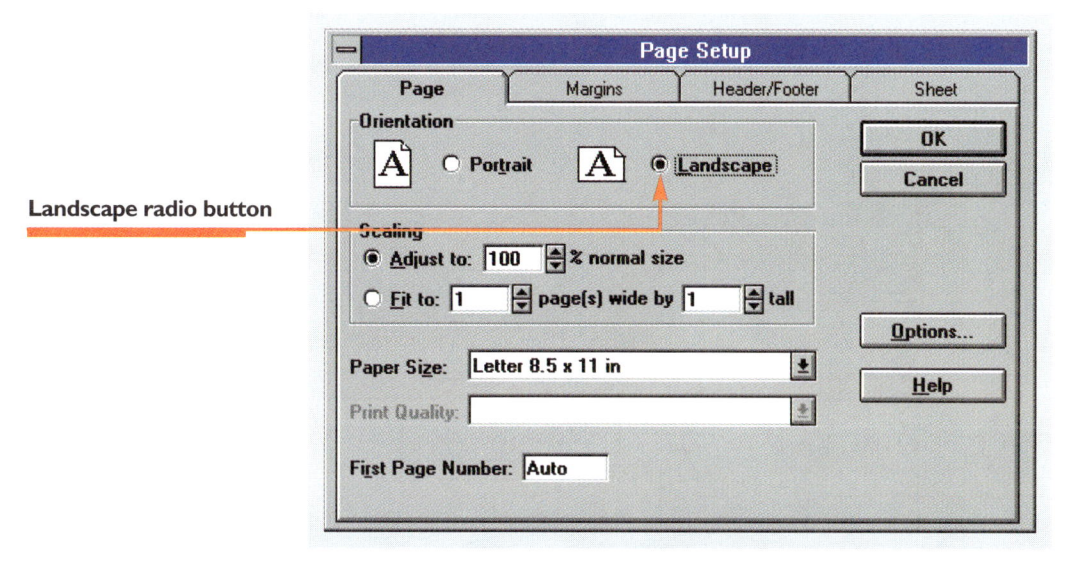

FIGURE 5-21: Chart and data ready to print

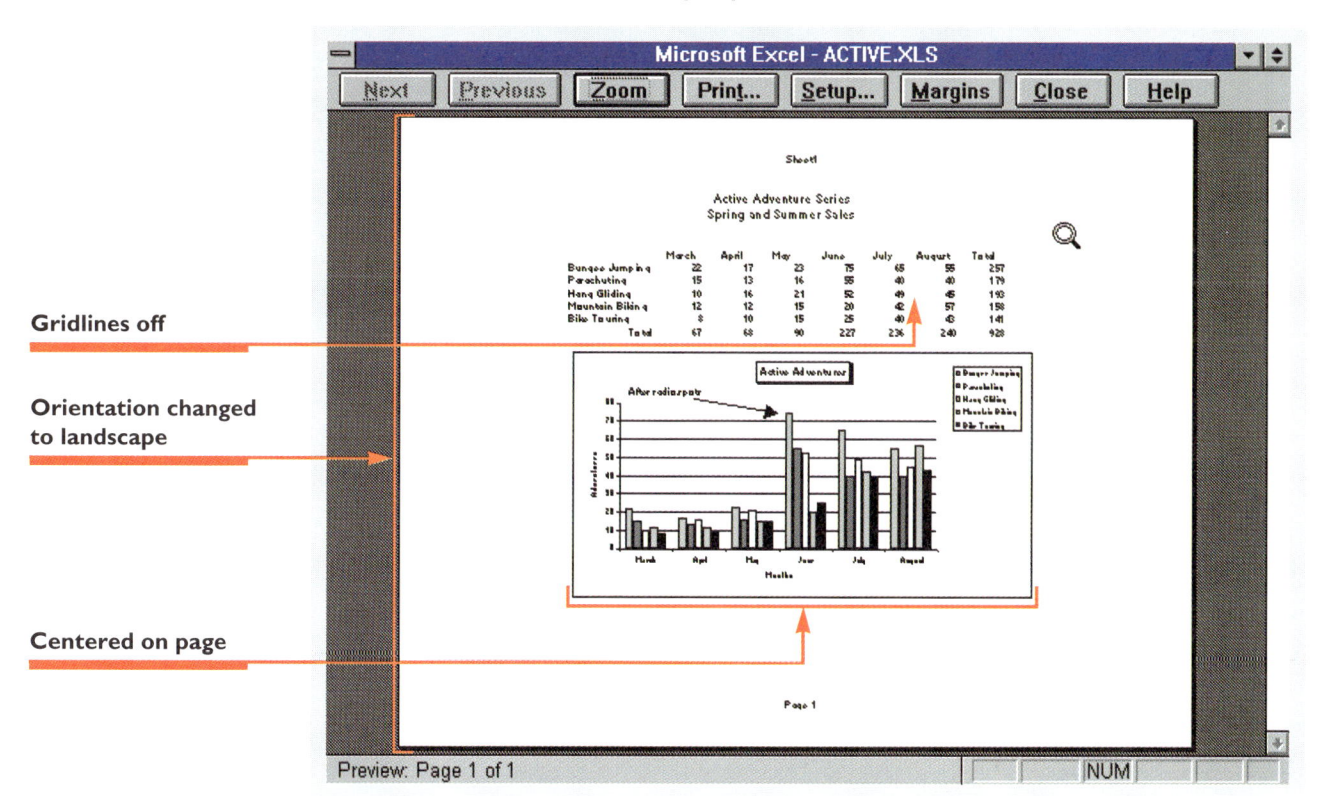

Gridlines off

Orientation changed to landscape

Centered on page

QUICK **TIP**

You can print charts and worksheets on transparencies for use on an overhead projector.■

CONCEPTS REVIEW

Label each of the Excel chart parts shown in Figure 5-22.

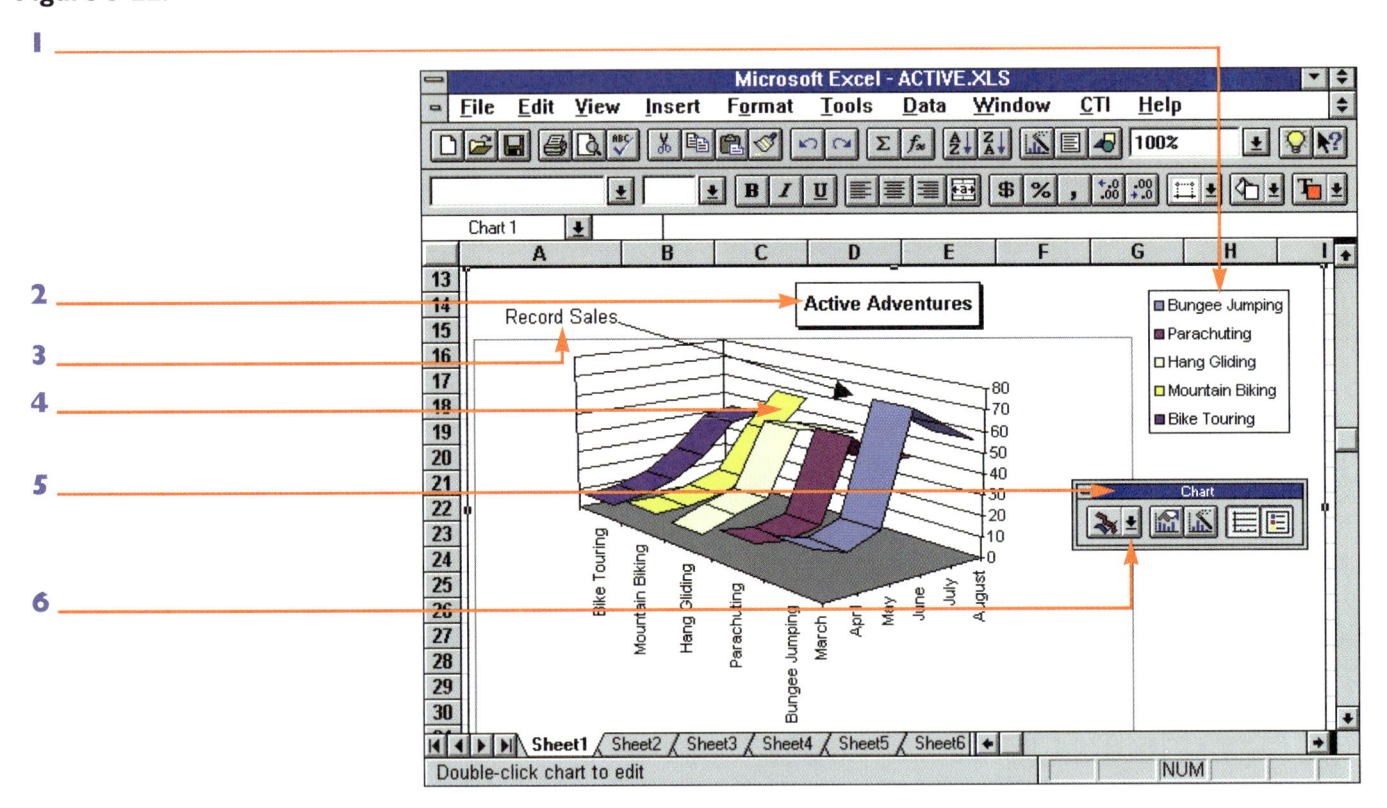

1.
2.
3.
4.
5.
6.

FIGURE 5-22

Select the best answer from the list of choices.

7. Use a pie chart when you want to show:
    a. Trends over a period of time
    b. Comparisons between data
    c. Relationship of parts to a whole
    d. Patterns between sets of data

8. The box that identifies patterns used for each data series is a:
    a. Data series
    b. Plot
    c. Legend
    d. Range

9. What is the term for a row or column on a chart?
    a. Range address
    b. Axis titles
    c. Chart orientation
    d. Data series

10. Which of the following charts is most effective for showing trends over time?
    a. Line chart
    b. Column chart
    c. Pie chart
    d. Area chart

11. The first step when creating a chart is to:
    a. Choose Chart from the Insert menu
    b. Select a cell
    c. Select a range
    d. Choose the ChartWizard

12. The tool used to add a drop shadow is:
    a.
    b.
    c.
    d.

APPLICATIONS REVIEW

1 Create a distribution report and then create a column chart beneath the data.

  a. Open a new workbook and use the Save As command to save it as SOFTWARE to your Student Disk.

  b. Enter the information from Table 5-4 in your worksheet.

  c. Save your work.

TABLE 5-4

	Microsoft Excel	Microsoft Word	WordPerfect	PageMaker
Accounting	10	1	9	0
Marketing	2	9	0	6
Engineering	12	5	7	1
Personnel	2	2	2	1
Production	6	3	4	0

  d. Select all the entered information, then click the ChartWizard tool on the Standard toolbar.

  e. Select the range in the worksheet where you want to insert the chart.

  f. Complete the ChartWizard dialog boxes and build a two-dimensional column chart with a different color bar for each department with the title "Software Distribution by Department."

  g. Drag the selection handles of the chart so the chart fills your screen.

  h. Save your work.

2 Change the chart type in the existing worksheet.

  a. Select the chart by clicking it.

  b. Click the Chart Type tool list arrow in the Chart toolbar.

  c. Click the 3-D Column Chart tool.

  d. Save your work.

3 Add a text annotation to the current chart.

  a. Double-click the chart to put it in Edit mode.

  b. Create a text annotation that says "Need More Computers."

  c. Drag the text annotation about 1" above the Personnel bar.

  d. Save your work.

4 Add an arrow to current chart.

  a. Click the Arrow tool on the Drawing toolbar.

  b. Click below the text annotation, drag down to the top of the Personnel bar, then release the mouse button. The arrow displays.

  c. Save your work.

5 Add axis headings to the current chart.

  a. Select the chart.

  b. Click Insert on the menu bar, click Titles, then click Category (X) Axis.

  c. Type "Department" in the selected text box below the x-axis,

  d. Click Insert on the menu bar, click Titles, then click Value (Y) Axis.

  e. Type "Number of Installed Packages" in the selected text box to the left of the y-axis.

  f. Save your work.

6 Move the legend and use color in the current chart.

  a. Make sure the chart is in Edit mode.

  b. Move the legend below the charted data.

  c. Change the color of one of the bars.

  d. Save your work.

7 Preview and print the current chart.

  a. Click the Preview tool. The Print Preview window opens.

  b. Examine the previewed image; remove gridlines.

  c. Select the chart, then click the Print Preview tool on the Standard toolbar.

  d. Center the chart on the page and change the paper orientation to Landscape.

  e. Click the Print Preview tool, then click Print after previewing the worksheet.

  f. Save your work.

INDEPENDENT CHALLENGES

You are the operations manager for the Springfield Municipal Recycling Center. The Marketing Department wants you to create charts for a brochure that will advertise a new curbside recycling program. Using the data provided, you need to create charts that show:

- How much of each type of recycled material Springfield collected in 1995 and what percentage of the whole each type represents. The center collects all types of paper, plastics, and glass from both business and residential customers.
- The yearly increases in the total amounts of recycled materials the center has collected since its inception three years ago. Springfield has experienced a 30% annual increase in collections.

To complete this independent challenge:

1 Prepare a worksheet plan that states your goal and identifies the formulas for any calculations.

2 Sketch a sample worksheet on a piece of paper, describing how you will create the charts. Which type of chart is best suited for the information you need to display? What kind of chart enhancements will be necessary?

3 Open the workbook SMRC.XLS on your Student Disk and save it as RECYCLE.XLS.

4 Create at least six different charts that show the number of recycled goods by total and by type of customer. Use the ChartWizard to switch the way data is plotted (columns vs. rows, and vice versa) to come up with additional charts.

5 Create the charts, then make the appropriate enhancements. Include chart titles, legends, and axis titles. Use the Color tool and the Font Color tool on the Formatting toolbar to help organize your chart information on the screen.

6 Before printing, enhance the appearance of the data, then preview the file so you know what the charts will look like. Adjust any items as needed.

7 Print the charts without printing the data. Then print a copy of the entire worksheet. Save your work before closing the file.

8 Submit your worksheet plan, preliminary sketches, and the final worksheet printouts.

As an administrator with the US Census Bureau, you are concerned with the distribution of the population by age and gender. Using the statistical data provided below, you need to create charts that show:

- How the population is distributed, by age and gender.
- How the population differs by gender.

AGE	MALE	FEMALE
65+	5%	7.5%
55-64	4%	4.5%
45-54	4.9%	5.2%
35-44	7.4%	7.6%
25-34	8.7%	8.7%
15-24	7.6%	7.3%
5-14	7.2%	6.9%
<5	3.9%	3.7%

To complete this independent challenge:

1 Prepare a worksheet plan that states your goal and identifies the formulas for any calculations.

2 Sketch a sample worksheet on a piece of paper, describing how you will create the charts. Which type of charts are best suited for the information you need to display? What kind of chart enhancements will be necessary?

3 Create a new workbook using the data above, and name it CENSUS.XLS.

4 Create at least six different charts that show the population in its entirety, by gender, by age, and by both age and gender. Use the ChartWizard to switch the way data is plotted (columns vs. rows, and vice versa) to come up with additional charts.

5 Add annotated text and arrows highlighting any data you feel is particularly important. Change colors to emphasize significant data.

6 Before printing, preview the file so you know what the charts will look like. Adjust any items as needed.

7 Print the charts with the data. Save your work before closing the file.

8 Submit your worksheet plan, preliminary sketches, and the final worksheet printouts.

UNIT 6

OBJECTIVES

- ▶ Plan a list
- ▶ Create a list
- ▶ Add records
- ▶ Find and delete records
- ▶ Sort records
- ▶ Find records using AutoFilter
- ▶ Use the PivotTable Wizard

Working WITH DATABASES

Now that you know how to build a worksheet and perform calculations, you are ready to use one of Excel's more powerful features—the database. A **database** is an organized collection of related information. A telephone book, a card catalog, and a list of company employees are all databases. Companies that distribute mass mailings and banks that manage customer accounts both rely on computer databases. Excel refers to databases as **lists**. ▶ Creating a list in Excel allows you to organize and manage worksheet information so that you can quickly find the data you need to work on projects or to use in reports and charts. In this unit, you'll learn how to plan and create a list, add and delete information, and locate specific information within a list. ▶ The Nationwide Travel Company uses lists for analyzing advertising expenses. Javier Yazzie from the Marketing Department needs to build and manage a list of customers to help decide where to focus Nationwide's advertising. ▶

Planning a list

When planning a list, you need to think about the information the list will contain and how you will work with the data now and in the future. Lists are organized into records. A **record** contains all the data about an object or person. Records are divided into fields. **Fields** are columns in the list; each field describes a characteristic about the record, like a customer's last name or address. Each field has a **field name**, a column label that describes the field. Field names can have up to 255 characters and can include spaces and uppercase and lowercase letters. ▶ You use a range of a worksheet called a **list range** to organize information into fields and records. The list range must fit on one worksheet; if your list contains more records than can fit on one worksheet, you should consider using database software rather than spreadsheet software. ▶ Javier Yazzie needs to compile a list of Nationwide customers so he can decide in which areas of the country the company should advertise. Before he enters the data into an Excel worksheet, he needs to plan the list. He uses the following planning guidelines.

Steps

1. **Identify the purpose of the list. Ask yourself what kind of information it should contain**
   Javier needs to use a list to find out from which areas of the country Nationwide customers are coming so he knows where to advertise.

2. **Plan the structure of the list. Determine the fields that will make up a record**
   Javier has information about each customer on customer cards. A typical card is shown in Figure 6-1. Each customer in his list will have a record. The fields will correspond to the information on the cards.

3. **Write down the names of the fields**
   Javier writes down field names that describe each piece of information as shown in Figure 6-1. Each customer will become a record. The fields will correspond to the information on the cards.

4. **Determine any special number formatting that will be required in the list. Most lists contain both text and numbers. When planning the structure of a list, you also need to consider whether any of the fields will require specific number formatting or prefixes**
   Javier notes that some zip codes begin with zero. Since a preceding zero is automatically dropped by Excel, he will need to add an apostrophe (') if the zip code begins with 0. The apostrophe tells Excel the cell contains a label rather than a value.

EXCEL 5 UNIT 6 WORKING WITH DATABASES

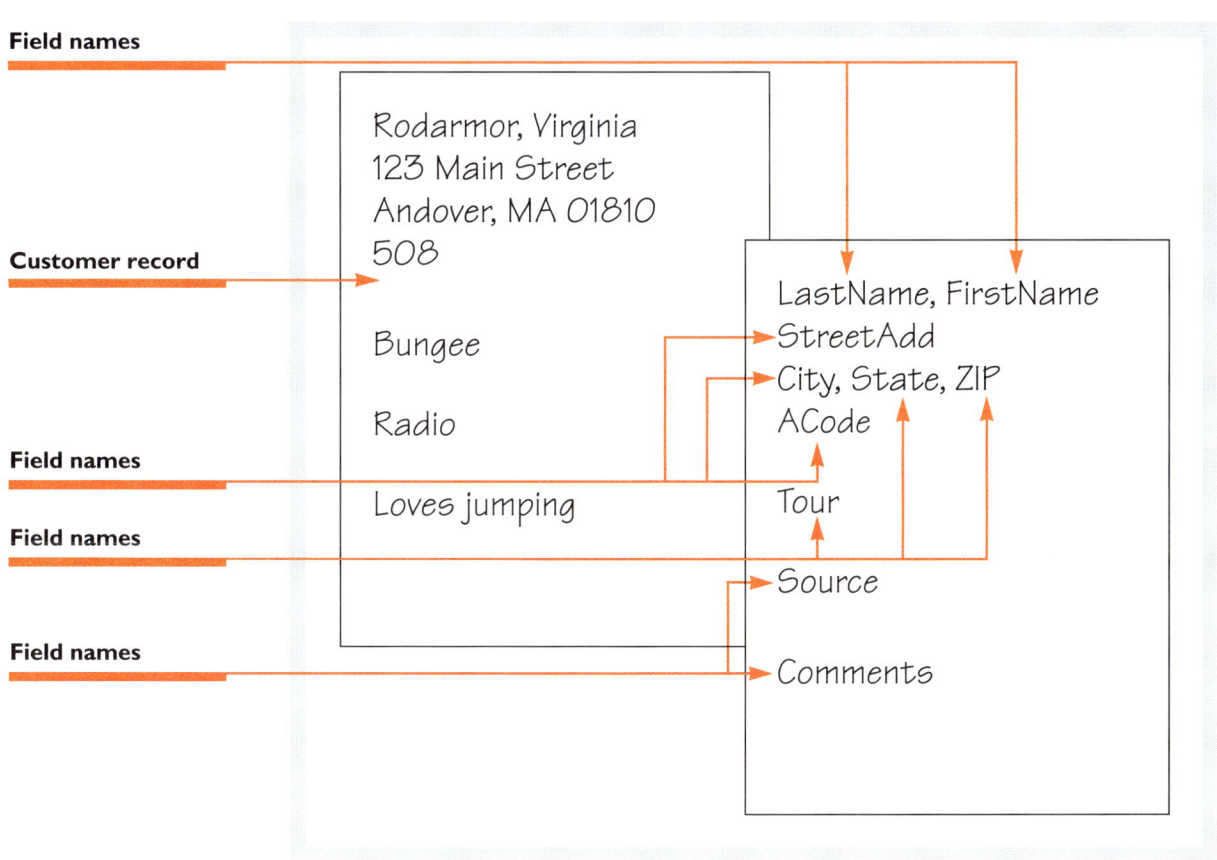

FIGURE 6-1: Customer record and corresponding field names

Field names

Customer record

Rodarmor, Virginia
123 Main Street
Andover, MA 01810
508

Bungee

Radio

Field names

Loves jumping

Field names

LastName, FirstName
StreetAdd
City, State, ZIP
ACode

Tour

Source

Field names

Comments

Creating a list

Once you have planned the structure of the list, the sequence of fields, and any appropriate formatting, you need to create field names. Table 6-1 lists field naming guidelines. ▶ Javier Yazzie is ready to create the list, using the field names he wrote down earlier. He will also select the range that the list will occupy on the worksheet.

Steps

1. **Open the workbook UNIT6.XLS from your Student Disk, save it as LISTDATA.XLS, then rename Sheet1 as Create**
   It is a good idea to devote an entire worksheet to your list.

2. **Beginning in cell A1 and moving horizontally, type each field name, as shown in Figure 6-2, in a separate cell**
   Always put field names in the first row of the list. When you finish entering all the field names, continue to Step 3, where you will format the field names. Don't worry that your field names are wider than the cells— you'll fix this in Step 5.

3. **Select the range A1:J1, then click the Bold tool B on the Formatting toolbar**
   Compare your worksheet to Figure 6-2. Next, you will enter three of the records in Javier's customer list.

4. **Enter the information from Figure 6-3 in the rows of cells immediately below the field names, using an apostrophe (') for zip codes beginning with 0**
   If you don't type an apostrophe, Excel will delete the first zero in the zip code. The data appears in columns organized by field name. Do not leave any blank rows. Now Javier wants to adjust the column widths so that each column is as wide as its longest entry.

5. **Select the range A1:J4, click Format on the menu bar, click Column, click AutoFit Selection, then click anywhere in the worksheet to deselect the range**
   This is a faster method of automatically resizing the column widths than double-clicking the column divider lines between each column. Compare your screen with Figure 6-4. Javier is now satisfied that his list is well-designed and that future data entry will be easy. He saves the list.

6. **Click the Save tool on the Standard toolbar to save the list**

TABLE 6-1: Field naming guidelines

SUBJECT	EXPLANATION
Use labels to name fields	Numbers and formulas can be interpreted as parts of formulas.
Do not use duplicate field names	Duplicate field names can cause information to be incorrectly entered and sorted.
Do not use punctuation or spaces	You can not use commas, periods, colons, tildes, number signs, hyphens, spaces, or +, –, *, / .
Use descriptive names	Avoid names that look like cell addresses, such as Q3.

FIGURE 6-2:
Field names entered and formatted in row 1

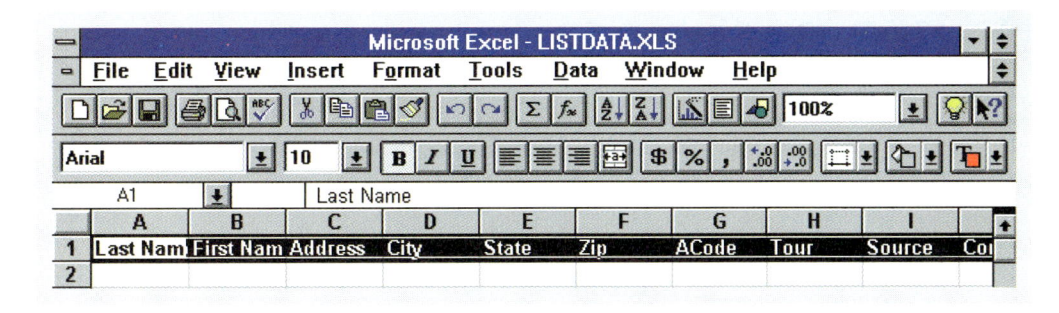

FIGURE 6-3:
Cards with customer information

Rodarmor, Virginia
123 Main St.
Andover, MA 01810
508

Bungee

Radio

loves jumping

Pacheco, Ralph
2120 Central NE
Albuquerque, NM 87105
505

Parachute

Magazine

loves our tours

Smith, Carol
123 Elm St.
Acton, MA 01776
508

Bungee

Magazine

likes jumping

FIGURE 6-4: List with three records entered

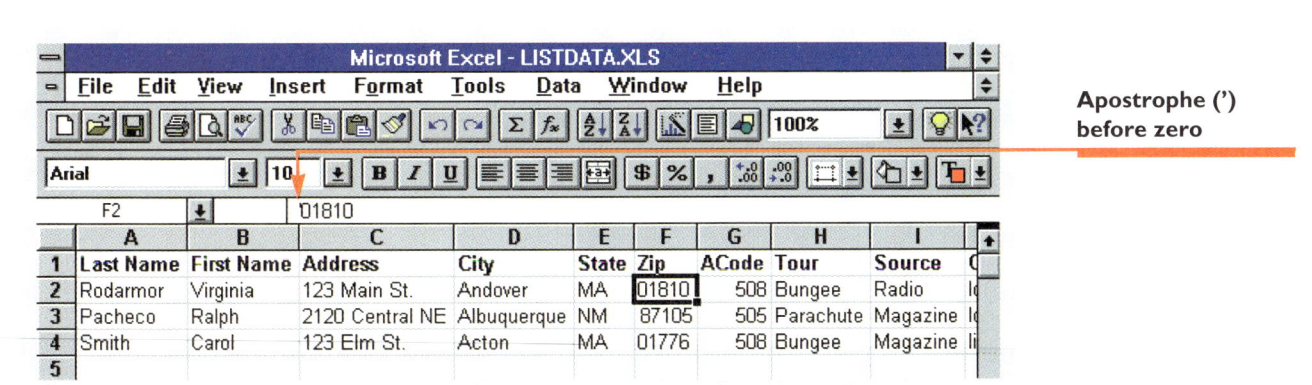

Apostrophe (') before zero

Maintaining the quality of information in a list

To protect the information, make sure that the data is entered in the correct fields. Stress care and consistency to all those who enter the data. Data entered in a haphazard manner might yield invalid results when manipulated.

EXCEL 5 UNIT 6 **WORKING** WITH DATABASES

Adding records

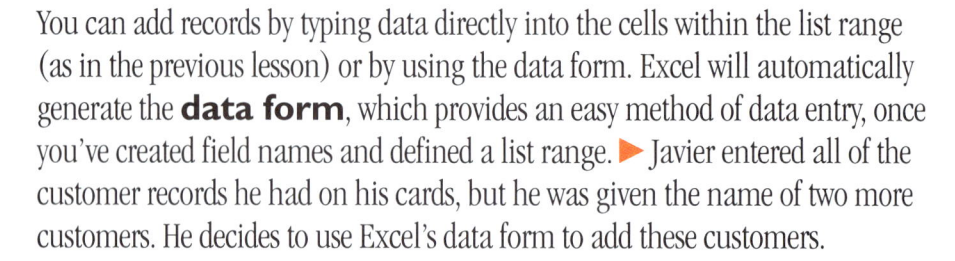

You can add records by typing data directly into the cells within the list range (as in the previous lesson) or by using the data form. Excel will automatically generate the **data form**, which provides an easy method of data entry, once you've created field names and defined a list range. ▶ Javier entered all of the customer records he had on his cards, but he was given the name of two more customers. He decides to use Excel's data form to add these customers.

Steps

1 **Make sure LISTDATA.XLS is open, then rename Sheet2 as Complete**
   Complete contains the nearly complete customer list. Before using the data form to enter data, you need to define the list range.

2 **Select the range A1:J38, click Insert on the menu bar, click Name, click Define, then type Database in the Names in Workbook text box, and click OK**
   The name displays in the name box. Javier will now enter a new record using the data form.

3 **Click Data on the menu bar, click Form, then click New in the Complete dialog box**
   A blank data form displays with the insertion point in the first field. See Figure 6-5.

4 **Type Chavez in the Last Name text box, then press [Tab] to move the insertion point to the next field**
   You could also click in the next field text box to move the insertion point there.

5 **Enter the rest of information in the data form, as shown in Figure 6-6**

6 **Click New**
   Jeffrey Chavez's record is added to the list, and a new, blank data form is opened.

7 **Enter the record shown in Figure 6-7**

8 **Click Close**
   The new record is added to the list and the data form closes.

FIGURE 6-5: Blank data form

Insertion point →

FIGURE 6-6: Data form with Jeffrey Chavez's record

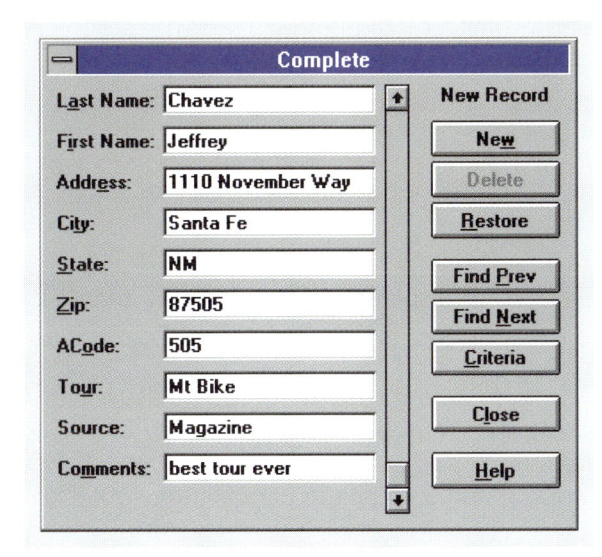

FIGURE 6-7: Data form with Cathy Relman's record

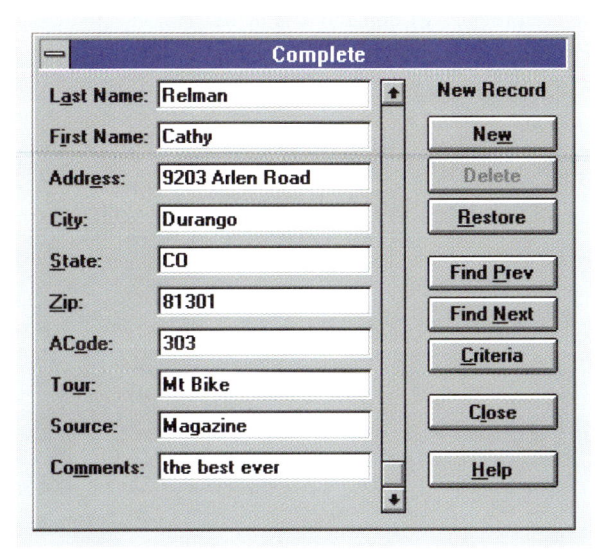

QUICK TIP

Once the list range is defined, any new records added to the list will be included in the list range. ■

EXCEL 5 UNIT 6 WORKING WITH DATABASES

113

Finding and deleting records

As you use a list, you need to keep it up to date by removing records that are no longer needed. To remove records, select the record and use the Delete command on the Edit menu, or use the Delete button on the data form. You can also tell Excel to delete all records that meet a certain **criteria**, that is, records that have something in common, such as a type of product. ▶ Susie Kwan, the owner of Nationwide Travel, told Javier that because so few people chose the Parachuting tour they are discontinuing it. Javier decides to use the data form to specify a criteria and delete all the customers who went parachuting.

Steps

1 Click **Data** on the menu bar, click **Form**, then click **Criteria**
The data form changes so that all fields are blank and "Criteria" appears in the upper-right corner. See Figure 6-8. You can set as many criteria to search for as you want. You want to search for records whose Tour field contains the label "Parachute."

2 Click the **Tour text box**, type **Parachute**, then click **Find Next**
Excel finds Ralph Pacheco's record, record 2, which is the first record of a customer who went on the Parachute tour. See Figure 6-9.

3 Click **Delete** then click **OK** in the alert box to confirm the deletion
Ralph Pacheco's record is deleted and all the other records move up one row. The new record 2, Carol Smith, is shown in the data form.

4 Click **Criteria** to display the Criteria form, then click **Find Next** to find the next record containing Parachute in the Tour field

5 Click **Delete** to delete record 9, Hope Miller's record, then click **OK** in the alert box to confirm the deletion

6 Repeat steps 4 and 5 to delete Pam Haughwout's record and Gail Paxton's record

7 Click **Criteria** then click **Find Next**
The computer beeps because it doesn't find any records that match the criteria, and the last record displayed appears in the data form.

8 Click **Close** to close the data form

9 Click the **Save tool** on the Standard toolbar to save your changes

FIGURE 6-8: Criteria data form

Click to find next record matching criteria

Type Parachute here

Identifies this as Criteria data form

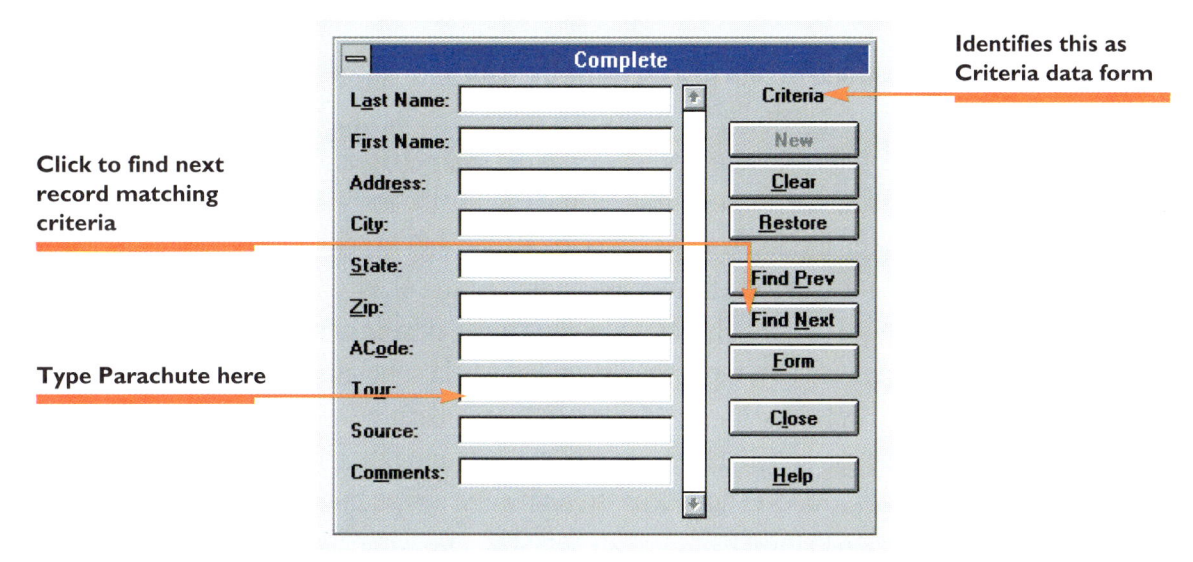

FIGURE 6-9: Finding a record using the data form

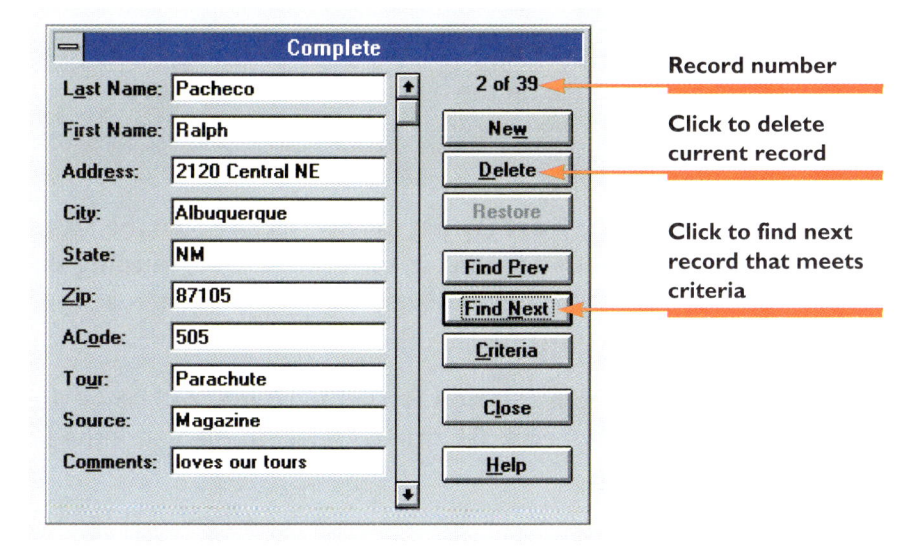

Record number

Click to delete current record

Click to find next record that meets criteria

Deleting records without using the data form

A record within a list can be deleted without using the data form. If you know which record should be deleted, click the row selector button for that record, click Edit on the menu bar, then click Delete.

EXCEL 5 UNIT 6 **WORKING** WITH DATABASES

Sorting records

When you add records to a list using the data form, the records are added to the end of the list. Usually, the records are entered in the order in which they are received, rather than in alphabetical order. **Sorting** allows you to rearrange the order in which the records display. You can use the toolbar to sort the records, or you can use the Sort command on the Data menu to perform more complicated sorts. ▶ You can sort an entire list or any portion of a list. Sorted information can be arranged in ascending or descending order. In **ascending** order, the smallest value appears at the top of the list, and in a field containing labels and numbers, numbers will come first. In **descending** order, the largest value appears at the top of the list, and in a field containing labels and numbers, labels will come first. Table 6-2 provides examples of ascending and descending sort orders. Lists can be sorted by up to three fields and are sorted by specifying a **sort key**, the criteria upon which the sort is based. ▶ Javier wants to sort the records by the Tour field, then sort within the Tour field by area code.

1 Click the **name box**, then select **Database**
The list becomes selected. Javier needs to sort the list by more than one field, and he will sort using the Sort command on the Data menu.

2 Click **Data** on the menu bar, then click **Sort**
The Sort dialog box displays. See Figure 6-10. Javier needs to sort the list by tour and then by area code.

3 Click the **Sort By list arrow**, scroll down the list until you see "Tour," click **Tour** to select it, then click the **Ascending radio button**
The list will be sorted first by the tour field in ascending order. Next, tell Excel to sort by the ACode field in descending order.

4 Click the first **Then By list arrow**, scroll down the list until you see "ACode," click **ACode** to select it, then click the **Descending radio button**
If you wanted to, you could sort by a third key by selecting a field in the second Then By list box.

5 Click **OK** to execute the sort, then click the **right arrow** on the horizontal scroll bar to see the effects of the sort
The list is sorted as requested, first alphabetically by tour, then within each tour, in descending order by area code. Compare your results to Figure 6-11.

6 Click the **Save tool** 🖫 on the Standard toolbar to save your changes

TABLE 6-2:
Sort options

OPTION	EXAMPLE
Ascending	7, 8, 9, A, B, C
Descending	C, B, A, 9, 8, 7

FIGURE 6-10: Sort dialog box

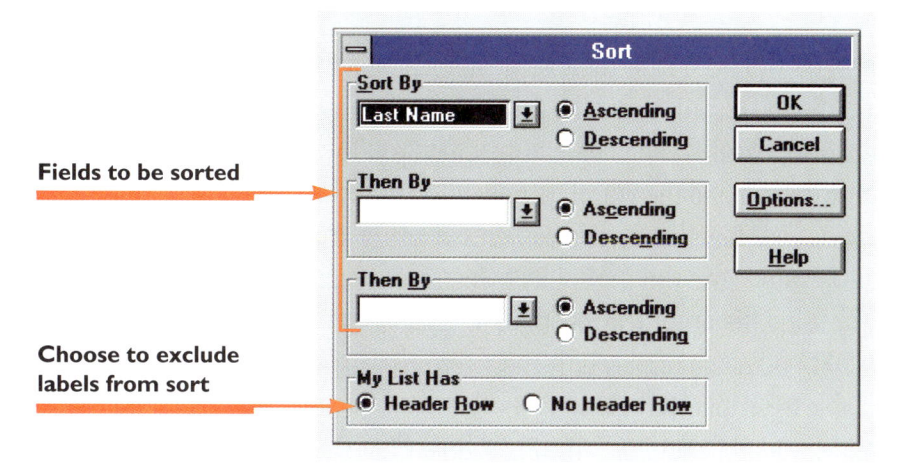

Fields to be sorted

Choose to exclude labels from sort

FIGURE 6-11: The sorted list

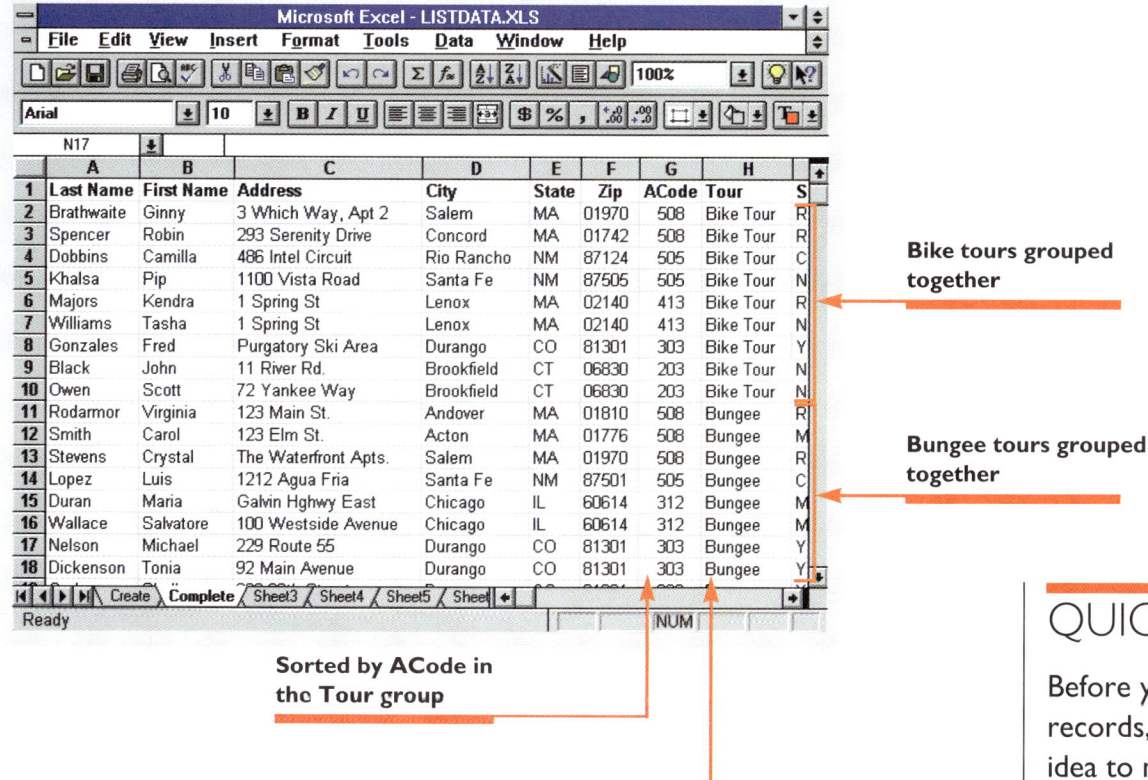

Bike tours grouped together

Bungee tours grouped together

Sorted by ACode in the Tour group

Sorted by Tour

QUICK TIP

Before you sort the records, it is a good idea to make a backup copy of your list or create a field which numbers records so they can be returned to their original order in case the sort doesn't work as planned.

EXCEL 5 UNIT 6 **WORKING** WITH DATABASES

117

Finding records using AutoFilter

Many times you will need to locate specific information in a list. You already know how to find specific records using the Criteria and the Find Next command buttons in the data form. Excel's AutoFilter feature allows you to search for records that meet specific criteria and then displays only those records meeting that criteria. ▶ You can refine your searches of field contents by using arithmetic operators. Arithmetic operators give you the ability to focus your search within a field. For example, by using the arithmetic operator for greater than (>) and specifying the value $10,000, you could display only those records with amounts greater than $10,000. Table 6-3 explains the arithmetic operators available. ▶ Javier wants to find and display all the customers having a zip code greater than 81000 (west of the Rockies), who learned about Nationwide Travel through magazine ads and then signed up for a Mountain Bike tour.

1 Click **Database** in the name box

2 Click **Data** from the menu bar, click **Filter**, then click **AutoFilter**
List arrows appear to the right of each field name in the list.

3 Click the **Zip list arrow**, then click **Custom**
The Custom AutoFilter dialog box displays. This dialog box allows you to customize the search parameters. Javier wants to see only those records having a zip code greater than 81000.

4 Click the **list arrow** next to = (equal sign), then click **>** (greater than sign) in the list of available operators

5 Type **81000** into the text box next to the greater than sign
See Figure 6-12.

6 Click **OK**
The dialog box closes and only records having a zip code greater than 81000 appear in the worksheet.

7 Click the **Tour list arrow**, then click **Mt Bike**
The list of records displayed reduces even further, as shown in Figure 6-13. Javier's criteria also includes only those customers who heard about Nationwide through a magazine ad, but all the records displayed have "Magazine" listed in the Source field so there is no need to specify that criteria. Javier wants to print this list.

8 Click the **Print Preview tool**, click **Print**, then click **OK**
Now turn off AutoFilter and display all the records.

9 Click **Data** from the menu bar, click **Filter**, then click **AutoFilter**
AutoFilter is turned off, and all records are displayed again.

TABLE 6-3:
Arithmetic operators used to find records

OPERATOR	EXPLANATION	OPERATOR	EXPLANATION
=	The specified field is equal to this value	<=	The specified field is less than or equal to this value
<	The specified field is less than this value	>=	The specified field is greater than or equal to this value
>	The specified field is greater than this value	<>	The specified field is not equal to this value

FIGURE 6-12: Custom AutoFilter dialog box

Click to display list of arithmetic operators

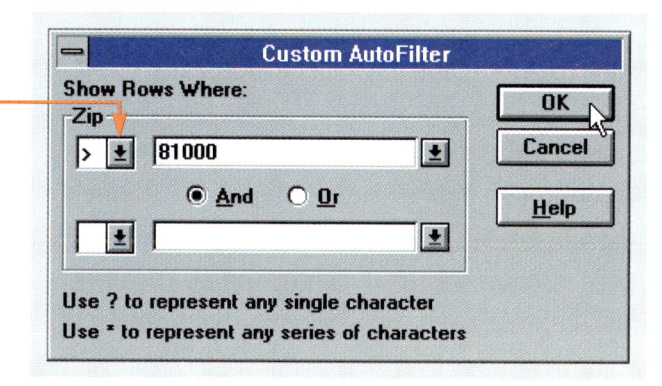

FIGURE 6-13: Using AutoFilter to search the list

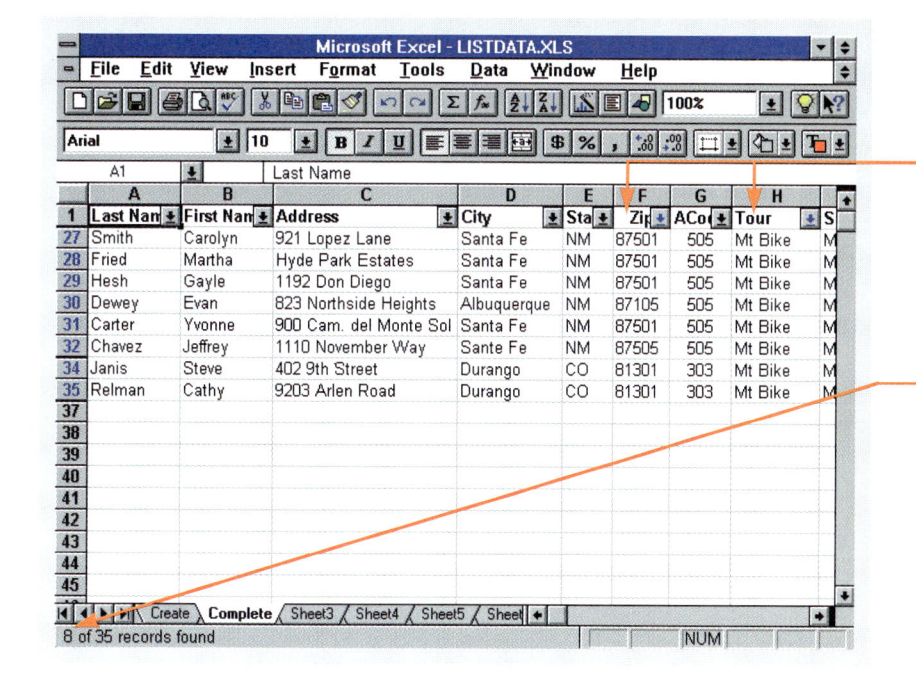

Search by these fields

Number of records found that match criteria

Using "And" or "Or"

AutoFilter can be used to narrow a search further using the Custom AutoFilter dialog box. Using the And or Or logical conditions enables you to create complex criteria, such as selecting records for those customers living in Colorado or New Mexico. See Figure 6-14.

Logical conditions

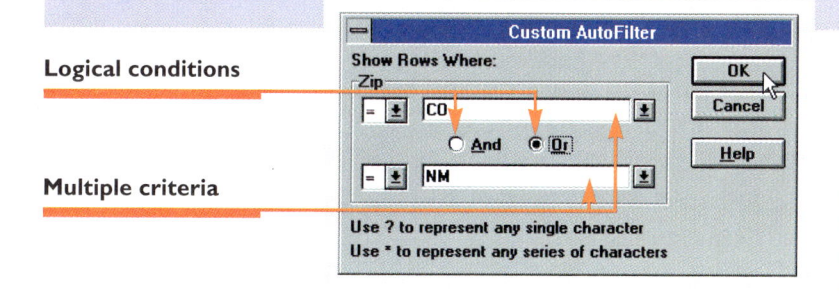

Multiple criteria

FIGURE 6-14: Using "Or" in the AutoFilter dialog box

QUICK TIP

Use the ? wildcard to specify any single character and the * wildcard to specify any series of characters. You can use wildcard symbols in your search criteria. For example, to search for last names beginning with "S," enter = (the arithmetic operator), followed by S*. To search for records when you are not sure of the exact spelling, enter Al l?n to find Allan, Allyn, and Allen.

EXCEL 5 UNIT 6 **WORKING** WITH DATABASES

Using the PivotTable Wizard

While the data form and AutoFilter features give you the power and flexibility to enter, find, and examine list information, Excel's **PivotTable** feature allows you to summarize your data in table form. It is similar to the ChartWizard as it leads you through a series of dialog boxes. For example, to find the number of tours which resulted from each advertising source, you would have to manually count the records once they had been sorted. The PivotTable Wizard does all this for you—all you have to do is select the fields you want to summarize. Once the PivotTable is created, the Query and Pivot toolbar displays. These tools, which are described in Table 6-4, enable you to make further enhancements in the table. ▶ Javier is happy with his list of marketing data, but he still needs an analysis of the number of tours in relation to advertising sources. He will use the PivotTable to obtain this information so he can formulate a marketing strategy that will be used to target and strengthen certain markets.

Steps

1. Make sure the range Database is selected

2. Click **Data** on the menu bar, then click **PivotTable**
   The first PivotTable Wizard dialog box displays and gives you the option of using an Excel List or external database as the data source.

3. Make sure the Microsoft Excel List or Database radio button is selected, then click **Next**
   The second PivotTable Wizard dialog box displays. Because you selected the range before you started, the Range text box indicates that the table will be created from the range named Database.

4. Click **Next**
   PivotTable Wizard Step 3 of 4 dialog box contains the fields within the list. You use this dialog box to describe how you want the data summarized within the table. See Figure 6-15. Javier wants to see which ad sources brought in tour business.

5. Drag the Tour field button from the list to the COLUMN box, then drag the Source field button from the list to the ROW box
   This will create a table with the tours as column headings and the source as row labels. The field in the DATA box is that information which will be analyzed. Javier wants the number of tours to be counted. Counting is different from summing—counting counts the number of records found that meet the criteria, and summing adds the contents in the fields of the records that meet the criteria. Counting is Excel's default form of analysis.

6. Again, click the **Tour field button** from the list on the right side of the dialog box, then drag it to the DATA box
   The field in the DATA box will be analyzed according to the specified columns and rows. See Figure 6-15. Continue to the next lesson to complete Javier's PivotTable, which helps him see which ad sources brought in which tour business.

FIGURE 6-15: Third PivotTable Wizard dialog box

Field buttons dragged to layout

Field buttons in list

TABLE 6-4:
Query and Pivot tools

TOOL	DESCRIPTION	TOOL	DESCRIPTION
	Starts PivotTable Wizard		Hides detail in table groupings
	Modifies PivotTable field		Shows detail in table groupings
	Ungroups selected rows or columns		Shows multiple workbook pages
	Groups selected rows or columns		Updates changes within the table

QUICK TIP

You can change the form of analysis by double-clicking the field in the DATA box and selecting a new form of analysis from the list.

EXCEL 5 UNIT 6 **WORKING** WITH DATABASES

121

Using the PivotTable Wizard continued

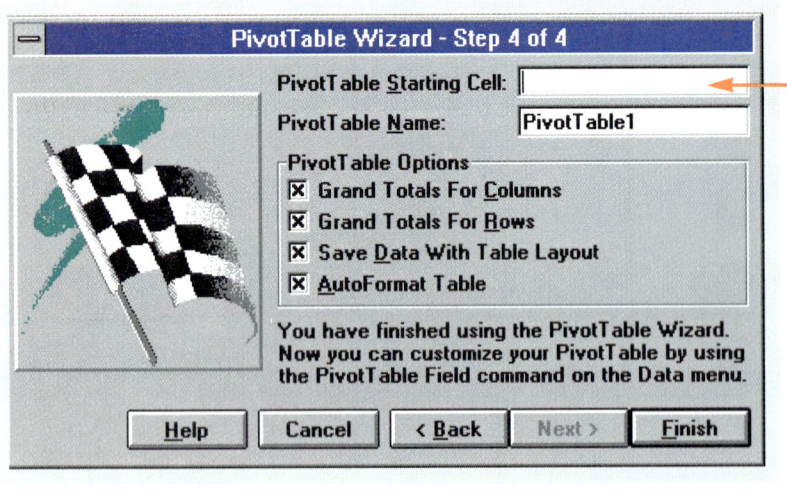

The PivotTable Wizard creates a table by allowing you to specify the fields you would like to see in the columns (the tour type in this example) and the fields that you would like to see in the rows (the advertising source in this example). What is selected as the column or row gives you a different perspective of the data. ▶ Javier's PivotTable is almost complete.

7 Click Next
The final PivotTable Wizard dialog box displays. See Figure 6-16. The PivotTable Starting Cell text box tells Excel where to create the table in the worksheet. If you leave this box empty, the table will be created on a new, blank worksheet.

8 Type A40 in the PivotTable Starting Cell text box, then click Finish
The PivotTable Wizard closes, and the PivotTable appears in the worksheet. Compare your completed PivotTable to the one in Figure 6-17. Javier examines the table and notes that magazine ads yield the best response, so he decides to recommend increasing advertising in specialty magazines aimed at each of the tour groups. Satisfied with his results, he saves and closes the workbook.

9 Click the Save tool 🖫 **on the Standard toolbar to save your changes, then close the workbook**

FIGURE 6-16: Last PivotTable dialog box

FIGURE 6-17: Completed PivotTable

Query and Pivot toolbar

Field name

PivotTable

Dramatize PivotTable data with a chart

A PivotTable can provide you with insightful information you might have missed. This data can be further dramatized by creating a chart using the ChartWizard. To do this, select the table. Do not include the totals columns, and be careful not to drag the field buttons. Then, click the ChartWizard tool on the Standard toolbar and complete the dialog boxes. The PivotTable you created in this lesson is charted in Figure 6-18.

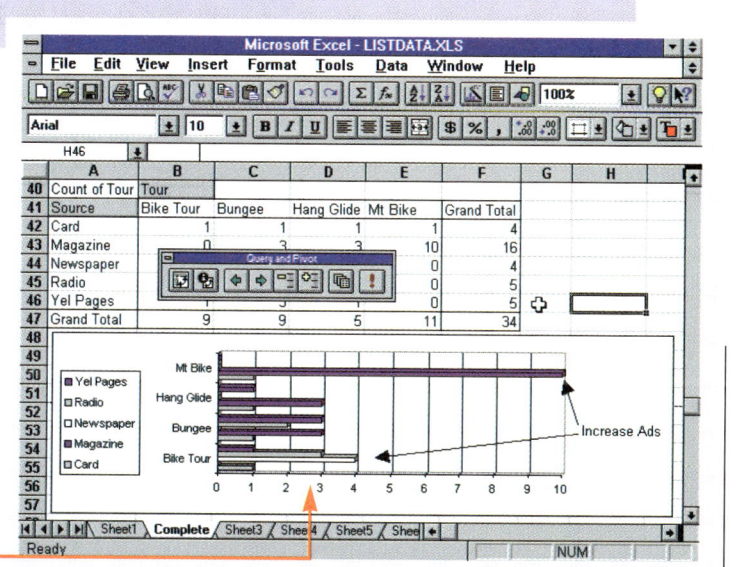

FIGURE 6-18: Charted PivotTable data

Charted PivotTable

QUICK TIP

Use AutoFormat to enhance the appearance of the PivotTable.

EXCEL 5 UNIT 6 WORKING WITH DATABASES

CONCEPTS REVIEW

Label each of the elements of the Excel list shown in Figure 6-19.

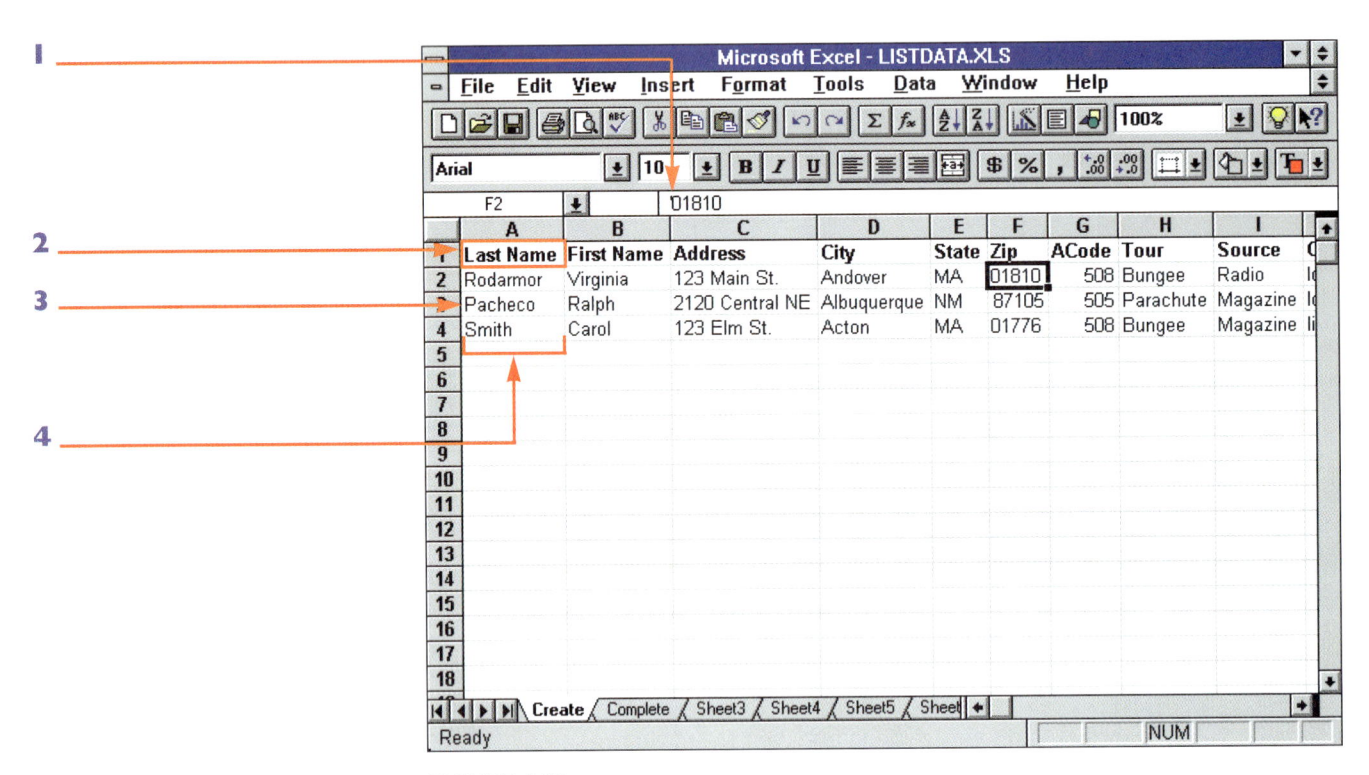

1. _____
2. _____
3. _____
4. _____

FIGURE 6-19

Match each of the statements with the term it describes.

5 To arrange records in a particular sequence

6 Organized collection of related information

7 Row in a Excel list

8 Column in a Excel list containing information related to a record

9 Label positioned at the top of the column identifying data for that field

a. Field
b. Record
c. List
d. Sort
e. Field name

Select the best answer from the list of choices.

10 Which of the following Excel sorting options do you use to sort a list of employee names in A-to-Z order?

a. Ascending
b. Absolute
c. Alphabet
d. Descending

11 Which of the following series of numbers is in descending order?

a. 4, 5, 6, 5, 4
b. 4, 5, 6, 7, 8
c. 8, 7, 6, 5, 4
d. 4, 6, 8, 6, 4

12 A PivotTable is used to:

   a. Twist the list so the columns turn into rows

   b. Count only numeric data

   c. Analyze and summarize any data within a list

   d. Turn values into labels

APPLICATIONS REVIEW

1 On paper, plan and design an employee list for M.K. Electric Sales.

   a. Column A will contain the Last Name field.

   b. Column B will contain the First Name field.

   c. Column C will contain the Years field.

   d. Column D will contain the Position field.

   e. Column E will contain the Pension field.

   f. Column F will contain the Union field.

2 Build the employee list.

   a. Open a new workbook and use the Save As command to save it as SALESEMP.XLS to your Student Disk.

   b. Type the title M.K. Electric Sales Employees at the top of the worksheet.

   c. Type the field names in the appropriate columns, using your planning sketch from Step 1.

   d. Enter the records in the appropriate fields using the information in Table 6-5.

   e. Save your work.

TABLE 6-5

LAST NAME	FIRST NAME	YEARS	POSITION	PENSION	UNION
Smith-Hill	Janice	8	Office Manager	Y	N
Doolan	Mark	3	Customer Ser.	N	N
Coleman	Steve	4	Senior Installer	N	Y
Quinn	Jamie	7	Junior Installer	N	Y
Rabinowicz	Sarah	11	Field Manager	Y	Y

3 Make formatting changes to the current list.

   a. Center the entries in the Pension and Union fields.

   b. Adjust the column widths of the Last Name and Position fields to make the data readable.

   c. Save and print the worksheet.

4 Using the data form, add records to the current list.

   a. Select all the records in the list, including the field names, and define the range as DATABASE.

   b. Open the data form and add a new record for David Gitano, a newly hired junior installer at M.K. Electric Sales. David is not eligible for the employee pension, but he is a member of the union.

   c. Add another new record for George Worley, the company's new office assistant. George is not eligible for the employee pension, and he is not a union member.

5 Find records of pension-eligible employees in the current list.

   a. Activate AutoFilter.

   b. Click the Pension list arrow and then click Y.

   c. Print this list.

   d. Turn off AutoFilter.

6 Sort the current list alphabetically by last name.

   a. Select the Database range from the name box.

   b. Use the toolbar to sort the list alphabetically in ascending order by last name and then by years.

   c. Save and print the sorted worksheet.

7 Create a PivotTable.

   a. Activate the PivotTable Wizard.

   b. The PivotTable data should examine Pension and Union field entries and Count of Pension should be analyzed.

   c. Use AutoFormat to create an attractive PivotTable.

   d. Create a chart of the PivotTable data.

   e. Save your work and then close the workbook.

INDEPENDENT CHALLENGES

You are the program director of Blair Cinema, an independent movie house that specializes in foreign and specialty films. One of your responsibilities is to compile a list of "movie buff" data about the artists who will be featured in an upcoming film festival, "Hollywood Greats: Pre-1960." The two-week event will honor Hollywood legends such as Katharine Hepburn, Joan Crawford, and Cary Grant whose performances in films before 1960 still dazzle audiences.

Plan and build a list of information a minimum of 10 movie legendary actresses and actors to be featured in the film festival. Enter your own data (based on what you know about your own movie favorites, or on information you make up), but make sure you include at least the following list fields:

- Name—What is the artist's professional name?

- Genre—Is the artist known primarily as a comic or dramatic artist?

- Films—In approximately how many films has the artist appeared?
- Most popular—For what film is the artist best known?
- Oscar—Has the artist won an Academy Award for his or her performance in a film?
- Title 1—Title of film in which the artist appeared.
- Title 2—Title of film in which the artist appeared.

To complete this independent challenge:

1. Prepare a list plan that states your goal, outlines the worksheet data you'll need, and identifies the list elements.

2. Sketch a sample worksheet on a piece of paper, indicating how the list should be built. Which actresses will you include? What information should go in the columns? In the rows? Which of the data fields will be formatted as labels? As values? If you have trouble compiling information about artists, check the movie section of your local newspaper or a movie guide for ideas.

3. Build the worksheet by entering the worksheet title and field names first, then entering the records. Remember you are creating and entering your own movie data. Save the data in a new workbook called CINEMA.XLS.

4. Make formatting changes to the list, as needed. For example, you might need to adjust the column widths to make the data more readable. Also, remember to check your spelling.

5. Sort the list alphabetically by last name, then by Genre, then by Oscar. Before printing, preview the worksheet so you know what it will look like. Adjust any items as needed, and then print a copy.

6. Next, use the AutoFilter to display records by genre so you can easily see how many comedic or dramatic actors/actresses are represented in the festival.

7. Create a PivotTable that analyzes the films in the list by Genre and Oscar. Count of Genre should be analyzed.

8. Preview the worksheet then print it. Save your work before closing the file.

9. Submit your list plan, preliminary sketches, and the final worksheet printouts.

Your advertising firm specializes in selling businesses the following specialty items imprinted with the customer's name and/or logo: hats, pens, and T-shirts.

Plan and build a list of information with a minimum of 20 records using the three items sold. Your list should contain at least five different customers. Each record should contain the customer's name, item sold, its individual and extended cost. You can use the data in UNIT4.XLS (supplied on your Student Disk or make up your own). Enter your data and make sure you include at least the following list fields:

- Item—Describe the item.
- Cost-Ea.—What is the item's individual cost?
- Quantity—How many did the Customer purchase?
- Ext. Cost—What is the total purchase price?
- Customer—Who purchased the item?

To complete this independent challenge:

1. Prepare a list plan that states your goal, outlines the worksheet data you'll need, and identifies the list elements.

2. Sketch a sample worksheet on a piece of paper, indicating how the list should be built. What information should go in the columns? In the rows? Which of the data fields will be formatted as labels? As values?

3. Build the worksheet by entering the worksheet title and field names first, then by entering the records. Remember you can make up your own data or you can use the data in UNIT4.XLS. Save the data in a new workbook called SPECILTY.XLS.

4. Make formatting changes to the list, as needed. For example, you might need to adjust the column widths to make the data more readable. Also, remember to check your spelling.

5. Sort the list in ascending order by Item, then by Customer, then by Quantity. Before printing, preview the file so you know what the worksheet will look like. Adjust any items as needed, and then print a copy.

6. Next, use the AutoFilter to display records whose Quantity is greater than 10 so you can see with which Customers you might want to increase business.

7. Create a PivotTable that analyzes the items in the list by Item and Customer. Count of Items should be analyzed.

8. Preview the worksheet then print it. Save your work before closing the file.

9. Submit your list plan, preliminary sketches, and the final worksheet printouts.

UNIT 7

OBJECTIVES

▶ Plan a macro

▶ Record a macro

▶ Run a macro

▶ Edit a macro

▶ Add a macro to a menu and a toolbar

Automating WORKSHEET TASKS

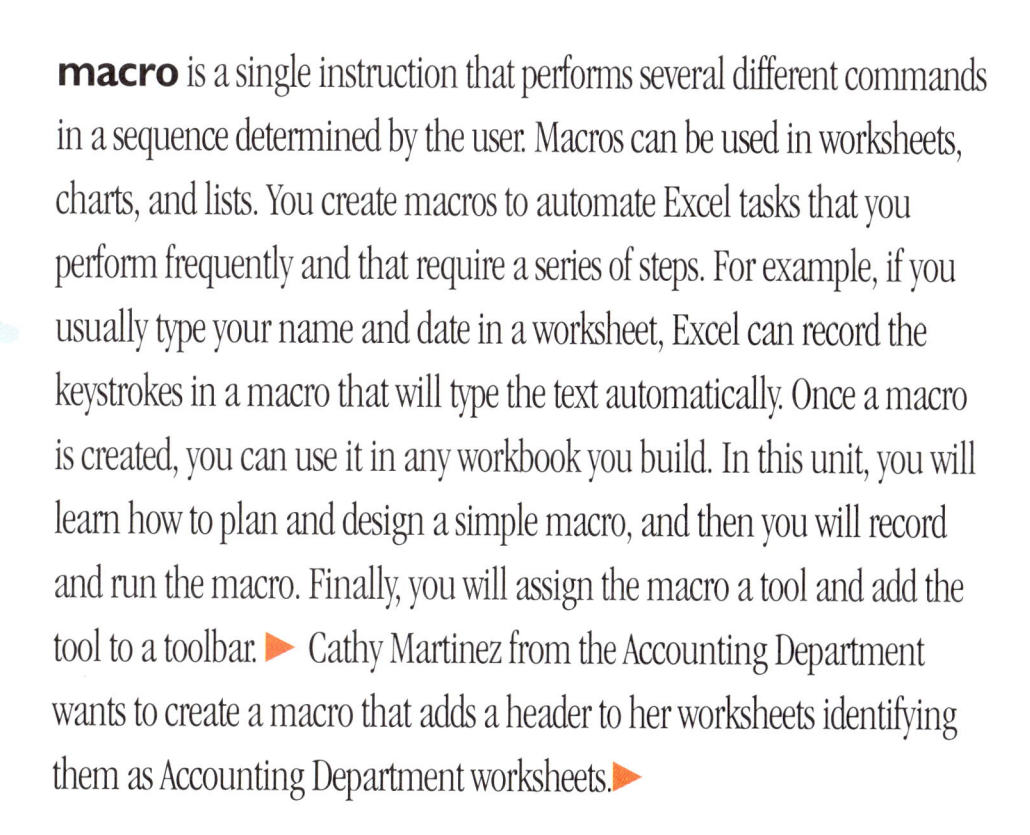

A **macro** is a single instruction that performs several different commands in a sequence determined by the user. Macros can be used in worksheets, charts, and lists. You create macros to automate Excel tasks that you perform frequently and that require a series of steps. For example, if you usually type your name and date in a worksheet, Excel can record the keystrokes in a macro that will type the text automatically. Once a macro is created, you can use it in any workbook you build. In this unit, you will learn how to plan and design a simple macro, and then you will record and run the macro. Finally, you will assign the macro a tool and add the tool to a toolbar. ▶ Cathy Martinez from the Accounting Department wants to create a macro that adds a header to her worksheets identifying them as Accounting Department worksheets. ▶

Planning a macro

Most tasks that you perform on a regular basis can be made into macros. A macro can enter and format text, for instance, or save and print a worksheet. ▶ You create a macro by recording the series of actions or by writing the instructions in a special format. Since the sequence of actions is important, you need to plan the macro carefully before you record it. Commands used to record, run, and modify macros are located on the Tools menu. ▶ Cathy puts a header, called a department stamp, on all her worksheets that identifies them as originating in the Accounting Department, and she wants to record a macro that automates this process. Cathy reviews the steps she needs to perform this task using the following guidelines.

1 Give the planned macro a descriptive name and write out a description of what it should do.
Cathy decides to call the macro DeptStamp and writes the description of the macro, as shown in Figure 7-1.

2 Decide how you will execute the commands you want to record. You can use the mouse or the keyboard or a combination of the two methods.
Cathy decides to use the mouse to click menus open and click commands.

3 Practice the steps you want Excel to memorize and write them down.
Cathy writes down the sequence of actions. Cathy is now ready to record and test the macro.

4 Decide where to locate the description of the macro and the macro itself. Macros can be stored in an unused area of the active workbook, in a new workbook, or in the **Personal Macro Workbook**, a special workbook that is always open and available.
Cathy decides to store the macro in a new workbook.

FIGURE 7-1: Paper description of planned macro

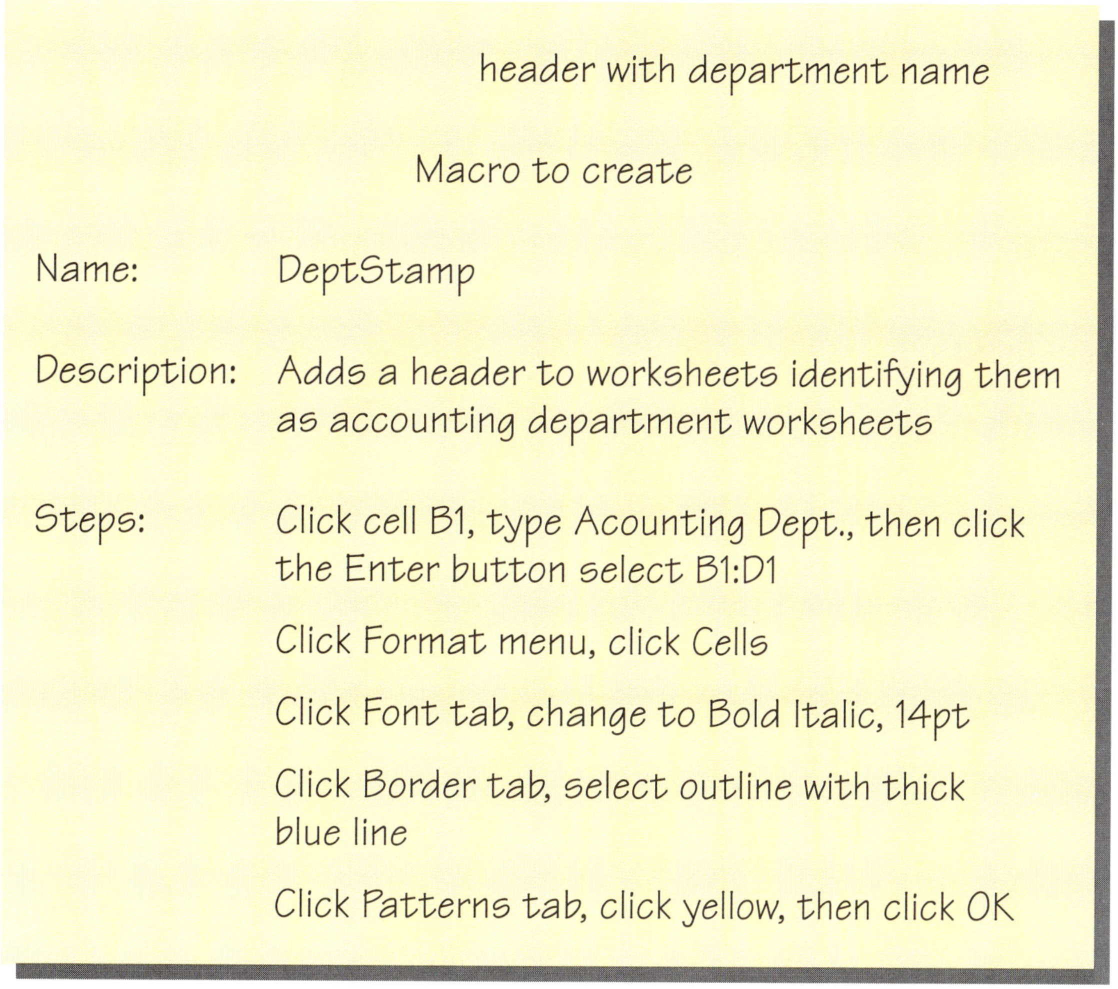

header with department name

Macro to create

Name: DeptStamp

Description: Adds a header to worksheets identifying them as accounting department worksheets

Steps: Click cell B1, type Acounting Dept., then click the Enter button select B1:D1

Click Format menu, click Cells

Click Font tab, change to Bold Italic, 14pt

Click Border tab, select outline with thick blue line

Click Patterns tab, click yellow, then click OK

Recording a macro

Recording is the easiest way to create a macro; you simply type the keystrokes and select the commands you want the macro to execute. As you record the macro, each action is translated into programming code, which you can later view and modify. To begin recording, select the Record New Macro command on the Record Macro submenu on the Tools menu, then enter your keystrokes and select commands as you would normally. When you have finished the procedure or set of keystrokes you want the macro to perform, click the Stop tool on the Stop Recording toolbar. The Stop Recording toolbar appears whenever you are recording a macro. ▶ Cathy Martinez wants to create a macro that will put a department stamp in cell B1 of her worksheets. She will create this macro by recording her actions.

Steps

1. Click the **New Workbook tool** on the Standard toolbar to open a new workbook, then save it as MYMACROS
   Cathy will begin to record actions that will create a department stamp in cell B1 in Sheet1.

2. Click **Tools** on the menu bar, click **Record Macro**, then click **Record New Macro**
   The Record New Macro dialog box appears.

3. Type **DeptStamp** in the Macro Name text box, as shown in Figure 7-2, then click **OK**
   The dialog box disappears, the small Stop Recording toolbar appears containing the Stop tool, and the word Recording appears below the Sheet1 tab. Use the keyboard, mouse, and menu commands to create the macro actions.

4. Click cell **B1**, type **Accounting Dept.**, click the **Enter button**, then select the range **B1:D1**

5. Click **Format** on the menu bar, then click **Cells**
   First, change the font style and point size.

6. Click the **Font tab**, click **Bold Italic** in the Font Style list box, then click **14** in the Size list box
   Next add a thick, blue outline to the cells containing the text.

7. Click the **Border tab**, click **Outline** in the Border section, click the **thickest line** in the Style section, then click the **Color list arrow text box** and click **blue** (the fourth color from the right in the top row on the palette)
   See Figure 7-3. Now add a bright background color to the cell.

8. Click the **Patterns tab**, click **yellow** (the third color from the right in the top row), then click **OK**
   All macro steps have been entered. Now turn off the macro recorder.

9. Click the **Stop tool** on the Stop Recording toolbar
   Compare your results to Figure 7-4. Excel automatically saves the macro.

FIGURE 7-2: Record New Macro dialog box

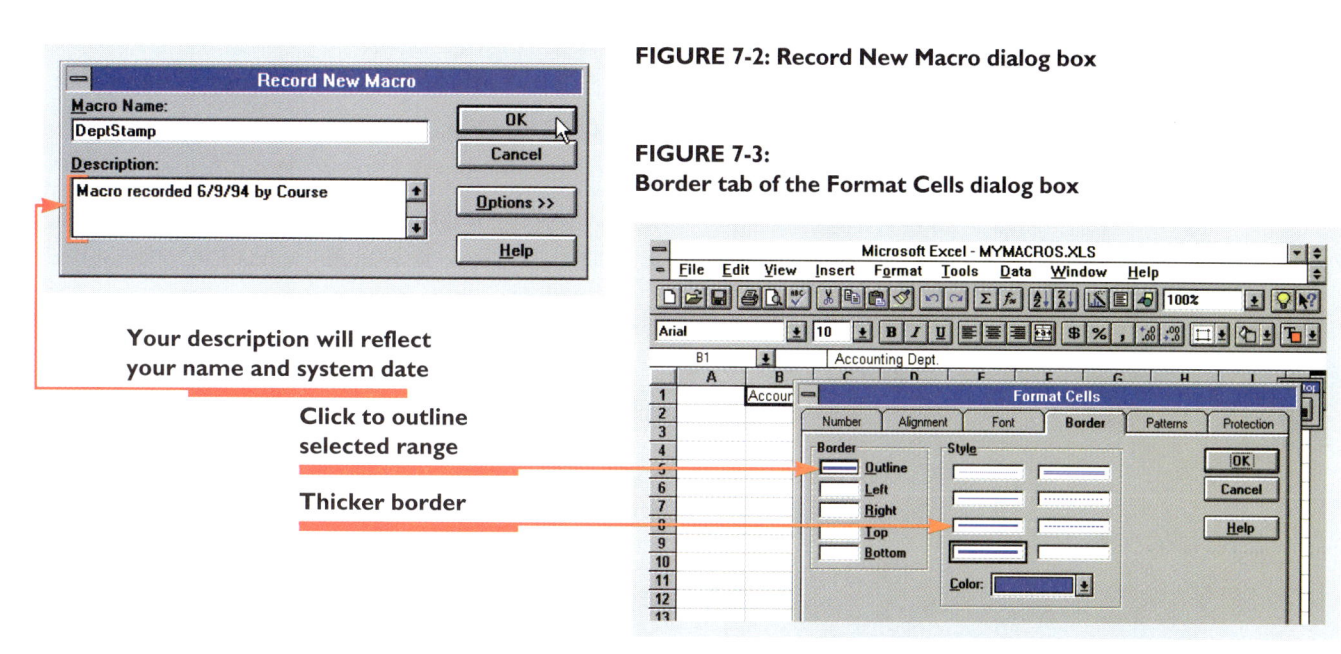

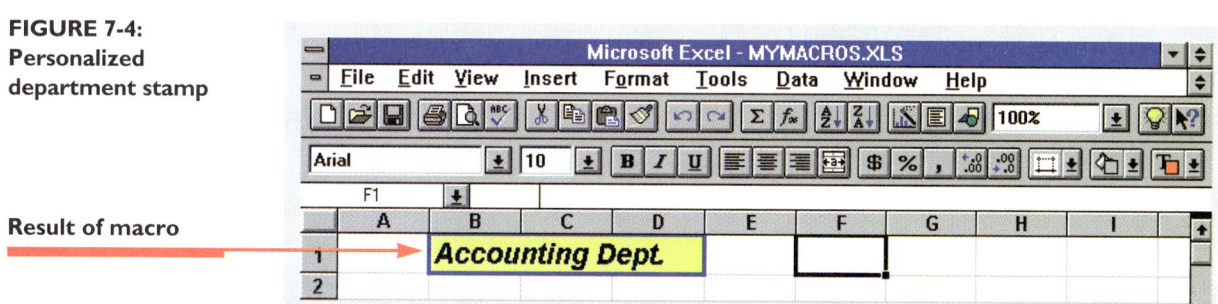

FIGURE 7-3:
Border tab of the Format Cells dialog box

Your description will reflect your name and system date

Click to outline selected range

Thicker border

FIGURE 7-4:
Personalized department stamp

Result of macro

Using the Personal Macro Workbook

Excel allows creation of macros in a Personal Macro Workbook. The Personal Macro Workbook is always open unless you specify otherwise and gives you access to all your macros at all times. Create macros in the Personal Macro Workbook by clicking Options in the Record New Macro dialog box, and then by clicking the Personal Macro Workbook radio button. See Figure 7-5. The Personal Macro Workbook is stored in a file called PERSONAL.XLS.

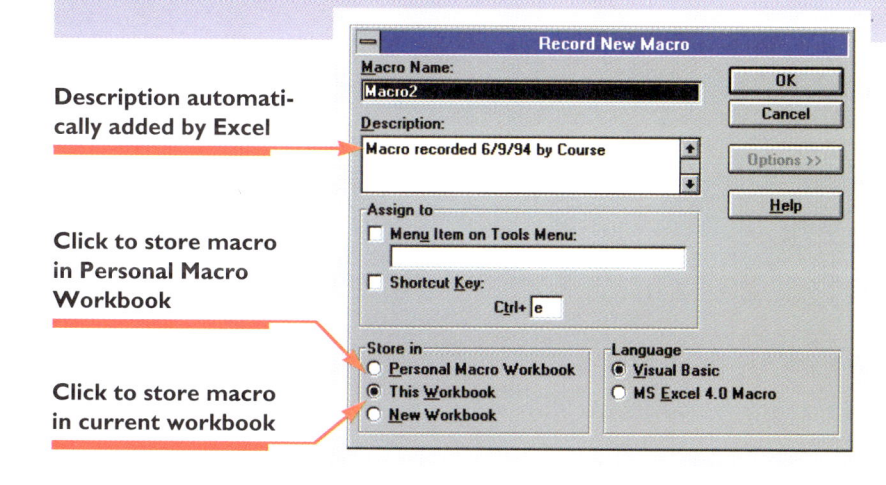

Description automatically added by Excel

Click to store macro in Personal Macro Workbook

Click to store macro in current workbook

FIGURE 7-5:
Record New Macro dialog box with available options

Running a macro

After you record a macro, you must test it to make sure that the actions you expect to see happen actually occur. To test a macro, you run it using the Macro command on the Tools menu. ▶ Cathy will test the DeptStamp macro to see if it works. After she runs the macro, she wants to look at the recorded steps stored in the workbook.

1 Click the **Sheet2 tab**
Use the Macro command on the Tools menu to run macros.

2 Click **Tools** on the menu bar, then click **Macro**
The Macro dialog box, shown in Figure 7-6, lists the macros contained in the workbook.

3 Click **DeptStamp** then click **Run**
Watch your screen as the macro goes through all the steps you recorded in the previous lesson. When it's finished, your screen should look exactly like your previous result. Macros are stored on **module sheets** named Module1, Module2, etc. Each macro is stored in a separate module sheet. All the commands entered during the recording session are listed in the module sheet for your macro. The module sheets appear after the regular worksheets in a workbook.

4 Click the **right tab scrolling button** on the status bar until you see the Module1 sheet tab, then click the **Module1 tab**
See Figure 7-7. The steps in the macro are listed in the Module1 sheet. A special toolbar called the Visual Basic toolbar appears. The Visual Basic toolbar contains tools that help you edit the macro.

5 Examine the steps in the macro
You can see your keystrokes and commands translated into words. For example, the line *.FontStyle = "Bold Italic"* was generated when you chose Bold Italic in the Format Cells dialog box. Now that you know the macro works, save your workbook.

6 Click the **Save tool** on the Standard toolbar

FIGURE 7-6: Macro dialog box

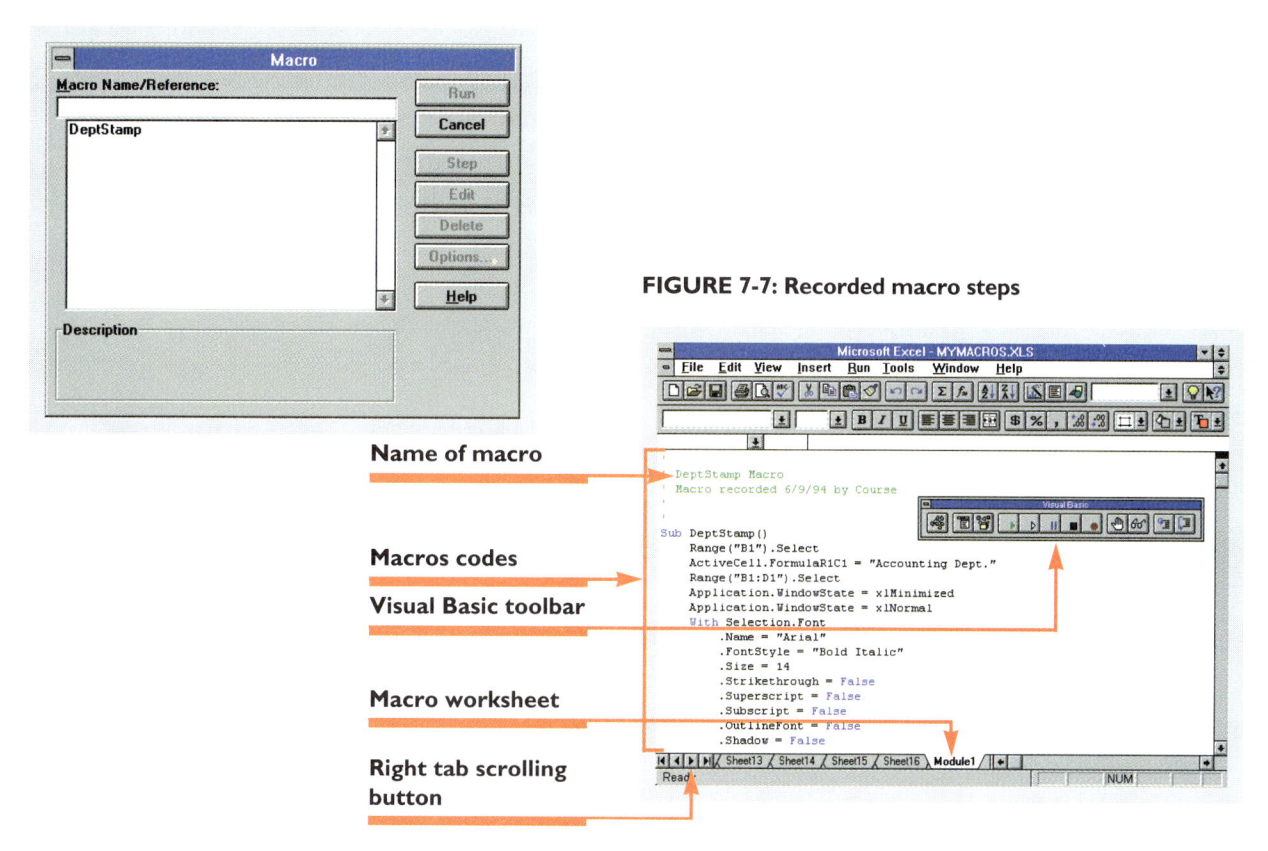

FIGURE 7-7: Recorded macro steps

- Name of macro
- Macros codes
- Visual Basic toolbar
- Macro worksheet
- Right tab scrolling button

Using step mode

If your macro doesn't do what you expected, you can run it using step mode. **Step mode** runs each line item in the macro one step at a time so you can watch each step as it is executed. To run a macro in step mode, make sure you are on a worksheet page rather than a module page, then click Step instead of Run in the Macro dialog box. In the Debug window that opens, click the Immediate tab, then start clicking the Step Into tool on the Visual Basic toolbar. With each click of , the macro completes the next line of code until the macro is finished. Figure 7-8 shows the macro being run in step mode.

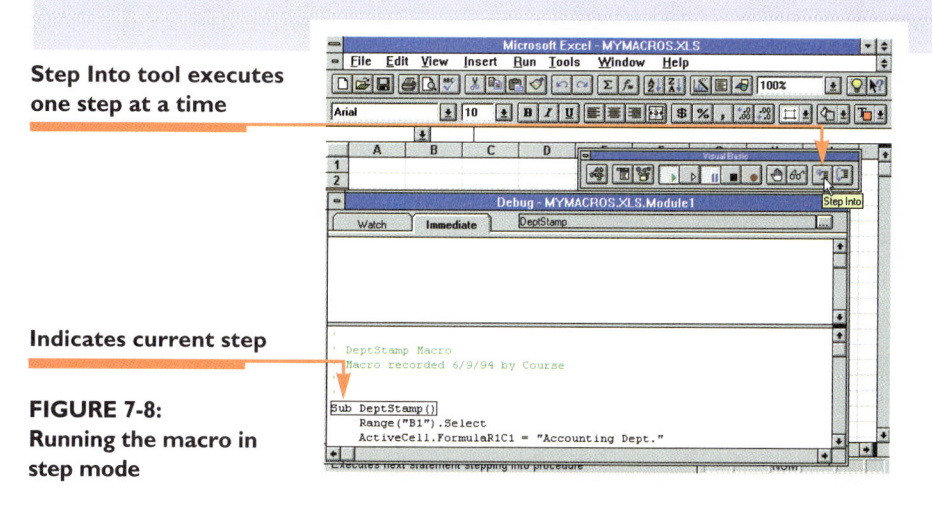

- Step Into tool executes one step at a time
- Indicates current step

FIGURE 7-8:
Running the macro in step mode

EXCEL 5 UNIT 7 **AUTOMATING** WORKSHEET TASKS

133

Editing a macro

After you record a macro, you might want to make some changes. If you have to make a lot of changes, you should record the macro again. If you need to make only minor adjustments, you can edit the macro code in the module worksheet. Macro code can be edited by typing directly in the code or by recording code directly into the existing macro. ▶ Cathy wants to modify her macro so that the point size of her department stamp is 18 points. She also decides to add the name of the company below the department name.

Steps

1. Click **Tools** on the menu bar, click **Macro**, click **DeptStamp** in the Macro dialog box, then click **Edit**
   The Module1 worksheet becomes active. You could also simply click the Module1 tab. First change the font size for the text from 14 to 18 and change the range that the border is drawn around.

2. Double-click **14** in the line *.Size = 14* within the macro code, then type **18**, then double-click **D1** in the line Range("B1:D1") *.Select* and type **E1**
   When you run the macro again, the larger point size will make the text spill into E1; you increased the selected range so the border would be drawn all the way around the text. See Figure 7-9. Next, add the company name in cell B3. You will make this modification by recording the steps directly in the macro. First, you need to move the insertion point in the code immediately before the point where the new recording will be placed.

3. Click in the vertical scroll bar once, then click the mouse pointer so the insertion point appears immediately to the right of the second End With, then press **[Enter]**
   See Figure 7-10.

4. Click **Tools** on the menu bar, click **Record Macro**, then click **Mark Position for Recording**
   You need to select the sheet where you want to make the additions. Sheet2 already has the department stamp on it.

5. Click the **Sheet2 tab**
   You are now ready to record the additional code.

6. Click **Tools** on the menu bar, click **Record Macro**, then click **Record at Mark**
   Now click a cell in which to start recording.

7. Click cell **B3**, type **Nationwide Travel Company**, click the **Enter button**, click the **Italic tool**, then click the **Stop tool**
   Test the macro again.

8. Click the **Sheet3 tab**, click **Tools** on the menu bar, click **Macro**, click **DeptStamp**, then click **Run**
   Compare your results to Figure 7-11.

9. Click the **Save tool** on the Standard toolbar

FIGURE 7-9:
Edited macro code

Code modified by retyping

Insertion point

FIGURE 7-10:
Ready to edit macro by recording

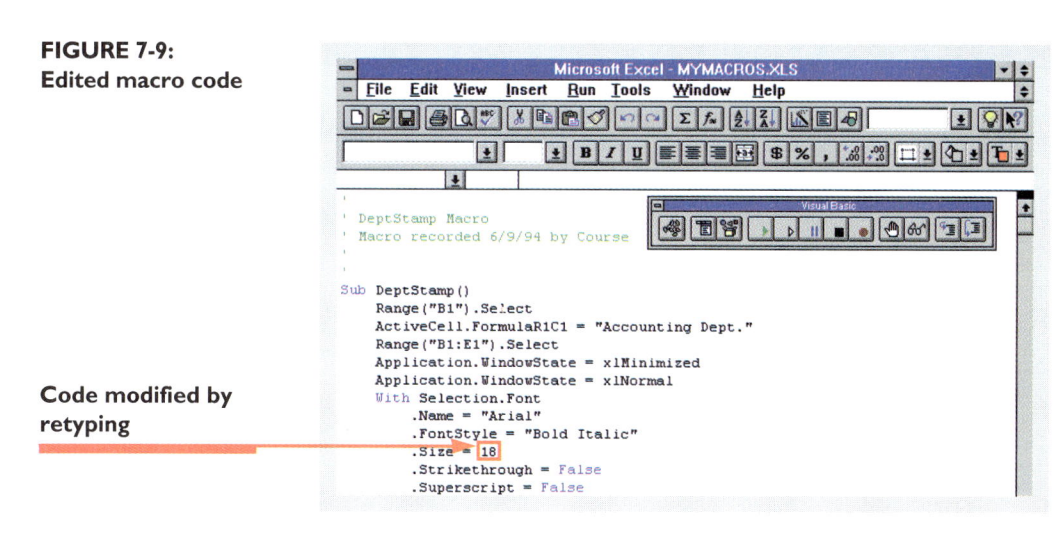

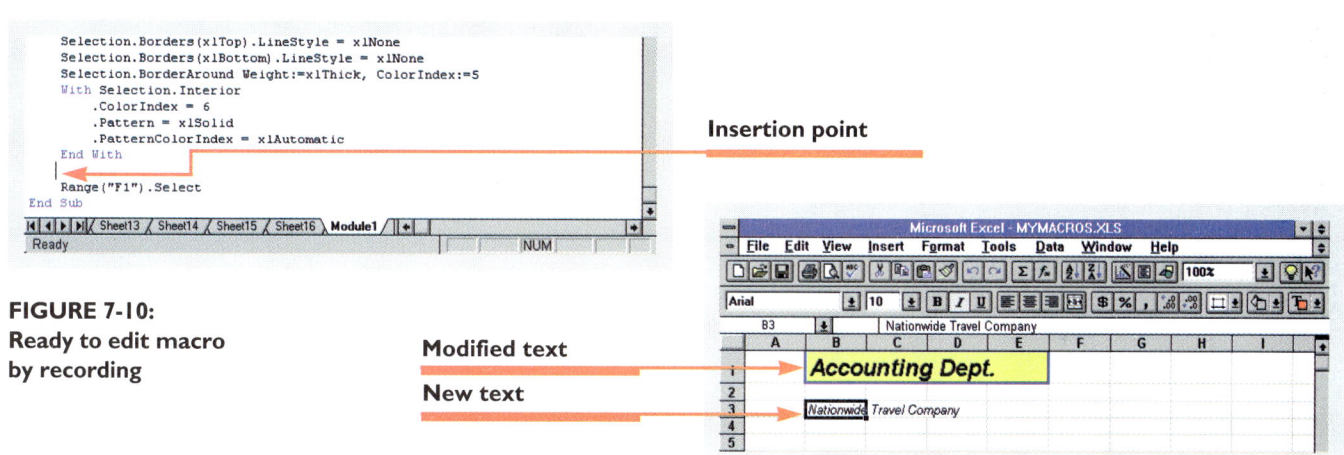

Modified text

New text

FIGURE 7-11: Results of modified DeptStamp macro

Adding comments to code

With practice, you will be able to interpret the actions of the lines of code within your macros. However, others who use your macro might want to know the function of a particular line. Comments are explanatory text added to the lines of code. When you enter a comment, type an apostrophe (') before the comment text. Figure 7-12 shows an example of a comment within a macro.

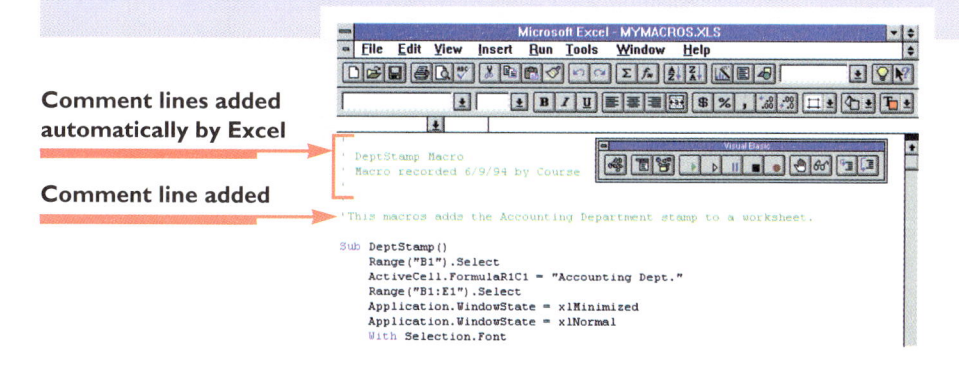

Comment lines added automatically by Excel

Comment line added

FIGURE 7-12: Comment added to macro

Adding macros to a menu and a toolbar

Once you have designed, created, tested, and modified your macro, you can add it as a new command to the Tools menu, and you can assign it to a tool and add it to a toolbar. ▶ Cathy decides try each of these options to see which she finds more convenient.

Steps

1. Click **Tools** on the menu bar, click **Macro**, click **DeptStamp**, then click **Options**
   You can be in any worksheet or module sheet in the workbook containing your macro when you perform these steps. The Macro Options dialog box displays. See Figure 7-13.

2. Click the **Menu Item on Tools Menu check box**, then in the text box below the check box, type **Add DeptStamp**, click **OK**, then click **Close**
   Now try the new menu command and insert the department stamp on a new worksheet.

3. Click the **Sheet4 tab**, click **Tools** on the menu bar, then click **Add DeptStamp**
   The department stamp is added to Sheet4. Cathy will now create a new toolbar for her macros, and then add the new macro to that toolbar.

4. Click **View** on the menu bar, click **Toolbars**, select **Standard** in the Toolbar Name text box, type **Macros**, then click **Customize**
   The Customize dialog box displays.

5. Scroll to the bottom of the **Categories list**, then click **Custom**
   See Figure 7-14.

6. Drag the balloon tool 🖼 to the Macros toolbar, then release the mouse button
   The new tool appears in the Macros toolbar and the Assign Macro dialog box displays.

7. Click **DeptStamp**, click **OK**, then click **Close** in the Customize dialog box
   See Figure 7-15. The new tool is on the Macros toolbar.

8. Click the **Sheet5 tab** then click the **DeptStamp tool** 🖼 on the Macros toolbar
   The department stamp is once again put into cells B1:E3. Cathy will now delete the Macros toolbar.

9. Click **View** on the menu bar, click **Toolbars**, click **Macros** in the Toolbars list, click **Delete**, click **OK**, click **OK** again, then click the **Save tool** 🖼 on the Standard toolbar
   The Macros toolbar disappears and your work has been saved.

FIGURE 7-13:
Macro Options dialog box

Select to add macro to Tools menu

Type name of menu command here

FIGURE 7-14: Customize dialog box

New toolbar

Tool to be added to toolbar

New tool

FIGURE 7-15:
New tool added to Macro toolbar

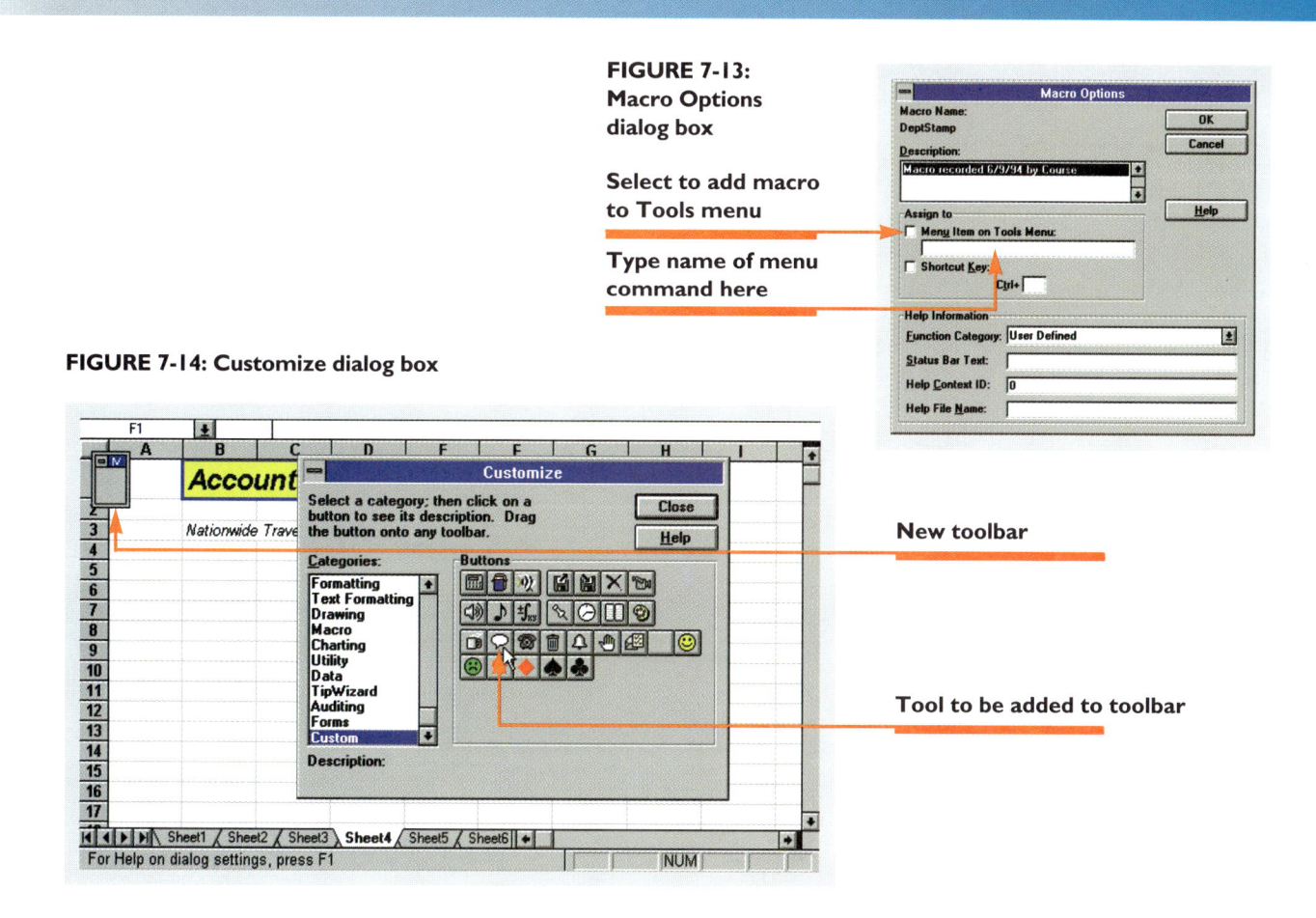

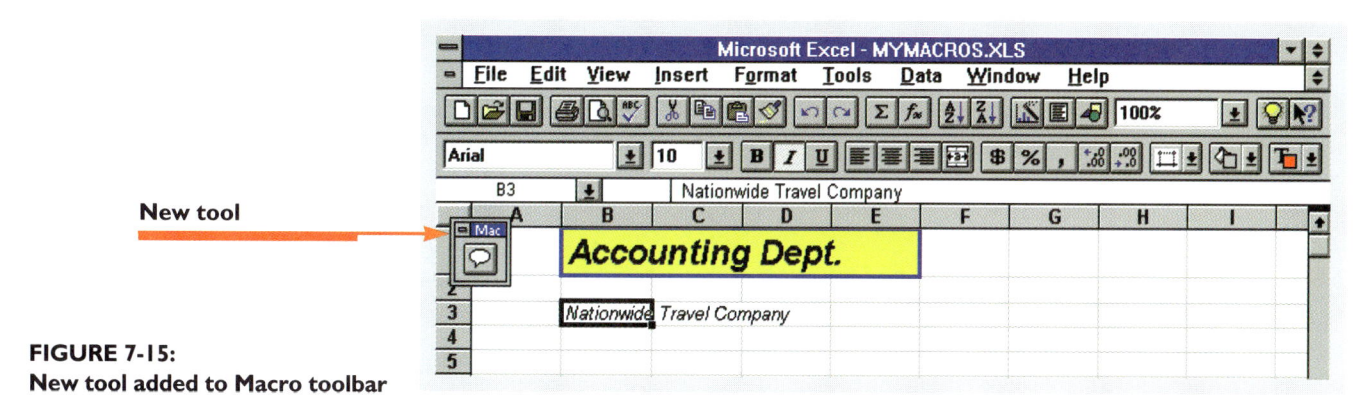

Creating and using templates

Macros can automate series of keystrokes and commands that you execute frequently, but what do you do if you find yourself creating the same workbooks over and over again? You can save a workbook as a **template**, a model workbook that contains the setup you use as well as labels, values, formulas, and formatting. When you open a template, Excel opens a copy of the file and leaves the original untouched so that you can use it again. To save a file as a template, click Save As on the menu bar, assign the template file a name, then click the Save File as Type list arrow and click Template.

EXCEL 5 UNIT 7 **AUTOMATING** WORKSHEET TASKS

CONCEPTSREVIEW

Label each of the elements of the macro shown in Figure 7-16.

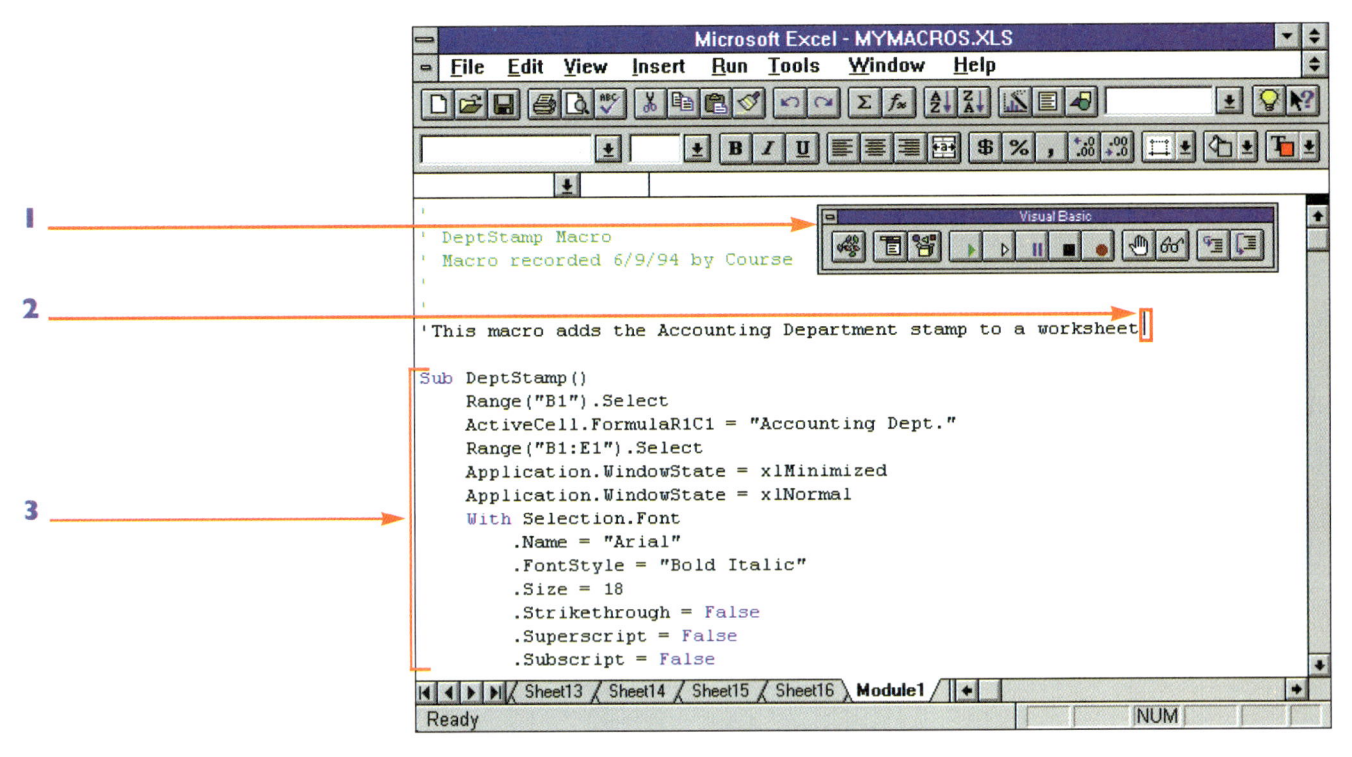

FIGURE 7-16

Select the best answer from the list of choices.

4 Which of the following would be the best candidate for a macro?

   a. Simple commands

   b. Often-used sequences of commands or actions

   c. Seldom-used commands or tasks

   d. Nonsequential tasks

5 When you are recording a macro, you can execute commands by

   a. Using only the keyboard

   b. Using only the mouse

   c. Any combination of the keyboard and the mouse

   d. Using only menu commands

6 A macro is stored in:

   a. The body of a worksheet used for data

   b. An unused area to the far right or well below the worksheet contents

   c. A module worksheet within a workbook

   d. A custom Work menu

7 Which of the following is *not* true about editing a macro?

   a. You can record changes directly in the existing macro code

   b. A macro cannot be edited and must be re-recorded

   c. You can type changes directly in the existing macro code

   d. You can make more than one editing change in a macro

8 Which of the following are ways to run a macro?

a. Clicking a new menu command

b. Choosing Run from the Macro submenu

c. Clicking a tool from a toolbar

d. All of the above

APPLICATIONS REVIEW

1 On paper, plan a macro that will enter and format your name, address, and telephone number.

a. The labels will be entered in A1:C4.

b. The labels will be 14-point Times.

c. Plan to add a border and color to the cells.

d. The macro will be named Address.

2 Record the Address macro.

a. Open a new workbook and save it as MACROS.

b. Click Record Macro on the Tools menu, then click Record New Macro to begin recording.

c. Type your address.

d. Select the range A1:C4.

e. Format the range as 14-point Times.

f. Add a border and color of your choice to the selected range.

g. Stop recording.

3 Run the macro to test it.

a. Make Sheet2 active.

b. Run the macro using the Run Macro command on the Tools menu.

4 Edit the macro

a. Make the Module1 worksheet active.

b. Locate the line of code that sets the font size.

c. Change the font size from 14 to 18 points.

d. Delete the line of code that enters the telephone number.

e. Increase the selected range by one column, and decrease it by one row so the border will adjust to the new size of the labels.

f. Add a comment line that describes this macro.

g. Test the macro in Sheet3.

5 Add the macro to the Tools menu.

a. Click Tools on the menu bar, click Macro, then click Options.

b. Click the Menu Item on Tools check box.

c. Type the description "Add Address" in the text box below the check box.

d. Test the menu command on Sheet4.

e. Save your work.

6 Add a tool to the toolbar

a. Click View Toolbars on the Edit menu, then select Customize.

b. Choose an attractive tool from the Buttons section, and drag it to the Standard toolbar.

c. Assign the Address macro to the tool.

d. Test the tool using Sheet7.

e. Save your work then close the workbook.

INDEPENDENT CHALLENGES

You are a new employee for a manufacturer of computer software. Your responsibility is to track the sales of different product lines and find out which types of computers sell the most software each month. Although sales figures vary from month to month, the format in which data is entered does not.

You need to streamline the way the sales are calculated and inserted on the worksheet used to create the report. The information will be contained in a workbook file that contains worksheets for Summary, Games, Business, and Utilities. Each worksheet will track the sales of programs for DOS, Windows, and Macintosh computers. Use Table 7-1 as a guide.

TABLE 7-1: Sales summary

SUMMARY

Games Software	DOS	Windows	Macintosh	Total
Space Wars 456				
Safari				
Flight School				
Total				
Business Software	**DOS**	**Windows**	**Macintosh**	**Total**
Word Processing				
Spreadsheet				
Presentation				
Graphics				
Page Layout				
Total				
Utilities Product	**DOS**	**Windows**	**Macintosh**	**Total**
Antivirus				
File recovery				
Total				

To complete this independent challenge:

1. Create a new workbook called PROGRAMS. Name Sheet1 through Sheet3 Games, Business, and Utilities, respectively.

2. Create a macro for each of the three types of software. The macro should create a grid similar to Table 7-1 that enters the labels for the appropriate type of software. For example, the Games macro should contain the following labels: Games Product, DOS, Windows, Macintosh, and Total (horizontally) and SpaceWars 456, Safari, Flight School, and Total (vertically).

3. Use colors and patterns to create an attractive look for each of the three macros.

4. Include a row below the last product in each group that totals the entries by type of computer.

5. Include a row below the total row that calculates the average number of products sold within that group.

6. Include a column to the right of Macintosh column that totals the entries by software product.

7. Add comment lines that describe the purpose of each of the macros.

8. Add each of the macros to the menu.

9. Create your own customized toolbar that contains a tool for each of your macros.

10. Print your work.

11. Submit your final worksheet printouts, including the macros and their descriptions.

As a computer support employee of an accounting firm, it is your job to be on the lookout for ways of making your fellow employees work more efficiently. Employees have asked for individual macros that would do the following:

- Delete the current row and insert a blank row.
- Delete the current column and insert a blank column.
- Format a selected group of cells with a red pattern, in Times 12-point bold italics.

To complete this independent challenge:

1. Plan the steps necessary for each of the macros in writing.

2. Create a new workbook called MOREMACS.

3. Create a new toolbar called Helpers.

4. Create a macro for each of the three suggestions described above.

5. Add descriptive comment lines to each of the macros.

6. Add each of the macros to the Tools menu.

7. Install a tool on the Helpers toolbar that will run each macro.

8. Test each of the macros to be sure each works from the Macro Run command, menu commands, and new tools.

9. Submit your written macro plans, as well as the printed code for each macro.

Glossary

Absolute reference A cell reference that contains a dollar sign before the column letter and/or row number to indicate the absolute, or fixed, contents of specific cells. For example, the formula $A$1+$B$1 calculates only the sum of these specific cells.

Active cell The current location of the cell pointer.

Address The location of a specific cell or range expressed by the coordinates of column and row; for example, A1.

Alignment The horizontal placement of cell contents; for example, left, center, or right.

Anchors Cells listed in a range address. For example, in the formula =SUM(A1:A15), A1 and A15 are anchors.

Application A software program, such as Excel or Word, that enables you to perform a certain type of task, such as data calculations or word processing.

Area chart A line chart in which each area is given a solid color or pattern to emphasize the relationship between the pieces of charted information.

Argument A value, range of cells, or text used in a macro or function. An argument is enclosed in parentheses; for example, =SUM(A1..B1).

Arithmetic operator A symbol used in formulas, such as + or -.

Ascending Data organized from A to Z or 0 to 9.

Attribute The styling features such as bold, italics, and underlining that can be applied to cell contents.

AutoFill A feature that creates a series of text or numbers when a range is selected using the fill handle.

AutoFilter A feature that allows you to search for records that meet criteria that you specify.

AutoFormat Preset schemes which can be applied to instantly format a range. Excel comes with sixteen AutoFormats which include colors, fonts, and numeric formatting.

Background color The color applied to the background of a cell.

Bar chart The bar chart displays information as the series of (horizontal) bars.

Border Edges of a selected area of a worksheet. Lines and color can be applied to borders.

Cancel button The X in the formula bar, the Cancel button removes information from the formula bar and restores the previous cell entry.

Cascading menu A subgroup of related commands that display beside a drop-down menu.

Cell The intersection of a column and row.

Cell address Unique location identified by intersecting column and row coordinates.

Cell pointer A highlighted rectangle around a cell that indicates the active cell.

Cell reference The address or name of a specific cell; cell references can be used in formulas and are relative or absolute.

Chart A graphic representation of selected worksheet information. Types include 2-D and 3-D column, bar, pie, area, and line charts.

Chart title The name assigned to a chart.

ChartWizard A series of dialog boxes which helps create or modify a chart.

Check box A square box in a dialog box that can be clicked to turn an option on or off.

Clear A command used to erase a cell's contents, formatting, or both.

Clipboard A temporary storage area for cut or copied items that are available for pasting.

Close A command that puts a file away but keeps Excel open so that you can continue to work on other workbooks.

Column chart The default chart type in Excel. The column chart displays information as a series of (vertical) columns.

Column selector button The gray box containing the column letter above the column.

Confirm button The check mark in the formula bar, the Confirm button is used to confirm an entry.

Control menu box A box in the upper-left corner or a window used to resize or close a window.

Copy A command that copies the selected information and places it on the Clipboard.

GLOSSARY

Criteria The information a user wants compared with the contents of a list or worksheet. Criteria are used with Find & Replace, Delete Record, Find Record, AutoFilter, and other commands. Criteria are also used to create PivotTables.

Cut A command that removes the contents from a selected area of a worksheet and places them on the Clipboard.

Data marker Visible representation of a data point, such as a bar or pie slice.

Data point Individual piece of data plotted in a chart.

Data series The selected range in a worksheet that Excel converts into a graphic and displays as a chart.

Delete A command that removes cell contents from a worksheet.

Delete records A command that removes records from a list.

Descending Data organized from Z to A or 9 to 0.

Dialog box A window that displays when you choose a command whose name is followed by an ellipsis (...). A dialog box allows you to make selections that determine how the command affects the selected area.

Directory A section of a disk used to store specific information, much like a folder in a file cabinet.

Drop-down menu A group of related commands located under a single word on the menu bar. For example, basic commands (New, Open, Save, Close, and Print) are grouped on the File menu.

Dummy column/row Blank column or row included at the end of a range which enables a formula to adjust when columns or rows are added or deleted.

Edit A change made to the contents of a cell or worksheet.

Electronic spreadsheet A computer program that performs calculations on data and organizes information. A spreadsheet is divided into columns and rows, which form individual cells.

Ellipsis A series of dots (...) indicating that more choices are available through dialog boxes.

Exploding pie slice A slice of a pie chart which has been pulled away from a pie to add emphasis.

Field A labeled column in a list; it contains the same kind of information for each record, such as a phone number.

Fill Down A command that duplicates the contents of the selected cells in the range selected below the cell pointer.

Fill handle Small square in the lower-right corner of the active cell used to copy cell contents.

Fill Right A command that duplicates the contents of the selected cells in the range selected to the right of the cell pointer.

Find A command used to locate information the user specifies.

Find & Replace A command used to find one set of criteria and replace it with new information.

Floating toolbar A toolbar within its own window; not anchored along an edge of the worksheet.

Font The typeface used to display information in cells.

Form A data entry method used when working with lists.

Format The appearance of text and numbers, including color, font, attributes, and worksheet defaults. See also number format.

Formula A set of instructions that you enter in a cell to perform numeric calculations (adding, multiplying, averaging, etc.); for example, +A1+B1.

Formula bar The area below the menu bar and above the Excel workspace where you enter and edit data in a worksheet cell. The formula bar becomes active when you start typing or editing cell data. The formula bar includes an Enter button and a Cancel button.

Freeze The process of making columns or rows visible.

Function A special predefined formula that provides a shortcut for commonly used calculations; for example, AVERAGE.

Function Wizard A series of dialog boxes that lists and describes all Excel functions and assists the user in function creation.

Gridlines Horizontal and/or vertical lines within a chart which makes the chart easier to read.

Input Information which produces desired results in a worksheet.

Insertion point Blinking I-beam which appears in the formula bar during entry and editing.

Label Descriptive text or other information that identify the rows and columns of a worksheet. Labels are not included in calculations.

Label prefix A character that identifies an entry as a label and controls the way it is displayed in the cell.

Landscape orientation Printing on a page whose dimensions are 11" (horizontally) by 8-½" (vertically).

Launch To start a software program so you can use it.

Legend A key explaining the information represented by colors or patterns in a chart.

Line chart A graph of data that is mapped by a series of lines. Line charts show changes in data or categories of data over time and can be used to document trends.

List A collection of information organized by fields and records. A telephone book, a card catalog, and a list of company employees are all lists. Also called a database.

List range A range of a worksheet that organizes information into fields and records.

Macro A set of recorded instructions that tell the computer to perform a task or series of tasks.

Menu bar The area under the title bar on a window. The menu bar provides access to most of the application's commands.

Mode indicator A box located at the lower-left corner of the status bar that informs you of the program's status. For example, when Excel is performing a task, the work "Wait" displays.

Module sheet A worksheet that stores all the actions made when you record a macro. Module sheets appear after regular worksheets in a workbook.

Mouse pointer A symbol that indicates the current location of the mouse on the desktop. The mouse pointer changes shapes at times; for example, when you insert data, select a range, position a chart, change the size of a window, or select a topic in Help.

Name box The left-most area in the formula bar that shows the name or address of the area currently selected. For example, A1 refers to cell A1 of the current worksheet.

Number format A format applied to values to express numeric concepts, such as currency, date, and percent.

Object A chart or graphic image which can be moved and resized and contains handles when selected.

Open A command that retrieves a workbook from a disk and displays it on the screen.

Order of precedence The order in which Excel calculates parts of a formula: (1) exponents, (2) multiplication and division, and (3) addition and subtraction.

Output The end result of a worksheet.

Pane A column or row which always remains visible.

Paste A command that moves information on the Clipboard to a new location. Excel pastes the formulas, rather than the result unless the Paste Special command is used.

Paste Special A command that enables you to paste formulas as values, styles, or cell contents.

Pie chart A circular chart that displays data as slices of pie. A pie chart is useful for showing the relationship of parts to a whole; pie slices can be extracted for emphasis.

PivotTable A feature that enables you to analyze data by simplifying list contents.

Point A unit of measure used for fonts and row height. One inch equals 72 points.

Print Preview window A window that displays a reduced view of area to be printed.

Program Manager The main control program of Windows. All Windows applications are started from the Program Manager.

Radio button A circle in a dialog box that can be clicked when only one option can be chosen.

Random Access Memory (RAM) A temporary storage area in a computer that is erased each time the computer is turned off or whenever there is a fluctuation in power. When a program is launched, it is loaded into RAM so you can work with that program.

Range A selected group of adjacent cells.

Range format A format applied to a selected range in a worksheet.

Range name A name applied to a selected range in a worksheet.

Record Horizontal rows in a list that contain related information.

Record command A command used to memorize all actions you want a macro to perform; it is one way to create a macro.

Relative cell reference Used to indicate a relative position in the worksheet. This allows you to copy and move formulas from one area to another of the same dimensions. Excel automatically changes the column and row numbers to reflect the new position.

Row height The vertical dimension of a cell.

Row selector button The gray box containing the row number to the left of the row.

Run To execute a macro.

GLOSSARY

Save A command used to save incremental changes to a workbook.

Save As A command used to create a duplicate of the current workbook.

Scroll bars Bars that display on the right and bottom borders of the worksheet window that give you access to information not currently visible in the current worksheet as well as others in the workbook.

Selection handles Small boxes appearing along the corners and sides of charts and graphic images which are used for moving and resizing.

Series of labels Pre-programmed series, such as days of the week and months of the year. Formed by typing the first word of the series, then dragging the fill handle to the desired cell.

Sheet A term used for worksheet.

Sheet tab scrolling buttons Enable you to move among sheets within a workbook.

Sort To arrange contents of a list or selected range in a particular sequence.

Sort key Any cell in a field by which a list or selected range is being organized.

Spell check A command that attempts to match all text in a worksheet with the words in the Excel dictionary.

Status bar The bar at the bottom of the screen that provides information about the tasks Excel is performing or about any current selections.

Text annotations Labels added to a chart to draw attention to a particular area.

Text color The color applied to the text within a cell.

Title bar The bar at the top of the window that displays the name given a workbook when it is saved and named.

Toggle button A button that can be clicked to turn an option on. Clicking again turns the option off.

Tool A picture on a toolbar that represents a shortcut for performing an Excel task. For example, you can click the Save tool to save a file.

Toolbar An area within the Excel screen which contains tools. Toolbars can be docked against a worksheet edge or can float.

Tooltip Description of a tool, which appears in a toolbar, under the tool.

Values Numbers, formulas, or functions used in calculations.

"What-if" Analysis Decision-making feature in which data is changed and automatically recalculated.

Window A framed area of a screen. Each worksheet occupies a window.

Workbook A collection of related worksheets contained within a single file.

Worksheet An electronic spreadsheet containing 256 columns by 16,384 rows.

Worksheet tab A description at the bottom of each worksheet that identified it in a workbook. In an open workbook, move to a worksheet by clicking its tab.

X-axis The horizontal line in a chart.

X-axis label A label describing the x-axis of a chart.

Y-axis The vertical line in a chart.

Y-axis label A label describing the y-axis of a chart.

Zoom Enables you to focus on a larger or smaller part of the worksheet in print preview.

Index

SPECIAL CHARACTERS
... (ellipsis), W 13, 11
' (apostrophe), 28, 31, 108, 110, 111
* (asterisk), 37, 38, 119
$ (dollar sign), 60, 71
= (equal sign), 36, 37, 40, 41, 118
>= (greater than or equal to sign), 118
<= (less than or equal to sign), 118
- (minus sign), 37
+ (plus sign), 37
? (question mark), 119
/ (slash), 37
\ (backslash), W 16
> (greater than sign), 118
< (less than sign), 118
<> (not equal to sign), 118

A
absolute cell reference, 60-61
Accessories group, W 6
Accessories group icon, W 6
Accessories group window, W 6, W 7
Accessories group window title bar, W 6
active cell, 8, 9
active window, W 6
adding. *See also* entering; inserting
   comments to macros, 137
   records to lists, 112-113
   worksheets, 55
Align Center button, 74, 75
Align Left button, 75
Align Right button, 75
alignment
   cell entries, 74-75
   charts, 99
Alignment tab, 10, 11
analysis, form, 121
anchors, 52
And logical condition, 119
apostrophe (')
   labels, 28, 31
   values in lists, 108, 110, 111
applications, W 1
   closing, W 8, W 21
   running, W 8-9

Applications group, W 6
area charts, 89
arguments, functions, 40
arithmetic operators, 36, 37, 118
Arrow button, 100
arrow keys, scrolling, W 7
arrows, scroll, W 7
ascending order, 116
asterisk (*)
   arithmetic operator, 37, 38
   wildcard, 119
attributes, cell entries, 74-75
AutoFilter, 118-119
AutoFit Selection command, 62
AutoFormat, 80-81
   PivotTables, 123
AutoFormat dialog box, 80, 81
AutoSum ToolTip, 41

B
Back button, 15
backslash (\), directory names, W 16
backup copies
   lists, 117
   worksheets, 43
bar charts, 89
blank rows, inserting, 52, 53
blink rate, cursor, W 12, W 13
Bold button, 12, 74, 75
Bold ToolTip, 12, 13
border tools, 78, 79
borders, worksheets, 78, 79
Borders button, 78
buttons. *See also specific buttons*
   command, W 12, W 13
   toggle, 12, 13

C
calculations, 4, 60-61. *See also* formulas
Calendar application, W 8
Cancel button, W 12, 33
Cardfile application, W 8
Cascade command, W 18
cell address, 8
cell entries
   attributes and alignment, 74-75

INDEX

copying and moving, 54-55
   editing, 29, 32-33
   fonts and point sizes, 72-73
cell pointer, 8
cell references, 36
   absolute, 60-61
   relative, 56
cells, 4, 5, 8
   active, 8, 9
   ranges. *See* ranges
   replacing contents, 55
Center Across Columns button, 74, 75
Center button, 12, 13
changing
   column width, 62-63
   dictionary, 65
chart tools, 92-93
Chart type tools list box, 93
charts, 4, 87-103
   alignment, 99
   creating, 90-91
   deleting, 91
   editing, 92-93
   fonts, 99
   formatting, 96-99
   legends. *See* legends
   moving and resizing, 94-95
   PivotTables, 123
   planning and designing, 88-89
   previewing and printing, 102-103
   rotating, 93
   text annotations, 100-101
   tools for enhancing, 96
   types, 89
ChartWizard dialog box, 90, 91
ChartWizard tool, 90, 91
check boxes, W 13, 10, 11
checking spelling, 64-65
clicking, W 4
Clipboard, copying and pasting, 54, 55
Clock application, W 8, W 9
closing
   applications, W 8, W 21
   dialog boxes, W 12
   Excel 5.0 for Windows, 20, 21
   menus, 11
   windows, W 12
   workbooks, 20, 21
color, worksheets, 78, 79
Color button, 78, 79
color palette, 78, 79

column charts, 89
Column command, 62
column selector buttons, 62
Column Width dialog box, 62, 63
columns, 8
   changing width, 62-63
   dummy, 53
   freezing, 82-83
   inserting and deleting, 52-53
combination charts, 89
Comma tool, 70, 71
command buttons, W 12, W 13. *See also specific buttons*
command prompt, W 2
commands. *See also specific commands*
   dimmed, W 13
   Format Column menu, 62, 63
   macros, 128
   selecting, W 12
comments, adding to macros, 137
computer, turning off, W 21
Contents button, 15
context-sensitive help, 15
control menu boxes, W 2, W 3, W 6, W 7, W 21
Control Panel icon, W 4
Copy button, 12, 54, 55, 56, 58
copying
   cell entries, 54-55
   drag and drop technique, 54, 55
   formulas, with absolute cell references, 60-61
   formulas, with relative cell references, 56-59
Create Directory dialog box, W 16
criteria. *See also* search criteria
   sort key, 116
Currency tool, 70, 71
cursor, W 12
   blink rate, W 12, W 13
Custom AutoFilter dialog box, 119
Customize dialog box, 76, 77, 136, 137
customizing toolbars, 76-77
   networks, 77
Cut button, 12, 54, 55, 58

D

data entry, 4
data forms
   adding records to lists, 112-113
   finding and deleting records, 114, 115
data markers, 88
data points, 88
data series, 88
databases. *See* lists

decimal places, space required, 71
Decrease decimal tool, 71
default values, column width, 62-63
Define Name dialog box, 35
Delete button, 115
Delete command, 114
deleting
    charts, 91
    records, 114-115
    rows and columns, 52-53
    worksheets, 55
descending order, 116
desktop, W 2-3
desktop accessories, W 2, W 8-9
dialog boxes, W 12, W 13, 10, 11. *See also specific dialog boxes*
    closing, W 12
dictionary, changing, 65
dimmed commands, W 13
direction keys, scrolling, W 7
directories, W 16, W 17
directory window, W 16, W 17
disk, saving files to, 42-43
displaying. *See* viewing
documents, W 14
dollar sign ($)
    absolute cell references, 60
    space required, 71
double-clicking, W 4
drag and drop technique
    copying, 54, 55
    sizing charts, 94
dragging, W 4, W 5
    files, W 16, W 17
Drawing button, 100, 101
drive icon, W 16, W 17
drives
    listing, 42, 43, 50, 51
    selecting, W 14, W 15, 42, 43
Drives list arrow, W 14, W 15
dummy columns and rows, 53

E

Edit mode, 32, 94
editing
    cell entries, 29, 32-33
    charts, 92-93
    macros, 134-135
    worksheets, 59
electronic spreadsheet, 4
ellipsis (...), W 13, 11
Enter button, 28, 29

Enter mode, 32
entering. *See also* adding; inserting
    data, 4
    formulas, 36-39
    labels, 28-29
    values, 30-31
equal sign (=)
    arithmetic operator, 118
    formulas, 36, 37
    functions, 40, 41
erasing. *See* deleting
error correction
    Cancel button, 33
    range names, 35
    spell checking, 64-65
Error mode, 32
Excel 5.0 for Windows
    exiting, 20, 21
    starting, 6-7
Exit command, 20, 21
Exit Windows command, W 20, W 21
exiting
    Excel 5.0 for Windows, 20, 21
    Windows, W 20-21
exploding slices, pie charts, 101

F

field names, 108, 109, 110-111
fields, 108
File Manager, W 16-17
File menu
    closing workbooks, 20, 21
    exiting Windows, W 20-21
filename extensions, 42, 43
filenames, 42
files
    backup, 43
    dragging, W 16, W 17
    listing, W 16, W 17
    saving, W 14-15, 42-43
    selecting, W 16, W 17
    selecting groups, W 17
    text, W 14
    workbooks. *See* workbooks
fill handle, 56, 57
Fill Series command, 57
filling ranges, 56, 57
Find command, editing worksheets, 59
finding records, 114-115
    AutoFilter, 118-119
floating toolbar, moving, 13

INDEX

Font tab, 72, 73
fonts
    charts, 99
    worksheets, 72-73
Format Axis dialog box, 99
Format Cells command, 73
Format Cells dialog box, 10, 11, 70, 73, 78
Format Column menu, 62, 63
Format Data Series dialog box, 96, 97
Format menu, 10, 11
Format Painter tool, 71
formatting, 70
    attributes and alignment, 74-75
    AutoFormat, 80-81
    charts, 96-99
    fonts and point sizes, 72-73
    non-contiguous ranges, 75
    PivotTables, 123
    ranges of cells, 70
    values, 70-71
Formatting toolbar, 12, 13, 73, 74, 75, 78
formatting tools, 74, 75
formula bar, 8, 9, 28, 29
formulas, 26, 36
    copying and moving with relative cell references, 56-59
    copying with absolute cell references, 60-61
    dummy columns and rows, 53
    entering, 36-39
    order of precedence, 39
freezing rows and columns, 82-83
Function Wizard dialog box, 41
Function Wizard tool, 41
functions, 40-41

G
Games group, W 6
Go To command, 16
Go To dialog box, 17
GoTo key, 75
graphic images, integrating into spreadsheets, 81
graphical user interface (GUI), W 1
graphics, 94. *See also* charts
greater than or equal to sign (>=), arithmetic operator, 118
greater than sign (>), arithmetic operator, 118
gridlines, 96
groups, Program Manager, W 6-7
GUI (graphical user interface), W 1

H
handles, 81
    selection, 90, 91
Help buttons, 15
Help tool, 15
Help utility, 14-15
Hide command, 62
History button, 15
How To window, 14, 15

I
icons, W 2, W 3
    arranging, W 18-19
    selecting, W 4-5
Increase decimal tool, 71
Index button, 15
input, 26
Insert dialog box, 52, 53
inserting. *See also* adding; entering
    rows and columns, 52-53
insertion point, W 5, 32, 33
    adding records to lists, 112, 113
Italics button, 74, 75

K
keyboard
    editing cell entries, 29
    pointer-movement keys, 10, 16, 17
    scrolling, W 7
keyboard shortcuts, W 13, 10
keystrokes, macros, recording, 130-131

L
labels, 26
    entering, 28-29
    filling ranges with series, 56, 57
    values as, 31
landscape orientation, 102
legend, 88
legends, 94
    moving, 94-95
    selecting, 94
less than or equal to sign (<=), arithmetic operator, 118
less than sign (<), arithmetic operator, 118
line charts, 89
Lines and Borders button, 75
list boxes, W 13

list ranges, 108
    adding records to lists, 113
listing
    drives, 42, 43, 50, 51
    files, W 16, W 17
lists, 4, 107-123
    adding records, 112-113
    backup copies, 117
    creating, 110-111
    finding and deleting records, 114-115
    finding records using AutoFilter, 118-119
    maintaining quality of information, 111
    PivotTable Wizard, 120-123
    planning, 108-109
    sorting records, 116-117
logical conditions, 119

M

Macro dialog box, 132, 133
Macro Options dialog box, 136, 137
macros, 127-137
    adding comments, 137
    adding to menus and toolbars, 136-137
    editing, 134-135
    planning, 128-129
    recording, 130-131
    running, 132-133
Main group, W 6
Main group icon, W 6
main menu bar, 8, 9
Maximize button, W 10, W 11
maximizing windows, W 10, W 11
menu bar, W 2, W 3, W 12
menus, W 12, W 13, 10, 11. *See also specific menus*
    adding macros, 136-137
    closing, 11
Microsoft Excel application icon, 6, 7
Microsoft Excel program icon, 7
Microsoft Office group icon, 6, 7
Microsoft Office window, 7
Minimize button, W 10, W 11
minus sign (-), arithmetic operator, 37
mistakes. *See* error correction
mode indicator, 32
modifying. *See* changing
module sheets, 132
mouse, W 4-5
    clicking and double clicking techniques, W 4
    drag technique, W 4, W 5
    moving in worksheet, 16
    pointing technique, W 4

mouse buttons, W 4
mouse pointer, W 2, W 3, W 4, W 5, 56, 57
    changing column width, 62
    creating charts, 90, 91
    insertion point, W 5, 32, 33
    painted formats, 71
    sizing charts, 94
    sizing windows, W 11
    text annotations in charts, 100
moving
    cell entries, 54-55
    charts, 94-95
    formulas, with relative cell references, 56-59
    icons, W 18-19
    scroll bars, W 7
    toolbars, 13
    using range names, 35
    windows, W 18-19
    in workbooks, 35
    in worksheet, 16-17
    between worksheets, 18, 19
    worksheets, 19
multiple worksheets, viewing, 8, 9, 95

N

Name box, 35
Name list box, W 12, W 13
name list box, 75
names
    fields, 108, 109, 110-111
    files, 42, 43
    ranges, 34, 35
    worksheets, 18-19
networks, customizing toolbars, 77
not equal to sign (< >), arithmetic operator, 118
Notepad application, W 8, W 14-15
Notepad window, W 14, W 15
numbers. *See* values

O

objects, 94. *See also* charts
OK button, W 12
on-line help, 14-15
Open button, 12
Open File dialog box, 50, 51
opening worksheets, 50-51
operators, arithmetic, 36, 37, 118
Or logical condition, 119
order
    of precedence, formulas, 39
    sorting records, 116-117

INDEX

output, 26
overhead projectors, printing transparencies, 103
Overview of Customizing Toolbars window, 15

P

Page tab, 102, 103
Paintbrush application, W 8
painting formats, 71
Panes, 82-83
paper spreadsheet, 5
Paste button, 12, 54, 55, 56, 58
pasting Clipboard contents, 54, 55
patterns, worksheets, 78, 79
Patterns tab, 78
Percentage tool, 70, 71
Personal Macro Workbook, 128
pie charts, 89
    exploding slices, 101
Pivot tools, 121
PivotTable Wizard, 120-123
    AutoFormat, 123
    charts, 123
PivotTable Wizard dialog box, 120, 121, 122
planning
    charts, 88-89
    lists, 108-109
    macros, 128-129
    worksheets, 26-27
plus sign (+), arithmetic operator, 37
Point mode, 32
pointer. *See* mouse pointer
pointer-movement keys, 10, 16, 17
pointing, W 4
points
    fonts, 72-73
    row height, 63
positioning. *See* moving
precedence, order of, formulas, 39
previewing
    charts, 102, 103
    worksheets, 44, 45
Print button, 12
Print dialog box, 44, 45
Print Preview button, 12
Print Preview window, Zoom button, 45
printing
    charts, 102, 103
    saving before, 45
    transparencies, 103
    worksheets, 44, 45

Program Manager, W 2, W 3
    exiting Windows, W 21
    groups, W 6-7
Program Manager window, W 3

Q

Query tools, 121
question mark (?), wildcard, 119

R

radio buttons, W 13, 10, 11
RAM (random access memory), W 14
range formatting, 70
range names, 34, 35
ranges, 34-35
    filling, 56, 57
    large, unnamed, selecting, 81
    lists. *See* list ranges
    non-contiguous, formatting, 75
    selecting, 34, 75
Ready mode, 32
recalculation, 4, 60-61
Record New Macro command, 130
Record New Macro dialog box, 130, 131
recording macros, 130-131
records, 108
    adding to lists, 112-113
    finding and deleting, 114-115
    finding using AutoFilter, 118-119
relative cell reference, 56
removing. *See* deleting
Replace command, editing worksheets, 59
Replace dialog box, 59
replacing cell contents, 55
repositioning. *See* moving
resizing. *See* sizing
Restore button, W 10, W 11
rotating charts, 93
row selector buttons, 52, 53
rows, 8
    dummy, 53
    freezing, 82-83
    inserting and deleting, 52-53
    specifying height, 63
running
    applications, W 8-9
    macros, 132-133

S

Save As command, 43
Save As dialog box, 42, 43, 50, 51, 139
Save button, 12, 74
Save Changes dialog box, 20, 21
Save command, 43
saving
   files, W 14-15
   frequency, W 14, W 15, 42
   before printing, 45
   workbooks, 42-43
scatter charts, 89
screen saver, W 12
scroll arrows, W 7
scroll bars, W 7, 16, 45
scroll box, W 7
scrolling buttons, sheet tab, 8, 9
Search button, 15
search criteria, 59
   complex, 119
   finding records, 114, 115
Search dialog box, 14, 15
searching
   editing worksheets, 59
   finding records, 114-115
selecting
   commands, W 12
   drives, W 14, W 15, 42, 43
   files, W 16, W 17
   groups of files, W 17
   icons, W 4-5
   large, unnamed ranges, 81
   legends, 94
   ranges, 34, 75
   text boxes, 98, 99, 100
selection handles, 90, 91
sheet tab scrolling buttons, 8, 9
sheet tabs, 8, 9
   naming worksheets, 18, 19
sizing
   charts, 94-95
   windows, W 10-11
sizing buttons, W 2, W 3
slash (/), arithmetic operator, 37
Sort dialog box, 116, 117
sort key, 116
sorting records, 116-117
specifying row height, 63
spell checking, 64-65
Spelling button, 12
Spelling dialog box, 64, 65

split bar, W 16, W 17
spreadsheets
   electronic, 4
   paper, 5
   uses, 5
Standard toolbar, 12, 13
Standard Width command, 62, 63
starting
   Excel 5.0 for Windows, 6-7
   Windows, W 2-3
StartUp group, W 6
StartUp group window, W 18, W 19
status bar, 8, 9
Step mode, 133
Student Disk, W 14
SUM function, 40, 41
Summary Info dialog box, 42
switching between applications, W 9

T

Tab scrolling buttons, 18, 19
tabs, 8, 9, 10, 11, 72, 73, 102, 103
templates, 139
Test button, W 12
text annotations, charts, 100-101
Text Box button, 101
text boxes, W 13
   selecting, 98, 99, 100
text files, W 14
3-D Chart tool, 92, 93
tick marks, 88
Tile command, W 18
title bar, W 2, W 3, 8, 9
toggle button, 12, 13
toolbars, 12, 13. *See also specific toolbars*
   adding macros, 136-137
   customizing, 76-77
   floating, 13
   positioning, 13
Toolbars dialog box, 76, 77
tools, 8, 12-13. *See also* buttons; *specific buttons*
Tools menu, 128
ToolTips, 12, 13, 41
transparencies, printing, 103
triangle, W 13
turning off the computer, W 21
2-D Chart tool, 92, 93
2-D Column Chart tool, 92, 93
type style and sizes, 72-73

INDEX

U
Underline button, 74, 75
underlined letters, W 13
Undo button, 58
Undo command, 33
Undo tool, 33
Unhide command, 62

V
values, 26
    entering, 30-31
    formatting in lists, 108
    formatting in worksheets, 70-71
    as labels, 31
viewing
    multiple worksheets, 95
    worksheet windows, 8-9

W
Wait mode, 32
what-if-analysis, 4
Width command, 62
wildcards, 119
Win command, W 2
Window menu, W 18, W 19
Windows
    exiting, W 20-21
    starting, W 2-3
windows, W 2, W 3. *See also specific windows*
    arranging, W 18-19
    closing, W 12
    sizing, W 10-11
workbooks, 8
    closing, 20, 21
    moving in, 35
    rearranging worksheets, 19
    saving, 42-43
worksheet area, 5
worksheet window, viewing, 8-9
worksheets, 4, 5, 69-83. *See also* cell entries; cells
    adding, 55
    attributes and alignment, 74-75
    AutoFormat, 80-81
    colors, patterns, and borders, 78-79
    deleting, 55
    editing, 59
    fonts and point sizes, 72-73
    formatting values, 70-71
    integrating graphic images, 81
    moving, 19
    moving between, 18, 19
    moving in, 16-17
    multiple, viewing, 95
    naming, 18-19
    opening, 50-51
    planning and designing, 26-27
    previewing, 44, 45
    printing, 44, 45
Write application, W 8

X
x-axis, 88
.XLS filename extension, 42
XY charts, 89

Y
y-axis, 88

Z
Zoom button, Print Preview window, 45